The American Dream: Reality and Illusion, 1945–1980

A/AS Level History for AQA
Student Book

Tony McConnell and Adam I.P. Smith

Series Editors: Michael Fordham and David Smith

CAMBRIDGE
UNIVERSITY PRESS

University Printing House, Cambridge CB2 8BS, United Kingdom

Cambridge University Press is part of the University of Cambridge.

It furthers the University's mission by disseminating knowledge in the pursuit of education, learning and research at the highest international levels of excellence.

www.cambridge.org
Information on this title: www.cambridge.org/ukschools/9781107587427 (Paperback)
                              www.cambridge.org/ukschools/9781107587540 Cambridge Elevate-enhanced Edition)

First published 2015

A catalogue record for this publication is available from the British Library

ISBN 978-1-107-58742-7 Paperback
ISBN 978-1-107-58754-0 Cambridge Elevate-enhanced Edition

Additional resources for this publication at www.cambridge.org/ukschools

Cambridge University Press has no responsibility for the persistence or
accuracy of URLs for external or third-party internet websites referred
to in this publication, and does not guarantee that any content on such
websites is, or will remain, accurate or appropriate. Information regarding
prices, travel timetables, and other factual information given in this work
is correct at the time of first printing but Cambridge University Press does
not guarantee the accuracy of such information thereafter.

Message from AQA

This textbook has been approved by AQA for use with our qualification. This means that we have checked that it broadly covers the specification and we are satisfied with the overall quality. Full details of our approval process can be found on our website.

We approve textbooks because we know how important it is for teachers and students to have the right resources to support their teaching and learning. However, the publisher is ultimately responsible for the editorial control and quality of this book.

Please note that when teaching the A/AS Level History (7041, 7042) course, you must refer to AQA's specification as your definitive source of information. While this book has been written to match the specification, it cannot provide complete coverage of every aspect of the course.

A wide range of other useful resources can be found on the relevant subject pages of our website: www.aqa.org.uk

Contents

About this Series

Cambridge A/AS Level History for AQA is an exciting new series designed to support students in their journey from GCSE to A Level and then on to possible further historical study. The books provide the knowledge, concepts and skills needed for the two-year AQA History A Level course, but it's our intention as series editors that students recognise that their A Level exams are just one step to a potential lifelong relationship with the discipline of history. This book has further readings, extracts from historians' works and links to wider questions and ideas that go beyond the scope of an A Level course. With this series, we have sought to ensure not only that the students are well prepared for their examinations, but also that they gain access to a wider debate that characterises historical study.

The series is designed to provide clear and effective support for students as they make the adjustment from GCSE to A Level, and also for teachers, especially those who are not familiar with teaching a two-year linear course. The student books cover the AQA specifications for both A/AS Level. They are intended to appeal to the broadest range of students, and they offer challenge to stretch the top end and additional support for those who need it. Every author in this series is an experienced historian or history teacher, and all have great skill in conveying narratives to readers and asking the kinds of questions that pull those narratives apart.

In addition to high-quality prose, this series also makes extensive use of textual primary sources, maps, diagrams and images, and offers a wide range of activities to encourage students to address historical questions of cause, consequence, change and continuity. Throughout the books there are opportunities to criticise the interpretations of other historians, and to use those interpretations in the construction of students' own accounts of the past. The series aims to ease the transition for those students who move on from A Level to undergraduate study, and the books are written in an engaging style that will encourage those who want to explore the subject further.

Icons used within this book include:

 Key terms

 Speak like a historian

 Voices from the past/Hidden voices

 Practice essay questions

 Taking it further

 Thematic links

 Chapter summary

About Cambridge Elevate

Cambridge Elevate is the platform which hosts a digital version of this Student Book. If you have access to this digital version you can annotate different parts of the book, send and receive messages to and from your teacher and insert weblinks, among other things.

We hope that you enjoy your AS or A Level History course as well as this book, and wish you well for the journey ahead.

Michael Fordham and David L Smith

Series editors

Introduction

The USA after 1945

In 1945 Americans who, 25 years earlier, had decided in the wake of the Great War more or less en masse to be **isolationist** – that is, not to participate in international affairs – found themselves citizens of one of the two world **Superpowers** that had won the Second World War. Their economy, which had fallen into depression in the 1930s and recovered only barely as a result of President Roosevelt's New Deal, which vastly increased the power of the presidency, was now running in overdrive because most of the other major economies of the world were either ruined by war, or vastly indebted to the Americans, or both. As Winston Churchill said in 1945, 'The United States stands at this moment at the summit of the world'. Its industrial and technological might gave it the ability to prosper in the new world formed in the aftermath of the Second World War; its experience of saving Europeans from two particularly all-consuming and barbaric conflicts gave it the impetus to do so.

From an American perspective, exerting massive influence over world affairs – assuming a position of leadership of the 'free' (as opposed to **communist** and controlled) world – now made perfect sense. American goods would find eager markets abroad – all the more so because America, at the end of the Second World War uniquely among major nations, had an intact and enhanced, indeed superpowered, manufacturing sector as well as the infrastructure necessary to

Key terms

New Deal: the name for President Franklin Delano Roosevelt's efforts to restructure and support the failing American economy in the 1930s. Historians are divided on whether there was one New Deal or three separate New Deals. In modern American thought the New Deal is seen as a cornerstone of liberal politics.

Figure 0.1: Map of the United States of America.

transport goods around the globe. American culture would be transmitted just as easily. To Hollywood movies would be added the even more ubiquitous output of American television. American commerce would follow, as anyone who has ever eaten a mass-produced burger washed down by a syrupy drink knows.

In 1945 the **president** was Harry S. Truman, who had come to office following the sudden death of his predecessor Franklin Delano Roosevelt. In 1981 his successor, Ronald Reagan, who had survived an assassin's bullet early in his term (he apologised to his wife with the words, 'Honey, I forgot to duck') presided over one of the two world Superpowers. The United States, led by its confident 40th president, used its long-established position as the leader of the democratic capitalist world to launch an ideological and economic attack upon its fellow Superpower, the communist Soviet Union, which Reagan branded an 'evil empire'. By 1990, in the presidency of Reagan's vice president and successor George H.W. Bush, the Soviet Union was collapsing: the United States stood alone as the only Superpower left.

This textbook is intended to show the student what happened between the moment Harry Truman became president, taking over from the man who won the war and changed the presidency, and the election that brought Reagan, the Republican figure whose memory is idolised by his party, to the **White House**. There is an idea expressed by both these men – and by many others who have held their high office – that America has a special, privileged place as leader of the democratic world. This is the idea of American Exceptionalism – America as the 'last best hope of earth', which often seems to dominate modern American politics and is rooted in history: the story of America is the story of becoming and remaining a force for good, the global Superman of 'Truth, Justice and the American Way'.

The textbook is arranged by president. It begins with Truman, whose triumphs have been overshadowed by the horror of the Korean War, and who remains the only man to have ordered the use of nuclear weapons in warfare. He was succeeded by Dwight Eisenhower, a Republican rather than a Democrat (although both parties had wanted to claim him as their own), and a war hero rather than a politician. He was followed in turn by John F. Kennedy, whose reputation, enhanced by his glamorous nature and early death, seems to outweigh his achievements, and by Lyndon Johnson, who was either a pernicious bully or an effective statesman, or both, and whose attempts to reform American society were partially successful but then thwarted by the national horror of the Vietnam War. He was succeeded by Richard Nixon, a man capable of subtle diplomacy and of cynical warfare, and of precise electioneering and criminal conspiracy. The presidents who followed, Gerald Ford and Jimmy Carter, inherited a damaged office and a damaged economy; the latter's admission that all was not well with America helped to give his successor Ronald Reagan a chance to restate the **American Dream** on his way to the White House.

By 1980 America was in a position to win the Cold War, although few except the incoming president seemed to have realised it. Its economy was strong even during a recession. Its culture dominated the western world. Its military was the world's finest. It had put a man on the Moon, and remains the only nation to

Key terms

American Exceptionalism: the idea that because America has geographical, economic and political advantages, it has a responsibility to use those advantages well and (sometimes) to assume a position of global leadership.

have done so. Communism was crumbling as an economic system, and although revolutionary socialism survived as a way of organising politics, the free market had begun to creep into communist economies. The recession of the 1970s, the degradation of politics by three presidents, one a criminal and two widely thought to be unfit for high office, the stalling of any real progress towards further civil rights, and humiliation in warfare in Vietnam, had prompted some Americans to think that the dream had become a nightmare. By the end of the so-called Reagan Revolution the Cold War was won, a new wave of prosperity was beginning and American culture was so dominant that historians such as Francis Fukuyama came to believe that serious historical change was over, because mankind had found in the American Way the best way to live. It was, it seemed, morning in America.

Major events and themes in American history to 1945

The United States of America had been formed in 1776 when 13 British colonies, arranged along the east coast of North America, had declared independence from the British government, which they perceived as **tyrannical** and oppressive of their rights. Under the leadership of men such as Thomas Jefferson, who wrote the Declaration of Independence, which asserted that all men had the right to 'life, liberty, and the pursuit of happiness', and George Washington, the general who won the Revolutionary War that accompanied the Declaration, a new nation was formed. In 1787 it reformed itself again with a written Constitution, which came into force in 1789.

The young nation soon came to take over the whole central section of the continent on which it found itself. A combination of diplomacy, force and the sense of entitlement that came from the American notion of Manifest Destiny allowed the United States to assume its present territorial boundaries by 1890, to the detriment of the **Native American** populations who already lived there.

The Constitution of the United States of America

In the aftermath of the Revolutionary War, American leaders produced a loose confederation of states, which did not really work. The Constitution produced to address these issues (see Figure 0.2) was designed specifically to strengthen the union between the states, and it was based upon various ideological principles which dated back in some cases to 17th-century England – where they had long-since ceased to operate. It has various key features:

- Separation of powers would ensure that no one branch of government – and no individual – could become too powerful.
- There would be a single executive, called a **president**, whose powers would be heavily limited by the legislature and by the judiciary, the **Supreme Court**.
- The Constitution would be federalist, which meant that the central Government would be sovereign, and so would the individual states – the Constitution would outline which body was sovereign on each particular issue. The polite fiction – and popular rhetoric – was of course that the people would be sovereign.
- The Constitution could be changed (by amendment) only when there was genuine general agreement that it should be.

Key terms

Cold War: the name for the undeclared hostility and tension between communists and capitalists that began after the Second World War and ended in 1990. During the Cold War the USA assumed a position of leadership of the free, democratic, capitalist world. The leading nation in the communist world was the USSR.

Key terms

Manifest Destiny: the idea that America was and is fated to dominate the continent of North America, the western hemisphere and the world. It drove expansion in the 19th century and helped to define America's foreign policy in the second half of the 20th.

Key terms

Constitution: the set of ideas about how a country should be governed – its institutions, and the **rights** and responsibilities of its government and people.

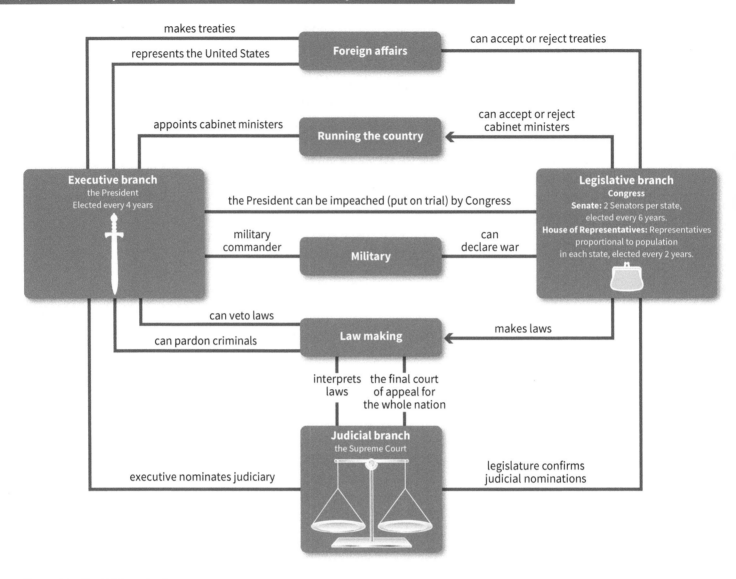

Figure 0.2: The US Constitution.

Race and society in America

The early prosperity of the United States had been partly founded on the institution of slavery; the slaves were black. From 1861 to 1865 there had been a civil war caused in large part by a disagreement over the question of whether slavery should continue; the northern states, in which slavery had stopped and where it was unprofitable, had emerged victorious over the southern states. The results for the South were catastrophic. White southern Americans had lost a destructive war fought mainly in their territory; their slaves had been emancipated, meaning that they had lost a considerable portion of their assets. They had, however, for the most part retained their land. Black Americans, increasingly to be identified as African Americans, had been left more or less at the mercy of the hostile white population. They owned no land, and had little education; they were not allowed to use many public facilities (a process known as '**segregation**' and based on 'Jim Crow' laws – see Figure 0.3) and there were large numbers of extra-judicial killings of black people – known as lynchings.

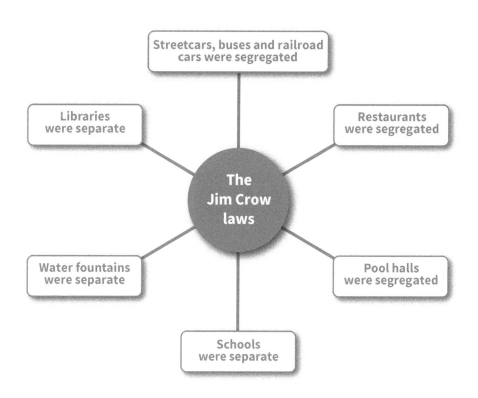

lynching: an extra-judicial killing by a mob. In the popular image, this usually meant the hanging of a young black man from a tree, although not all lynchings were hangings. The vast majority of victims were black; many who were not were Hispanic. More than a hundred lynchings occurred every year in the South throughout the 1890s.

Figure 0.3: Jim Crow laws in the South.

By 1945 the position of African Americans in the South had barely changed, but millions of African Americans had moved to the North. There was certainly racism among white populations in the North, and there was lynching; African Americans were more likely than not to live in poverty, but conditions were still better in the North than in the South. Black leaders had sought and suggested a number of solutions – from the development of black leadership, to wholesale acquiescence, to leaving America entirely to go back to Africa (a policy that was of some alarm to African governments).

A New York City play of 1909 had been the first to refer to that city as a 'melting pot'. This meant that people of different races met in New York City and mixed together freely. Very little could have been further from the truth. Lower Manhattan was (and is) a patchwork quilt of ethnicities – Chinese here, Italians there, and so forth. There was always the potential for conflict between nationalities in the great cities, which were largely in the more urbanised North.

In the South, the ethnic divisions were even clearer. There, segregation was commonplace and legally protected; lynching went unpunished; the black community was itself divided over what to do about it. Those whose families had been slaves in the 1860s were free in 1945, but their freedom was circumscribed by violence, racism and an almost complete lack of civil rights. The South, although urbanising, was still largely agricultural.

The American West, home of the cowboy in the late 19th century, was very badly affected by the Depression. Overfarming and drought turned parts of Oklahoma and Texas into a dustbowl. There was still, out West, plenty of room for expansion.

The Depression and the New Deals

The Wall Street Crash of 1929 had started a chain of events that had led to a serious economic depression in America. It had also led to the election of President Franklin Delano Roosevelt (FDR), whose philosophy was to be as active as possible in addressing America's economic problems, see what worked and continue those policies. His economic policies are known together as the New Deals (as in, 'A New Deal for the American people'). From 1933 to 1939 he stabilised the American economy through a combination of economic stimulus, infrastructure spending and social security; most importantly, though, he established a number of federal agencies that both altered the balance of American federalism, taking power away from the individual states, and increased the power of the president himself. Whether the New Deals would have worked in stabilising the American economy long term is an interesting but moot point; American economic progress was faltering on the eve of the Second World War, but vastly helped by the outbreak of hostilities. America became able to lend money and sell weapons to the Allies; unemployment, which had been high in the 1930s, was all but eliminated.

American politics

From 1865 to 1945 there were only two political parties with a realistic chance of winning either the presidency of the United States or control of **Congress**. These were the Republicans and the Democrats. The Republicans were the more right-wing party, but they were also the party of African Americans as they had been the party of Lincoln, the northern Republican president who had emancipated the slaves in the Civil War. Since the Civil War the Democrats had barely won the presidency, needing some form of crisis to help them to beat the Republicans. In 1932, in the midst of the economic crisis, they had won again: Franklin Roosevelt was a Democrat. He created a 'New Deal coalition' of voters who voted for him again and again (he won four presidential elections; nobody else had won more than two). The Democrats were becoming the party of the urban North, with its poor immigrants and internal migrants, many of whom were African American. They still retained the support of the South.

America 1945–1980: major themes

As you read this book, you will be able to build a narrative – in fact several narratives, should you choose – of American history. There are also certain themes to draw out:

- What did the American Dream mean, and how did that change over time? How far did people in America actually live it?
- How prosperous was America, and was that prosperity shared equally, if shared at all?
- What did it mean to be American? Was it solely defined in opposition to being 'un-American'?
- What made American **democracy** distinctive, and how did it develop?

You should attempt to trace these themes, where appropriate, throughout your studies.

How far was the American Dream a reality?

The American Dream was defined in 1931 like this: 'Life should be better and richer and fuller for everyone, with opportunity for each according to ability or achievement'. Where a person was born, or to whom, should not matter. The American Dream is about liberty and prosperity. In 1941, nearly half of all white families and almost 90% of black families lived in poverty. One in seven workers was unemployed. By 1945 unemployment was negligible. The US commanded half the world's manufacturing capacity and more than half the world's electricity, owned two thirds of the world's gold stocks and half of all its monetary reserves. It produced twice as much petrol as the rest of the world combined. It had the world's largest merchant fleet, a near monopoly of the emerging industries of aerospace and electronics – and, for a time, a monopoly of the technology of atomic power. The seeds of the coming consumer boom had been sown. The American Government was also able to set itself at the centre of a (western) world system of finance. The Bretton Woods System, set up in 1944 and activated in 1945, stabilised world finance by pegging currencies to gold and to each other and created the World Bank and International Monetary Fund. The general idea was to ensure that trade could carry on openly, without countries seeking to put undue pressure on one another. From an American point of view this was perfect as it gave the country access to more markets for its economic surplus – and this money could be used to ensure that the American Dream came true.

 Thematic link: American Dream

How far was American prosperity shared by all Americans?

Some Americans benefited from all this cash – many Americans, in fact, and the numbers of Americans in dire poverty decreased. The Servicemen's Readjustment Act, known informally as the GI Bill of 1944, enabled massive government-funded expansion of higher education and government-backed mortgages, spurring home ownership for the many, many young Americans who had fought in the Second World War. Poverty remained, though, and some were excluded from participation in the rising tide of prosperity.

One of the most famous dreams of the period was 'a dream deeply rooted in the American Dream', expressed by the African-American civil rights leader Martin Luther King, Jr, that segregation would end and that people of all races would live in harmony in an integrated American community. Life for African Americans has improved dramatically since 1945; they have access to justice, can vote, are not formally excluded from any part of civil society, and are no longer brutally and randomly attacked. All this is theoretically true – but there are dramatic counter examples even from the 21st century. Moreover, African Americans are disproportionately poor, and even without the influence of the racism still endemic in American society, poor Americans did not experience the American Dream to anything like the extent of the rich.

Thematic link: prosperity

How did Americans view themselves at home and abroad?

If America's new position in the world made geopolitical and economic sense, and the example of American **isolationism** after the First World War made it clear that, this time, the victory had to be exploited, that was well enough: there were also other reasons for America to accept her place as the leading nation of the democratic world. During the American Civil War of 1861–65, President Abraham Lincoln had fought to keep the United States united, declaring that American democracy served as an example to all mankind. This was just one reason why America was exceptional. In the 19th century many Americans had accepted America's 'Manifest Destiny' to dominate the continent and the hemisphere, to create a nation founded on the ideology of individual freedom. Here, now, was America's chance to spread that ideology around the world.

The new world order was one of constant though undeclared war. The Cold War pitted the United States against another country that had emerged from the Second World War victorious: the Union of Soviet Socialist Republics. The USSR had been severely damaged by German invasion in a way that America had not, and started off behind in the race for global supremacy. The alliances of wartime turned very quickly to rivalry. It was clear that only the USSR could challenge the Americans, and they had economic and ideological reasons to do so. If the USA sought world domination for its ideological system of democracy, so did the USSR, which saw itself as the first stage in a programme of socialism for the entire world. Free-market capitalism, with limited safeguards designed to prevent the disaster of another stock market crash, was incompatible with centrally planned communist economies. The Cold War was an ideological and economic struggle, given extra spice by the presence of nuclear weapons, and led in the West by America's president. In his **inaugural address** in 1961 the new president, John F. Kennedy, addressed the whole world as he accepted the challenge of world leadership on behalf of the USA. By the 1980s President Ronald Reagan was happy to characterise the USSR as the 'evil empire' of dangerous atheists who would like nothing more than to subvert Americans away from truth, justice and the American Way.

Being 'American' had always mattered. To be un-American was inherently suspicious. Perhaps, if you were not American, you were a communist – a spy sent by the 'evil empire'. Perhaps, if you questioned the legitimacy of a war that was achieving nothing other than the deaths of young men, you were un-American. How far did the soldiers of the Vietnam War, whose average age was 19, live the American Dream? And how much of a crisis did defeat in Vietnam pose to American identity?

Thematic link: identity

What was the nature of American democracy?

The Cold War era was an era of protest. It was an era of extraordinary public condemnation of the government of a kind that seems commonplace to us but was not at the time. We tend to remember the occasions on which protestors were attacked by dogs, or shot, or locked up, but the remarkable thing about American protest was how many people were involved and how much effect it actually had. One of the fundamental contradictions of the period is this: the American government could during the Cold War deploy troops across the world and exercise moral leadership for the majority of the most developed nations of the world, but it still had to listen to protests in its own cities. Soviet leaders in the USSR would never have put up with this kind of behaviour, and they said so.

There is also a story to tell about high politics during this time. The dominance of the Democratic Party was based on a **New Deal** coalition of white southerners, organised labour and northern workers. It was formed in 1932, consolidated by FDR, held together by Truman and appealed to by every subsequent Democratic presidential candidate in this period. Over time this coalition fractured and became harder to put together, most clearly in the white South, with Reagan's election marking, overtly, the end of the Democratic 'Solid South' and making it harder for Democrats to win the White House and, eventually, Congress.

 Thematic link: democracy

How to use this book

This book is intended to provide a chronological and thematic overview of American history from 1945 to 1980. Inevitably, some topics and events are left out, or given slightly less weight than others. The authors hope that this book will be a starting point for your study, rather than its end. We would encourage you to look at the past from different perspectives. In particular, you should remember that the vast majority of Americans who lived during the hundred years you are studying were not presidents or members of Congress. Although leaders can be very important, particularly in times of crisis, the culture and prosperity of any country are built upon its ordinary people.

As you read, remember that we, as authors, are historians like any other. We present a version of the past that we believe to be accurate. Because we are writing a textbook, we also present alternative views of American history, and try to give you a flavour of the additional reading you might find, and what it might tell you. If we present something as a fact, it means that we have checked it and believe it to be true. If we present something as an opinion, it is just that: our opinion, and it is no more or less valid than anyone else's opinion simply because we have put it in a textbook.

The individual chapters of the textbook are arranged by presidency: it is up to the reader to decide whether this is a helpful way of arranging their thoughts. The chapters are then further arranged into thematic sections about politics, economics, international relations, etc. Many of the themes of American history transcend particular periods; the four themes outlined in the section entitled 'America 1945–1980: major themes' are identified when they occur in the textbook, to help you to build up your own picture of how much America changed from 1945 to 1980, and what caused these changes. As you work through this course you should consider these themes, and when you revise you might wish to revisit them.

Although candidates for the AS examination need only work through this book to the end of Chapter 3, they are encouraged to read through Chapter 4 as well to gain some idea of what happened next; they should take care to base their answers only on events up to the end of Kennedy's presidency in November 1963.

America in 1945 was richer than it had ever been before, and it successfully maintained its prosperity. The consumer boom of the 1950s, which was based on that prosperity, improved American lives and enabled many more Americans to live the American Dream securely. Not everyone benefited all the time. By 1963, calls for civil rights for African Americans had reached fever pitch. In the world as a whole, the American policy of Cold War **brinkmanship** had nearly resulted in a nuclear conflagration. Meanwhile, the consensus in American society – those parts of American society that were not seeking civil rights – was on the verge of collapse amidst a sea of protest. It had not collapsed yet. America's leadership of the free world had, by 1963, reached its apex.

However, the prosperity that came in the 1950s, and which in many ways came to define it, was not universally shared. The growing American middle class dominated the growing American culture to the extent that their dominance became overstated; not every American drove an automobile, responded to advertising and lived in suburbia. Nor did every American teenager watch rebellious movies, listen to rock and roll music and read the Beat poets. There were still a number of competing ideas about what it was to be American; some of them, though, were drowned out to an even greater extent than they had been before. Nor was the image of the United States as the champion of the free world entirely unsullied abroad. Its management of its 'own' sphere of influence, the Americas, was not entirely smooth in the 1950s and 1960s; the growth of communications satellites ensured that the various outrages committed by those opposing civil rights gave pause to those worldwide who would see the United States as the leaders of the free world, and the 'them or us' narrative of the Cold War was openly challenged as countries such as Egypt declared themselves 'non-aligned'. The America that Lyndon Johnson inherited when his predecessor John F. Kennedy was assassinated had more problems than the myths surrounding Kennedy might suggest.

We will evaluate the extent of and reasons for the changes in American society from 1945 to 1963. We will analyse and evaluate source material from a range of Americans and observers of American life from 1945 to 1963. We will examine different ideas about the successes and failures of American presidents in addressing the needs of America from 1945 to 1963. In this part of the book you will build a sense of the way in which the American economy continued to grow – and grow, and grow, and grow – leaving America a place in which the consumer society had taken hold. You will think about the way in which that economic growth at home led to changes in American views about how fairly that wealth should be distributed, and you will consider whether the other social changes that were occurring, particularly in the sphere of civil rights, were prompted by that economic growth. To refer to the metaphor often used to describe the distribution of wealth within a society, it is far easier to argue about who should have the biggest slice of the pie when there is enough pie to go around. Finally, you will think about how America's global position and its domestic politics were linked.

1 Truman and Post-war America, 1945–1952

In this section, we will examine the presidency of Harry S. Truman. More powerful in global terms than any president had been before, Truman assumed leadership of the free world in the global conflict that arose between the two principal victors of the Second World War. We will examine the way in which hostility to communism, the political system espoused by America's opponents, came to dominate political life. We will also examine the legal (and therefore perhaps apparently insubstantial) gains made by African Americans in this period. We will look into:

- The United States in 1945 and the legacies of the world war: the powers of the presidency; the main political parties; post-war prosperity; regional, ethnic and social divisions.

- The USA as a Superpower: Truman's character and policies; post-war peace making; the Cold War and 'containment' in Europe and Asia; the response to the rise of communism in Asia.

- Truman and post-war reconstruction; the economy; political divisions and domestic problems; the rise of McCarthyism.

- African Americans in North and South: the impact of the Second World War; campaigns for civil rights; the responses of the federal and state authorities.

Introduction: an accidental president

Harry S. Truman was the seventh accidental president – a vice president promoted following the death of his predecessor – but unlike the elevations of the previous six accidental presidents, his accession to the presidency cannot have come as much of a surprise. Franklin Delano Roosevelt (FDR) had seemed unwell for the whole of 1944, and there had been speculation that he would not stand again in the election of that year. Truman had not been a consistent supporter of Roosevelt; he had opposed his seeking a third term, let alone a fourth. He did, however, admire his predecessor for his war leadership and for his New Deal. Truman's career in charge of the **Senate** Special Committee to Investigate the National Defense Program had gained him an excellent reputation as someone who could negotiate to ensure that neither Big Business nor **Organized Labor** could be allowed to inflate defence costs during the war. His influence was recognised by *Time* magazine; he gained his nomination off the back of his administrative ability rather than his great ideas.

Truman's reputation is a difficult one to quantify. He himself had despaired of re-election in 1948, before committing himself to the campaign; in 1952, although eligible to run again, he recognised that he had no hope of victory. Following, as he did, the longest-serving president in US history – whose reputation was only enhanced by the victories that so swiftly followed his death – he was always likely to struggle to gain the affection of the public. As the man responsible for realigning the economy following an all-out ('total') war, he was always likely to shoulder the blame for disruption that would be caused. And as the first president to fight the Cold War, he found himself making some of the rules for a game the other major player of which, Soviet leader Josef Stalin, was ruthless, obtuse and opportunistic.

The United States in 1945 and the legacies of the world war

Truman, for much of the war, had been the man responsible for ensuring that America's wartime production was well directed and free from waste. Now he found himself in the Oval Office – not entirely unexpectedly given Roosevelt's obvious ill health. The war he inherited was rapidly replaced by another, this one undeclared, and then ultimately by a real shooting war on the other side of the world in Korea. He found himself with real domestic problems to face – real reconstruction to be done – but also with wars to win, communists (both real and imagined) to deal with, and a hostile Congress all too aware that his presidency had been delivered by a Democratic back-room fix and the infirmity of a revolutionary president already counted among the honoured dead of a righteous war.

When Roosevelt died on 12 April 1945, Truman was thrust into the steepest learning curve in history. He found a war machine directly managed by the president – Roosevelt had been the only member of the Cabinet with an overview of national security or of defence. Worse, Truman was briefed early in his presidency on the existence of the atomic bomb, which he would use less than four months after assuming office. Truman faced the difficulty of following a great president whose record had got him reelected three times and whom he could

Figure 1.1: Truman had this sign on his desk.

1. List the major issues or problems that you think Truman faced when he inherited the presidency. Discuss with the rest of your class which of these issues might have been:

   - the most urgent
   - the most difficult for Truman to deal with.

2. As you read this chapter, make a note of the occasions on which Truman used his presidential powers. Do you agree with his assessment that he had only the power to persuade?

Key terms

Executive Orders: the use by the president of his power as head of the executive branch to make things happen, not by ordering people as their president, but by ordering them as their boss.

hardly attempt to emulate for fear of being compared unfavourably with the great man; nor could he abandon Roosevelt's agenda. He trod carefully for his first half-year, winning the war before turning his attention to the peace.

Truman's agenda at home was centred on keeping the USA as economically sound as he could while bringing the country back from its war footing, and not risking the economy's helpful forward momentum. This was quickly joined by an agenda abroad; the uneasy alliance with the USSR had degenerated into suspicion and then into outright hostility. There were certainly communist spies in the States; there were more in the public's imagination, and Truman found himself dealing with a **Red Scare** in which enemy infiltrators were seen at the heart of American life. Truman was the president who, more than any other, would set the tone for the Cold War.

The powers of the presidency

The formal, constitutional powers of the presidency had not been changed since 1789, but the presidency Truman inherited in 1945 was more powerful than it had ever been. In theory, while presidents were entitled to propose legislation, that was really the prerogative of Congress. FDR had created an entire programme of legislation, the New Deal, designed to give the **federal government** the power to manage the economy and stimulate growth when necessary. That the federal government should do this was controversial; that the president should be in charge of it was more so. By 1933, when Roosevelt had taken over, the situation in America was so desperate because of the Depression that a radical solution was needed. His solution – the creation of federal agencies to coordinate and carry out economic policy – created a large amount of work. Truman inherited a presidency with more to do than ever before, and the civil service around him was not big enough to do it.

Roosevelt had then been faced with the Second World War. He had run the war without much reference to Congress or the Supreme Court, sometimes using Executive Orders to do so. The bigger the federal government, the more people were affected by Executive Orders. The precedent set by Lincoln in the Civil War and renewed by Wilson in the First World War was now established: in wartime the president had very great powers over foreign policy, and was expected to use them. The Cold War would ensure that the United States existed in a state of constant war for generations to come. The president's military power as commander-in-chief is constitutionally enshrined, but heavily circumscribed, as only Congress is allowed to declare war, and only Congress controls the military budget. So it was that the Cold War was undeclared and the Korean War was referred to as a 'police action'.

And still, the presidency was not as powerful as one might imagine. Presidents do not have, as prime ministers do, an automatic majority in their legislature. Truman found neither the Democratic Congress he inherited nor the Republican one that replaced it in 1947 to be amenable to his wishes. The man who remains the only leader ever to order the detonation in war of a nuclear device bemoaned his lack of power thus: 'I sit here all day trying to persuade people to do the things they ought to have sense enough to do without my persuading them. That's all the powers of the President amount to.' With Truman began the image of the president as persuader-in-chief. His eventual successor Lyndon B. Johnson would go further: 'The only power I've got is nuclear, and I'm not allowed to use it.'

The main political parties

The main political parties in America remained, in Truman's time, the Democrats and the Republicans. The Republicans had taken the blame for the Depression because they had controlled all the branches of government throughout the 1920s. The Democrats, led by FDR, had won back the White House, the House of Representatives and the Senate in 1933, and in 1945 they retained them still. The Democratic Party was not entirely united – FDR had campaigned in the congressional elections of 1938 against some members of his own party. Broadly, the 'New Deal coalition' consisted of farmers from the Midwest, southerners and workers in the cities. Encouraged by the gains made in the New Deal, some black people had also begun to vote Democratic.

It is now fashionable to stress the importance of the anti-New Deal politics of the immediate post-war years, seeing the astonishing Republican gains in 1946 as evidence of this (the Republican slogan was 'Had Enough?'). While the Second World War had greatly aided the ability of the government to do things ('state capacity' in the jargon of political science) it also rehabilitated big business who had been the arsenal of democracy and gave them huge power to achieve goals such as an end to price controls and limits on labour power as soon as peace came. The 1946 Republican intake were in a powerful position, having taken control of Congress. They were able to pass the Taft–Hartley Act, which enabled states to pass 'right to work' laws. At the same time the liberal New Deal alliance was fracturing – with social democrats such as Henry Wallace on one side and conservative southerners on the other.

The New Deal coalition seemed to have broken apart in the 1948 election, when Truman faced two rebellious factions, both of whom put up presidential candidates. In the 'miracle of 1948' he nevertheless defeated the Republicans. The main policies identified by each party at this election can be seen in Table 1.1. The media and opinion pollsters entirely overestimated the extent to which Truman would lose votes, and predicted a Dewey victory.

Henry Wallace, Truman's left-wing Democratic opponent who identified as a progressive, opposed him largely on the issue of foreign policy – which meant communism. He had announced his candidacy in 1947, not long after leaving the cabinet. Wallace's candidacy rested on assumptions that gained more traction at the time than they have among historians. First, Truman was overreacting in his aid programme to the countries of Europe that had suffered in the Second World War, and wasting American money. Second, Stalin would not be all that bad an opponent if only handled properly, and Truman did not handle him as well as Roosevelt. Truman was therefore being too tough on international communism, to the detriment of the United States. Early polls suggested that Wallace might get over 5% of the Democratic vote; with the benefit of hindsight we can see that his candidacy helped Truman by allowing Truman to demonstrate, in the midst of the Red Scare, that he (unlike the conciliatory Wallace) was tough on Reds.

Truman's other opponent, Strom Thurmond, identified himself as a **Dixiecrat**, a '**States' Rights**' Democrat, and opposed Truman because Truman had begun to advocate civil rights and supported the state of Israel. Thus began the movement that would ultimately see the Solid South re-align itself with the Republican Party, while African Americans voted Democratic instead. Moderate support for civil rights turned at the 1948 Democratic Party Convention, at which the party's presidential candidate would be nominated, to radical support. This was a political decision: Democratic bosses knew that it would split their party, but calculated that gains among African-American populations in the northern cities would more than make up for the loss of parts of the South. Meanwhile, Truman's unsuccessful attempt to **veto** the anti-labour Taft–Hartley Bill in 1947, which had been overwhelmingly popular in Congress, had given him the labour vote. The Democrats had realigned themselves to become the party of the cities. The Republicans, on the other hand, were in disarray. With no threat that their party would split they were forced into an uneasy compromise. There had been no member of Congress able to win the nomination; the compromise candidate, Thomas Dewey, was more liberal than the rest of his party, which did not approve of his agenda. Truman highlighted this by calling a special session of the 80th Congress, which he had labelled 'Do Nothing', and inviting them to pass their own candidate's legislation. They declined.

With the splits in the Democratic Party in 1948, the issue of what Democrats believed had been set for a generation: those who did not accept Truman's positions would gradually be squeezed out of the party. In the Republican Party, all that was clear was that the party was deeply split over the role of the government in regulating the economy and society. In the country, 'Do Nothing' turned out to be an unpopular position for Congress to have taken.

Voices from the past

The 'Do Nothing' Congress

Extracts from 'Turnip Day in Washington' by Michael Straight, *New Republic* magazine, 26 July 1948, an article about Truman's decision to recall the 80th Congress for a special session in 1948.

On three key issues, housing, inflation and civil rights, the 80th Congress so far failed utterly …

Housing. Four million American homes must be provided for this year. Passage of the Taft-Ellender-Wagner bill which provides for 15 million new homes in 10 years by public housing, slum clearance and aid to private construction, is the first priority … Full hearings have been held on the bill. It was passed months ago by the Senate. Obeying the orders of the National Association of Real Estate Boards and the National Association of Home Builders, the House Republicans … have prevented the bill from coming to the House for a vote. Instead, they jammed through a fake housing bill. …

Civil-rights legislation … Both parties are absolutely committed to passage of such legislation. The Republican Party platform calls for "prompt enactment" of an anti-lynching law, and federal legislation to abolish discrimination, the poll tax, and segregation in the armed forces. The Democratic platform supports all these proposals and more …

Inflation … Wholesale and retail prices reached all-time peaks this month … 13 million American families have been forced by inflation to use up most or all of their savings.[1]

Democratic policies 1948 (Truman and whole party)	Republican policies 1948 (Dewey)	Republican policies 1948 (Congressional leadership)
Civil rights are very important – abandons the idea of states' rights to segregate	No need to modify civil rights laws	No need to modify civil rights laws
Workers' rights, delivered by the New Deal, must be preserved	Expansion of social security and increased funding for public housing	Restriction of labour rights
Communism should not be allowed to spread abroad	Anti-communism	Anti-communism at home and abroad
Farmers should be supported to ensure their prices remain high	Price controls should be enacted	Protective tariffs should be enacted
Expansion of healthcare as part of social security	Federal government to take control of health and education	Reduce income taxes to stimulate growth
The president and Congress should be active in government	The president and Congress should be active in government	Government should be small and not do very much

Table 1.1: Main policy platforms of the main parties in 1948.

Figure 1.2: The *Chicago Tribune*'s inaccurate headline, 3 November 1948.

ACTIVITY 1.2

Look at Table 1.1. To whom do you think Truman's policies would have appealed, and why?

Post-war prosperity

The USA had many advantages after the Second World War. Its competitors were crippled economically. The best-off of the European powers was probably Britain, and it was on the verge of economic collapse, shedding its empire as it collapsed. During the war Americans had saved $140 billion as war bonds; although releasing this money back to the savers would affect the government's own finances, it would also provide them with spending power to stimulate demand in the economy, and help military producers to adapt their assembly lines for consumer goods.

The economic boom of the United States was not a given in 1941. The first issue was what to do with returning servicemen, who would need jobs which did not yet exist. The $13 billion provided in the GI Bill of Rights of 1944 for returning soldiers to start businesses or go to college created two groups neither of which added to unemployment; both groups in different ways repaid the investment in them by bringing skills or productivity to the economy. Although he had his differences with Congress over the best way in which to manage post-war reconstruction, Truman was able to run for re-election on an economic platform, pointing to low unemployment.

Regional, ethnic and social divisions

America in 1945 had distinct regions. The Northeast, centred culturally around New England but financially on New York City, was the commercial hub. Its cities had an ethnic mix founded on decades of immigration into New York; there were also substantial communities of African Americans who had migrated to the northern cities in the 20th century. There was in this region a tension between the **White Anglo-Saxon Protestant** (WASP) communities that had existed in the area from deep in the 19th century and some of the other communities. New York City, sometimes described as a 'melting pot', was no such thing: its communities were widely dispersed, and different ethnic and cultural groups had their own areas of town – Jewish tailors in the garment district and Italians in Little Italy, for example.

The American Midwest, centred around Chicago, had much in common with the Northeast, and its cities were similarly mixed. Farming concerns carried more weight out here, and miners too. The area was also the home of the American auto industry. General Motors and Ford were based in Detroit, Michigan. There were tensions between Big Business and Organized Labor, inevitably, and also between the productive heartland of America and the financiers to the East.

The West, those lands west of the Mississippi that had been settled in the 19th century at the expense of the Native Americans, was as ever the land of farmers and ranchers, the modern-day cowboys. The small farms originally settled by the pioneers had tended to agglomerate into larger farms. Truman himself had suffered the indignity of the foreclosure of his family farm and its absorption into something larger. Agribusiness was being born. The major concern of westerners was that farm prices should be sufficiently high that farmers could make a living. The far West – the Pacific states of Washington, Oregon and California, shared many of these characteristics, although Los Angeles, CA, in particular, had similar ethnic diversity to a northern city. It was otherwise very different – western urban living had none of the high-density tenements and slums that were so common out East.

The final region, the South, had until recently relied on an agricultural system of tenant farming and sharecropping. Devastated by the Oklahoma and Arkansas dustbowls, but at least partly reinvigorated by the Tennessee Valley Authority, the agency that had, under President Roosevelt's direction, sought to bring electrical power and other infrastructure to the region, it was clear that the South would need economic development in addition to the massive transformation caused by military spending in the Second World War – most of the training camps were in the South (or the far West). The South was the home of most of the African-American population; it was also the home of segregation – although segregation happened in the North as well. The economic crisis of the 1930s and the Second World War had taken the focus away from the issue of African Americans' rights in the South, but it seemed by 1945 that this would be a problem requiring some form of action soon.

 Thematic link: prosperity

Americans had tended to pull together during the Second World War. This is not to say that Roosevelt found that his countrymen were entirely united; there were strikes, which Roosevelt solved, and there was still tremendous poverty across the nation. By 1946, though, any sense of national emergency had dissipated. So, too, had Truman's political honeymoon. The strikes of 1946 (which are discussed in more detail in the section on Political divisions and domestic problems) were caused by a combination of inflation and consistently low wages. The depression and war that had persuaded workers to accept such conditions had gone: instead, there were fears from those who were in work (nearly everyone) that soldiers returning from the front would take the jobs of those who had stayed behind. Even in a situation of nearly full employment there were tensions between those whose position in society still seemed tenuous; these were eased by the GI Bill of Rights of 1944, which kept so many returning soldiers away from the jobs market.

That was the situation in the more industrial parts of the country. In the agricultural areas, things were slightly different. Roosevelt's New Deal policies had barely helped the worst-off farmers, and a long-standing trend continued: smallholders came under pressure to sell out to larger landowners, and 'agribusiness' – large, conglomerated farms – came to the fore. This disrupted traditional communities across the Midwest and Plains states. The concept of the family farm came to be undermined, and with it the job security of millions of Americans in states such as Iowa, Kansas and Nebraska. Southern small farms went the same way; in the South, though, the question of social standing was coming to be tied up with the question of ethnic origin. There were poor whites in the South, and there were poor blacks; the separateness caused by their different ethnicity was more important than any common feeling caused by their common poverty.

The USA as a Superpower

The USA was a Superpower because it had emerged so strongly in military and economic terms from the Second World War. That status was not impregnable, as Truman quickly realised. British sea power had now gone, meaning that the USA could not rely upon their ally to protect their interests in the Atlantic and to police the Indian Ocean; the USA would have to take on the British role, which had essentially been to ensure the balance of power in Europe and Asia. Had any one hostile nation – Germany, say – taken over Europe, US interests would have been threatened. They were no less threatened by potential Soviet dominance. From a Soviet point of view, Stalin, the leader of the Union of Soviet Socialist Republics (USSR, or Soviet Union – a communist state founded out of the ruins of the old Russian Empire), was convinced that there would soon be a conflict between the communist and capitalist worlds. This conviction persuaded him to take actions that would help to cause this conflict. The USA had to act fast to preserve its Superpower status, preferably embedding its new status while it still possessed exclusive access to nuclear weapons.

Superpower status seemed also to bring a particular sense of responsibility with it. One area in which this was expressed was the Middle East. In 1948 the British had retreated from control there, unable to sustain their power because of their failing post-war economy. There were, in the aftermath of the Holocaust, persuasive calls for a Jewish homeland to be established in Israel. Truman backed these calls for domestic electoral reasons, as well as out of a sense of American guilt over turning Jewish refugees away in the late 1930s and in order to, as he said, see that justice was done. The identification of America as Israel's greatest ally, and the importance of the Jewish vote in New York, New Jersey and ultimately Florida, have been compelling themes in American foreign policy ever since.

Truman's character and policies

Truman had a reputation for plain-speaking honesty and high moral standards, but he was also a pragmatic politician seeking to further the interests of America and the Democratic Party, in that order. His foreign policies can be seen in this light. His presidency was largely defined – perhaps haunted – by one of his earliest decisions, which was to drop an atomic bomb on Japan not once, but twice. The bomb that destroyed Hiroshima on 6 August 1945 killed around 150 000 people. Truman used it as a way to end the war quickly; he believed that continuing the slow dismantling of the Japanese Empire would take another year and cost at least half a million lives. He did not imagine that another bomb would be needed, three days later. The ethical justification for what Truman did is debated still, and the moral significance of his decision was clear to him from the very start. In 1946, through the United Nations, he attempted to surrender the USA's atomic weapons capability to the UN, and open up to weapons inspectors, on condition that the USSR abandoned their own research and did the same. Stalin refused.

Truman had learnt about nuclear weapons only on becoming president. This was part of the reason for his creation of a **National Security Council** (NSC), of which the vice president was a member, so that no future vice president would be so unaware of something so vital, and might have more of an opportunity than

Truman himself had had to prevent such a long-term plan from going ahead. The NSC also helped to pull together the work of the new **Central Intelligence Agency (CIA)**, which had been created as an agency of war, and the **State Department**, in monitoring intelligence reports. Truman created the Department of Defense, realising that under Roosevelt only the president had commanded both the Army and the Navy. His professionalisation of the American war machine was partly a response to the Second World War, and partly a realisation that the Cold War was becoming embedded in American life. Just like any conventional war, there were other effects on American life: the military draft continued; military spending grew; a national-security state based on secrecy grew up, which demanded public trust without public accountability.

Post-war peace making

Truman's first overseas mission was to attend the second victors' conference of 1945, in July and August at Potsdam. His problem there was that FDR had misrepresented the first, in February at Yalta. He had told Congress that the decisions made at Yalta 'ought to spell the end of the system of unilateral action, the exclusive alliances, the spheres of influence, the balances of power, and all the other expedients that have been tried for centuries and have always failed'. In fact, Yalta divided up Europe, producing a clear path for Stalin to create a sphere of influence for himself out of the countries of Eastern Europe. Stalin had perceived an impending conflict between capitalism and communism, and in that sense was more responsible than Truman for the build-up of tensions after 1941. He was not intent on provoking war, but in a long-term build-up of communist power, and in an age-old Russian goal of having some strongly defended states between the USSR and Germany, he sought to forestall any further German invasions. The imposition of communist dictatorships in eastern Europe was the most destabilising thing he did, but it had been foreordained at Yalta. Truman's problem was that he could hardly say so without accusing Roosevelt, his heroic predecessor, of lying.

The conference at Potsdam came a month after the San Francisco Conference to establish the United Nations, at which the Soviet point of view was largely ignored: the United Nations was to be founded on democratic and capitalist principles, and there was certainly no mention of the long-term Russian goal of building up a 'buffer zone' of friendly states in Eastern Europe designed to keep the Germans at bay. At Potsdam, Truman was forced to tell Stalin about the impending atomic attack on Japan – Stalin had known about the existence of nuclear weapons for some time, and did not even bother to pretend to be surprised. Truman was also forced to concede that the plans made at Yalta for free and fair elections in liberated Europe would not be honoured – there would certainly be elections, but Stalin had no intention of allowing them to be free in the countries that the Russians had liberated. The Russians did not play any part in helping to reconstruct Germany, which was divided into four zones of conquest (the others held by Britain and France). Indeed, the Soviets did not believe that the reconstruction of Germany – its planned rebuilding to ensure that it would be able to develop properly and along peaceful lines – should occur. Instead, Truman antagonised Stalin, perhaps by trying to hold him to agreements which, FDR's public statements notwithstanding, had not actually been made at Yalta.

The Potsdam Conference was always supposed to be about thrashing out the detail of the broad agreements made at Yalta; Germany had been defeated, and the general course of the war (not to mention the atomic bomb) made it clear that Japan would soon follow. On almost every major decision made at Potsdam, the Soviet point of view prevailed. Stalin was allowed to impose his will upon eastern Europe, creating a buffer zone of friendly states between the USSR and the old enemy, Germany. For his part, Truman emerged from the conference with a clear path to the end of the war and without reneging on any of Roosevelt's agreements. Perhaps Roosevelt himself might have emerged with more, had he still been alive – or perhaps not. The Soviet 'Red' Army had made more impressive progress through eastern Europe and Germany than had the allies; by Potsdam, all Stalin really had to do was to hold onto what he had already gained through force of arms.

Figure 1.3: Clement Attlee, the new British Prime Minister, Harry Truman and Josef Stalin at Potsdam. Their facial expressions, and the body language of their aides, are interesting.

The Cold War and 'containment' in Europe and Asia, and the response to the rise of communism in Asia

In the early years of the Cold War, Truman had two main aims. The first was to prevent further expansion of the communist (Soviet) sphere of influence. The former British prime minister Winston Churchill had announced in a speech in Missouri, Truman's home, in 1946, that 'an Iron Curtain has descended across Europe'. American strategy was to prevent the **Iron Curtain** from moving any further west. Truman's rhetoric was cloaked in the language of American Exceptionalism, but he stated a simple geopolitical reality: America intended to ensure that it had influence over Europe, and that the Soviet Union's influence was limited. Truman formulated the **Truman Doctrine** in January 1947. He did this to justify his subsequent actions, and also because as a Democratic president faced

	Yalta Conference	**Potsdam Conference**
Date	February 1945	July 1945
Location	Yalta, USSR	Potsdam, Germany
Leading negotiators	Roosevelt (USA), Churchill (UK), Stalin (USSR)	Truman (USA), Churchill then Attlee (UK), Stalin (USSR)
Attitude to Germany	Germany to be divided into four zones of occupation at agreed points.	Germany to be divided at slightly different points as the Soviet army had reached further than expected.
Attitude to Japan	Stalin agreed to enter the war against Japan at some point.	Japan was called upon to surrender; Stalin was asked not to invade Japan (because the Americans did not want to drop the atomic bomb on Soviet troops).
Attitude to eastern Europe	Free and fair elections would be conducted in eastern Europe; the Soviet army would be allowed a free hand there.	USSR would supervise elections in eastern Europe, especially in Poland (where the USSR absorbed some Polish territory). It had already imposed a communist government in Romania.

Table 1.2: The agreements made at Yalta and Potsdam.

with a Republican Congress, he had broad freedom of action in foreign policy, and very little freedom in his domestic policy. The domestic consequences of his rhetoric included the ramping up of the Red Scare. He was trying to avoid turning the situation in Europe into a global anti-communist crusade. He was careful to say that he was not trying to eliminate communism: Stalin was not another Hitler. Instead, he intended to contain it, to prevent it from spreading beyond its borders. His rhetoric was strong enough, though, to speak to Congress in March 1947 of the imposition of totalitarian regimes 'against their [the people's] will', and to make it American policy 'to assist free peoples to work out their own destinies in their own way'. He established a key part of Cold War rhetoric by setting the Americans up as the leaders of the 'free'.

This Truman Doctrine was first tested in Greece. The British had announced that they were withdrawing support for Greece and Turkey because they simply did not have the resources to support them any more. They could not repair the massive damage to their infrastructure – roads, railways, even farmland – which had been caused during the war. The USA stepped up to the plate, and democratic capitalism – or capitalism, at least, was preserved. Truman referred to Greece as potentially the first domino to fall. **Domino theory** would be a key rationale for US policymaking in the Cold War. Truman had seen the pattern in Poland and Hungary: the politics and economies of the newly liberal states would fail; the Soviet Red Army would step in to keep the peace; 'free and fair' elections would then return a communist government. In June 1947, Truman asked the new **Secretary of State** George Marshall to come up with a plan for the reconstruction of Europe using American money; that winter, Congress demurred, unhappy at the cost, but the Czechoslovak communist coup, and the prospect of the same occurring in Italy, focused Congressional minds.

 Key terms

Truman Doctrine: Truman's statement that America would support free peoples resisting subjugation, by which he meant communist rule.

 Key terms

Domino theory: the idea that if a country became communist, other nearby countries might also 'fall' to communism, like dominoes.

Speak like a historian

Arthur M. Schlesinger, Jr, on the Truman Doctrine

The menace of unexpected crisis hung over the world, demanding, it was supposed, the concentration within government of the means of instant decision and response. All this, reinforcing the intellectual doubt about democratic control of foreign relations, appeared to argue more strongly than ever for the centralization of foreign policy in the Presidency.

Such centralization came in stages. The new President had been a senator himself. This was less of an advantage in dealing with Congress than sometimes supposed … [W]hen Truman required congressional consent in foreign policy either because of the need for appropriations (the British loan, the Greek-Turkish aid program, the Marshall Plan) or for treaty ratification (NATO), he succeeded in rallying the necessary support. He also paid a price: to get the policy he had to overcolor the crisis. Thus Senator Vandenberg told him that if he wanted to enlist Congress behind aid to Greece and Turkey, he would have to scare hell out of the country. Truman therefore elevated a reasonable and limited program into a transcendent principle. The result was the Truman Doctrine … Truman himself did not construe his Doctrine in any crusading way, applying it neither to China nor to Eastern Europe, for example, as he applied it to Greece and Turkey. But the sweeping language remained, as did the technique of scaring hell out of the country.[2]

ACTIVITY 1.3

How far are you persuaded that Truman invented the Truman Doctrine for short-term political reasons?

The Marshall Plan was approved on 3 April 1948. Eventually Congress would approve $17 billion in aid between 1948 and 1952. This money went to any country in Europe that wanted it; Britain was a major recipient of aid, and was effectively saved from economic collapse by American help. Marshall Aid was offered to the USSR, with the intention that they should refuse; of course, they did. Italy received aid, which seemed to make the difference between a communist government coming to power there and being resisted. There was also Point Four Plan to spend $400 million in Asia and Latin America in 1949. These were specific counter-measures to Stalin's tactic of sending money into Eastern European countries and allowing local communist parties to distribute it, while also sending in the Soviet army to 'oversee' elections – a tactic that delivered a number of communist governments. This attempt to prevent the expansion of communism was called containment. Truman's second aim, which was linked, was to reconstruct western Europe as quickly as possible to prevent a further war. He was doing the same in Japan. The lessons of the First World War, after which Germany had been punished rather than reconstructed, only to start another war 20 years later, had been learnt.

Figure 1.4 shows the events of this period in Europe. The key crisis came in Berlin in 1948. France, Britain and the USA united their zones of Germany into the Federal Republic of Germany, known as West Germany. Because of the deals done at Yalta and Potsdam, the capital, Berlin, had been divided between those three powers and the USSR, although it was firmly in the Soviet zone of occupation. West Berlin was also unified. This improved the economy of the newly unified German state, and also provided a challenge to Stalin. Stalin's response was to blockade Berlin, cutting transport and power links, on a flimsy pretext. He wanted to take the rest of Berlin as a propaganda victory. Truman was determined not to allow this, and an airlift of fuel and supplies was mounted that lasted 11 months. Stalin lifted the blockade when he had tired of it – or perhaps when he had something else with which to annoy Truman, for in the middle of 1949 the USSR successfully tested its own atomic bomb. In direct response, Truman formed the North Atlantic Treaty Organization (NATO), a defensive alliance stating that if any member country was attacked, all other member countries would support it. This meant that if Stalin attempted to spread communism in Europe the Americans would treat it as a declaration of war on America. The Iron Curtain was fixed in place.

The formation of NATO had not been entirely Truman's idea. He had been working with Senator Arthur Vandenberg, a Republican from Michigan, to form what appeared to be a **bipartisan** foreign policy in 1948. This culminated in the 'Vandenberg Resolution' that passed the Senate in June of that year (see Voices from the past: The Vandenberg Resolution). This advised the president, essentially, to seek to create NATO. The timing of this resolution, which was written by Vandenberg and Undersecretary of State Robert Lovett (Marshall's deputy) in the month following the beginning of the Berlin Crisis, clearly suggests that the two are linked. For 1948 was an election year, and even Truman was not entirely expecting to win – at one point he had entertained persuading General Eisenhower, the Allied Supreme Commander in Europe during the Second World War, to run for president as a Democrat with Truman as his vice presidential running mate. Vandenberg had been mentioned by some, not just in his home state, as a potential candidate for the Republican nomination. Perhaps Truman was trying to ensure that America's foreign policy would have continuity regardless of who was in the White House. Perhaps his administration was working with Vandenberg on foreign policy to highlight the rifts within the Republican Party (Vandenberg was opposed to the influential Republican senator Robert Taft). Or perhaps he wished to show that he, Truman, was willing to step above party politics (unlike the majority of Republicans in this 'Do Nothing' Congress) by working with Vandenberg, who had had a series of dramatic conversions from isolationism (a position that dissolved overnight, he said, because of the Japanese attack on Pearl Harbor on 7 December 1941 that brought the USA into the Second World War) to full internationalism – he had, in 1941, made some of the running in the Senate to bring about the formation, in 1945, of the United Nations.

The Red Scare that Truman faced was the first cultural expression of the Cold War in the United States. There were other real features of this part of foreign policy. The permanent state of war led to a growth in presidential authority; there was, after all, a constant emergency. The military draft was continued, and dissenters were branded as unpatriotic, or traitors. Military spending was also an important factor. The military spending for the Second World War had decisively ended the Great Depression; now many members of the political and economic elite regarded Cold War military spending as a necessary means to forestall the return of depression. Moreover, the 'military-industrial complex' (Eisenhower's term) had grown powerful, and the national security state actively resisted public accountability – especially when those who might do the scrutiny were publicly suspected of communist sympathies. American patriotism developed along the lines of Cold War prestige, pride in the army, and right-wing anti-socialism.

The Cold War in Asia

In Europe, a peaceful solution had been found. In Asia, that would prove less easy. To the horror of the Truman administration and US Congress, the capitalist leader of China, Chiang Kai-Shek, had lost the civil war in his country to Mao Zedong, a communist. By the middle of 1949 the capitalist government had effective control only of the island of Taiwan; there were two Chinas. The communist one, the

People's Republic, immediately set about joining the communist world. Mao had been a revolutionary leader in China for 20 years. He was happy to defer, to an extent, to the leader of the USSR, which had after all managed the first successful communist revolution. He also wanted to spread communism further.

The obvious place was in Korea. The USSR had liberated it from Japanese rule at the same time as the Americans; they had met at the 38th parallel, a line of latitude, and the country had been divided into two zones with different systems of government. By 1950 communist North Korea felt that it might be in a position to take over the whole country. Mao, Stalin and the North Korean leader Kim Il-Sung met in Moscow in January 1950. We do not know exactly what transpired, although a best guess looks something like this: Stalin permitted Kim to invade the South, with Chinese assistance, so long as he, Stalin, and the USSR did not have to become directly involved. In America, meanwhile, the NSC had issued a memorandum, NSC-68, which advocated a more active **containment** – now, communism should be actively contained everywhere, not just in Europe, and not just in opposition to the Soviet Union. The new Secretary of State, Dean Acheson, mindful of this highly secret debate, had appeared to suggest that the Americans

Voices from the past

The Vandenberg Resolution

The Vandenberg Resolution was passed in the Senate on 11 June 1948, a month after it was published. Sections 3 and 4 are particularly relevant to the formation of NATO. The key point about this Resolution is that it was written by a Republican senator and a Democratic member of the State Department.

Whereas peace with justice and the defense of human rights and fundamental freedoms require international cooperation through more effective use of the United Nations: Therefore be it *Resolved*, that the Senate reaffirm the policy of the United States to achieve international peace and security through the United Nations so that armed force shall not be used except in the common interest, and that the President be advised of the sense of the Senate that this Government, by constitutional process, should particularly pursue the following objectives within the United Nations Charter:

1   Voluntary agreement to remove the veto from all questions involving pacific settlements of international disputes and situations, and from the admission of new members.

2   Progressive development of regional and other collective arrangements for individual and collective self-defense in accordance with the purposes, principles, and provisions of the Charter.

3   Association of the United States, by constitutional process, with such regional and other collective arrangements as are based on continuous and effective self-help and mutual aid, and as affect its national security.

4   Contributing to the maintenance of peace by making clear its determination to exercise the right of individual or collective self-defense... should any armed attack occur affecting its national security.

5   Maximum efforts to obtain agreements to provide the United Nations with armed forces as provided by the Charter, and to obtain agreement among member nations upon universal regulation and reduction of armaments under adequate and dependable guaranty against violation.

6   If necessary, after adequate effort toward strengthening the United Nations, review of the Charter at an appropriate time by a General Conference ... or by the General Assembly.[3]

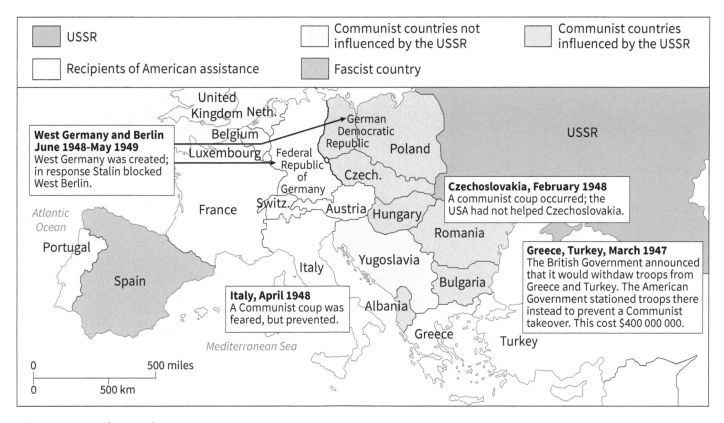

| USSR | Communist countries not influenced by the USSR | Communist countries influenced by the USSR |
| Recipients of American assistance | Fascist country | |

West Germany and Berlin June 1948-May 1949
West Germany was created; in response Stalin blocked West Berlin.

Czechoslovakia, February 1948
A communist coup occurred; the USA had not helped Czechoslovakia.

Italy, April 1948
A Communist coup was feared, but prevented.

Greece, Turkey, March 1947
The British Government announced that it would withdaw troops from Greece and Turkey. The American Government stationed troops there instead to prevent a Communist takeover. This cost $400 000 000.

Figure 1.4: Map of Europe from 1949.

might be willing to leave Korea alone – after all, with China communist they no longer had an ally to protect in the Yellow Sea. Certainly, Kim expected that he would succeed.

The Korean War, when it came in 1950–53, cost millions of dollars and millions of lives. It caught Truman, who was taking a break from Washington, by surprise. His response was to initiate a 'police action' under the auspices of the United Nations; in America, nobody was fooled. He himself lacked the power (reserved for Congress) to declare war. In Berlin, there had been an uneasy stalemate – and nothing changed. In Korea, nothing changed despite the fighting, which was brutal. In June 1950 the North Koreans pushed the South Koreans back so far they nearly won; the Americans responded in force that autumn and nearly destroyed North Korea entirely. By 1951 the war had become a muddy stalemate in the rough vicinity of the original border. Truman had a public row with his commander, General MacArthur, whom he relieved of command. As a result of this Truman confirmed that nuclear weapons were to be for strategic use only, and were to be controlled directly by the civilian authorities – the president. He also confirmed that **rollback** – MacArthur's preferred alternative to containment – would not be acceptable. The Korean War would ultimately ruin the careers of both men: it was so unpopular that Truman was forced to accept that he would not be re-elected if he ran for the presidency in 1952.

Thematic link: identity

27

Figure 1.5: The Iron Curtain Look. This advertisement from *Life* magazine in 1952 shows how the Cold War had become a part of American culture. The text reads: 'On this American model and hanging alongside her is a complete and stylish Soviet wardrobe. The total cost, excluding hat, is $461. … U.S. envoy's wife finds Moscow modes high priced, wide shouldered, not very handsome … The slender gams [thighs] of the girl above give her away as American.'

There are three main interpretations of the causes of the Korean War, which is sometimes known as the Forgotten War because historians paid so little attention to it in its immediate aftermath.

John Lewis Gaddis (*The Cold War*; 1997), a historian who has had tremendous access to the Soviet archives and has also worked in the US Department of Defense, is a leading proponent of the orthodox view that the Korean War was started by the North acting under Stalin's instructions.

Kathryn Weathersby (*To Attack or not to Attack?*; 1995) argues that Kim Il-Sung was to blame, and that Stalin was far too risk averse for such an adventure.

William Stueck (*Rethinking the Korean War*; 2002) argues that the Korean War was a local war whipped up by the Red Scare into something more serious when the USA intervened.

The key questions for historians to consider are:

1. Who started it, and who wanted it?

Kim Il-Sung, the North Korean leader whose family would go on to form a dynasty, would be a clear beneficiary. Any conflict would bolster his personal position, and if the North Koreans succeeded in unifying the country it would double his territory. Mao, the newly confirmed Chinese leader, would certainly benefit from the prestige of being a major actor in the Cold War, if he could provide military support for a successful invasion of South Korea. Removal of the capitalist presence from the Yellow Sea would also be a great help to the geopolitical situation in China. Besides, Mao had no love for the United States, which had supported the government of Chiang Kai-Shek that Mao had overthrown. Stalin, meanwhile, would certainly benefit from the provision for the United States of another distraction from the situation in Europe.

2. Why were the Americans so surprised?

Perhaps the Americans had assumed that the presence of an overwhelming American force in Japan would discourage any communist action on the Korean peninsula. Perhaps they had assumed that the statement in the Truman Doctrine that communism would be contained very obviously applied to Korea – whatever relaxed noises the State Department had been making about the situation in the Yellow Sea. It seems clear that the USA had absolutely no idea what was about to happen.

Truman and post-war reconstruction

Truman was unpopular when he left office, and his reputation was initially poor because he did not seem to have achieved a great deal. In fact, his time in office had been subtly important for a number of reasons. He moved forward with the ideas of the New Deal. He contributed towards civil rights, and towards the Democrats' identification as the party of civil rights. He established some important Cold War principles. He also began the misleadingly named process of post-war reconstruction. In fact, it is more helpful to think of what he did as a

ACTIVITY 1.4

Suggest some reasons why the Cold War so quickly became an integrated part of American culture.

form of realignment, repurposing or perhaps even confirmation that the changes wrought in the 1930s and 1940s were to be permanent.

The economy

The economy Truman inherited was booming. America had massive productive capacity, and complete dominance of the world market. **Lend-lease** meant that the West was in debt to America; war bonds meant that the American people had financed their government, and had plenty of savings. The economic realignment that was needed was to convert wartime production into domestic production, ensuring that American people could buy consumer goods, that new markets were developed in liberated countries (Germany and Japan, liberated from their own governments, would be among these, in contrast to what had happened in 1919) and that momentum was maintained. Meanwhile the Bretton-Woods System, set up in 1944 as a way of managing the post-war world economy, was very favourable to American aims. In particular:

- The newly created International Monetary Fund stabilised world finance.
- A fixed exchange rate stabilised world currencies.
- The General Agreement of Tariffs and Trades (GATT), which came into being along with the United Nations, helped to keep tariffs down and promoted free trade.

The net effect of all this was very favourable for the United States, the only major country with a sizeable manufacturing sector left that was not either massively indebted, ravaged by war, or both. It made trade dependably profitable. If the United States could rebalance its economy to capitalise on this, living standards across America would go up. In the immediate aftermath of the war came that very problem: how to convert the economy from war to peace. A $6 billion tax cut provided a stimulus for growth, but there was immediate discontent among workers. Miners and railroad workers wanted higher wages as they had lost their wartime overtime, thereby reducing their take-home pay. Worse, inflation was running high – around 20% in food prices – and government-imposed price controls on some food stuffs, that were intended to benefit consumers in fact hit farmers, who refused to market their goods at artificially low prices. The issue became even worse when Truman's efforts to get Congress to agree to price controls did not work; Truman, the Missouri farmer, was looking after his own. He was ultimately forced to concede defeat in the face of a serious meat shortage. Truman and Congress were unable to manage the situation, and the cost of living went up by 30% in the second half of 1946. Meanwhile Truman was threatening legislation to draft striking workers into the army so that he could order them to return to work. No wonder the Democrats were hammered in the **mid-term elections** of that year.

Truman's overriding aims appear to have been to ensure domestic stability and to avoid the slump he feared would be coming; the Roaring Twenties had not roared loudly for farmers, and Truman feared that this might happen again, undoing a lot of the work of the New Deal. He also wished to avoid rolling back the gains of the New Deal for labourers, ultimately unsuccessfully vetoing the Taft–Hartley Act of 1947 that diluted the power of the Social Security Act, the New Deal-era legislation that established social security in America.

Thematic link: prosperity

Political divisions and domestic problems

Truman governed in 1947 and 1948 as a president in opposition to the 'Do Nothing' Congress, run by Republicans for the first time in more than a decade. With the cooperation of some southern Democrats, Congress slashed taxes even further and cut government spending – they were trying to roll back the New Deal, and in particular move away from the idea that government spending should be used as a direct economic stimulus. Truman's response was to put forward the 'Fair Deal' – a social programme that was doomed to failure but enabled Truman to be seen to be promoting New Deal ideas such as a national health insurance bill, which was branded 'socialist.' He did achieve a little more in building social security and low-cost housing. 'Levittown' homes were named after the administrator William J. Levitt, who built houses at the rate of 1.5 million a year on the grounds that new houses were needed, especially in the growing suburbs; the policy was also popular among those who thought that nobody who owned his own house could possibly be a communist.

Apart from his difficulties with Congress, Truman's most obvious problem was dealing with industrial unrest. He found himself at odds with the Republicans, anti-New Deal Democrats, and even the Supreme Court. There were 5000 separate strikes in 1946, representing 4.5 million workers. The strikes were not just caused by rising prices. On the whole, both the corporations and the workers believed that they had behaved quite honourably during the Second World War, putting the national interest above their own advantage. Truman had led the Senate Committee, which ensured that this happened. The United Auto Workers strike at General Motors in December 1945 sparked a number of other strikes. Truman became so frustrated that he seized the steel mills on the grounds that the steel was a vital national asset; in 1952 the Supreme Court found this unconstitutional, the first such condemnation of a presidential action since 1866. Truman broke the miners' strike by seizing the mines – the coal strike had paralysed the economy and threatened to do considerable damage. John L. Lewis, the miners' leader, was later fined $10 000 (and his union $1.5 million) by an unsympathetic judge. This was not an all-out attack by Truman on the unions, although it was interpreted as such. It was an attack on Lewis, whom Truman viewed as a racketeer who intended to hold the country to ransom. Truman wanted to sort the situation out and was prepared to use any means to do so; he even tried to persuade Congress to let him draft striking railway workers into the army so that he could order them to work. Truman had also floated the idea of gagging the press on national security grounds. His detractors – both contemporaries and historians – saw in all this an attempt to create a 'National Security State' under which basic freedoms could be denied in the cause of fighting the Cold War. Some saw in his actions an attempt to create a state of constant emergency; others pointed out that the Korean War was in fact very serious and merely temporary.

The post-Second World War relationship between corporations and organised labour reflected the opportunities and needs of Cold War era American capitalism: in essence, the leadership of the American Federation of Labor and Congress of Industrial Organizations (AFL-CIO) agreed to back domestic and international anti-communism in exchange for wage, benefit and job security improvements for the unionised workforce. This, in turn, enhanced the ability of the United States to make Cold War foreign policy an instrument through which to construct a system of post-colonial economic and political dependency in the Third World. Truman was perfectly happy with this – his ideological position regarding labour was that it should be harnessed to make the United States stronger. The Taft–Hartley Act (Labor Management Relations Act) of 1947 was another factor in this: Truman vetoed this bill – an attempt by the Republican Congress to roll back the pro-workforce provisions of the 1935 Wagner Act – but Congress overrode his veto and the bill was passed. The ideological battle lines were now clear; the election result of 1948, in which the Republicans were utterly defeated, suggested that Truman's pragmatic acceptance of the New Deal labour reforms was popular.

The rise of McCarthyism

McCarthyism is named after Senator Joseph McCarthy, Republican of Wisconsin, who made his name as an anti-communist campaigner. From the moment in February 1950 when McCarthy claimed that he had a list of communists working in the State Department, the anti-communist movement was associated with him. Throughout his career, McCarthyism did not uncover a single actual spy.

There was a long history of anti-radicalism in the USA: in their intensity the anti-communist network mirrored the communist fanatics they persecuted. It was a diverse movement (see Table 1.3), a loose coalition, more effective in appealing to different constituencies in different ways than a single campaign would have been, but indisputably a movement of the political right. There had been a Red Scare in the early 1920s; by the 1930s, with the rise of Stalin to power in the USSR, it seemed that communism could become a global nightmare for the Americans. A cartoon of 1938 depicted Stalin as a giant octopus spreading his tentacles around the world. Nazi Germany had been seen in America as a potential bulwark against the spread of communism by, for example, the ambassador to the United Kingdom, Joseph Kennedy.

Communists were, in the popular imagination, everywhere. The opening of the Soviet archives in the 1990s made it clear that they had been. The historian Christopher Andrew has calculated that in 1941 the Soviets had 221 agents in every major branch of Roosevelt's government, one of whom was Alger Hiss, indirectly convicted of treason in a libel trial in 1950 after he challenged Representative Chambers to repeat his (Chambers's) claim that Hiss was a communist, outside Congress. When Chambers had said this in Congress he was protected by **Parliamentary Privilege**. When he repeated it outside Congress (adding that Hiss was not just a communist, but also a spy) he could be sued for libel, with a lower standard of proof than it would have taken to put him on trial for spying; Hiss sued him, and lost, going to jail for several years for perjury. By Truman's time, however, the spy ring had largely collapsed.

This fear of communist infiltration was not irrational. Stalin's plans for nuclear weapons were greatly helped by clandestinely gaining access to the Americans' blueprints, for example. The cure for this infiltration was, however, in some ways just as damaging as the disease. The House Un-American Activities Committee raised the issue, and the profile of its leader Richard Nixon, and they did correctly accuse Hiss. It also focused on Hollywood – where the movie industry was suffering as television became more popular, and where studio bosses blamed communists for industrial unrest. The Hollywood Ten, not celebrities but left-leaning writers and producers, attacked HUAC in 1947; they were jailed and barred from working in Hollywood. Many other Hollywood workers would be asked to declare all previous communist leanings over the next few years. There were several prominent Jews in Hollywood – often of eastern European origin – and HUAC's activities came to resemble a WASP crusade against them.

The Red Scare involved some tremendous violations of civil liberties. The Immigration and Naturalization Service was rounding up foreign-born communists in the late 1940s. Putting communist labour leaders on trial allowed the government to raise the issue of industrial sabotage. Initiating deportation proceedings against foreign-born communists emphasised the alien nature of the Communist Party and its ties to the USSR. For Truman, this made political sense at home and abroad. His efforts to rein in anti-Communist feeling were not entirely successful. The McCarran Internal Security Act of 1950 was passed by Democratic senators over Truman's veto. This Act:

- Forced organisations to provide membership lists and financial statements.
- Barred communists from employment in defence plants.
- Made it a crime to conspire to establish a totalitarian government in the USA.
- Authorised the arrest and detention of any person who there was reason to believe might engage in acts of espionage or sabotage.

Big Business	'Red-baiting' made it possible to confront unions without having to address economic and social issues. Business leaders assumed labour organisations were communists.
Liberals such as the Kennedys	Liberals were anti-communist because communism opposes free speech and free markets. Men such as the Kennedys also thought in foreign policy terms.
Congressional leaders	The House Un-American Activities Committee (HUAC) was led by Representative Richard Nixon, a Republican of California. The Senate's Subcommittee on Investigations was led by Senator Joseph McCarthy, Republican of Wisconsin.
The Federal Bureau of Investigation under J. Edgar Hoover	The FBI had a carefully concealed right-wing agenda. Hoover targeted any voice of criticism from the left, which he saw as contrary to old-fashioned small-town values.
Veterans' associations	Communism seemed to exist in opposition to the nationalism that was common among soldiers and veterans.
Labour leaders	Keen to stress the distinction of **liberalism** from communism, the leader of the Socialist Party, Norman Thomas, said that communists should not be allowed to teach because they had 'given away (their) freedom in the quest for truth'.

Table 1.3: The anti-communist network.

ACTIVITY 1.5

1. Make a list of all the reasons people opposed communism during Truman's presidency. You might wish to perform some additional research on McCarthy to see what motivated him.

2. Do you think that any of the reasons why Americans opposed communism at this time were good reasons? Explain.

3. Assess the value of McCarthy's speech at Wheeling to an historian studying the Red Scare.

Senator Joseph McCarthy entered the fray in 1950 with a speech in Wheeling in which he produced a piece of paper on which, he claimed, was written the names of the 205 communists working in the State Department. He mixed his anti-communist rhetoric with anti-establishment rhetoric implying that government workers had been 'born with a silver spoon in their mouths' and were not like real Americans. He abused the **Fifth Amendment**, undermining its presumption of innocence, saying, 'A witness's refusal to answer whether or not he is a communist on the ground that his answer would tend to incriminate him is the most positive proof obtainable that the witness is a communist'. McCarthy's Senate committee did not have to obtain proof of a legal standard; suspicion was quite enough to ruin a career. Blind to parallels with the totalitarian regimes he claimed to oppose, McCarthy also ordered the suppression from American centres abroad of books and art by communists or communist 'fellow travellers' including, bizarrely, work by Mark Twain.

The anti-Semitic nature of the Red Scare was further boosted by the event that led to McCarthy's dramatic revelation – the arrest in February 1950 of Julius and Ethel Rosenberg. They were accused of stealing information from Ethel's brother, who worked on nuclear weapons. They were convicted and executed in 1953. Although it was not known at the time, the FBI had secured a Soviet code book that demonstrated their guilt. McCarthy made a series of accusations of communism over the next four years, both general and specific, against people working at the State Department and in the army: they were working for the Soviets; they were homosexual and subject to blackmail; they were 'un-American'.

Some have seen anti-communism as a manifestation of a long-standing backlash against the modern, secular world and deep-seated anxieties about individual autonomy, gender identity and the perceived loss of community. These issues were centered on what it meant to be 'American' in the modern world, and had been driving factors in the earlier Red Scare of the 1920s. J. Edgar Hoover, the Head of the Federal Bureau of Investigation, had made his name then, targeting left-wing critics of the government as well as communists themselves. Truman realised that for years Hoover had been defying his superiors in the Justice Department and had secretly put people under surveillance without authorisation. The president did not have sufficient political clout to deal with the problem: Hoover was more popular, and his small-town values of family, flag and church resonated with the American public more clearly than did Truman's more nuanced approach. Truman recognised that the Cold War created a geopolitical situation in which the major enemy happened to be communist; the American public as a whole generalised from this to the idea that all communists were the enemy.

 Thematic link: identity

African Americans in North and South

In 1945 African-American communities across America hoped for advancement. Voting rights for black people were patchy in the North and non-existent in the South. Lynching was still commonplace. Black people were disproportionately poor. Over the next 30 years the Civil Rights Movement reached its famous heights; the legal barriers to black participation in society were removed, and lynching stopped. The story of civil rights was the story of legal struggle, direct action, peaceful protest and violent revolution.

During his presidency, Harry Truman did very little for African Americans, but what he did was hugely important. It was not his initial intention to campaign for civil rights in 1948 in anything more than a moderate way, but he embraced the ideas of the mayor of Minneapolis, Hubert Humphrey, in calling for real civil rights in North and South. He began the transformation of the Democratic Party into one that would fight for civil rights, and deliver major changes two decades later. There were cynical political motives involved – he certainly benefited from the black vote in northern cities, offsetting the lost white votes in the South. In the South, too, there were rumblings of change. In 1941 the Supreme Court had outlawed the whites-only primaries in Texas, and one million African Americans had registered to vote. By embracing civil rights as a Democratic issue, Truman also made it into a northern issue as well as a southern one.

 Voices from the past

Speech of Joseph McCarthy, Wheeling, West Virginia, 9 February 1950

The great difference between our western Christian world and the atheistic Communist world is not political, gentlemen, it is moral … The real, basic difference … lies in the religion of immoralism … invented by Marx, preached feverishly by Lenin, and carried to unimaginable extremes by Stalin. This religion of immoralism, if the Red half of the world triumphs—and well it may, gentlemen—this religion of immoralism will more deeply wound and damage mankind than any conceivable economic or political system …

Today we are engaged in a final, all-out battle between communistic atheism and Christianity. The modern champions of communism have selected this as the time, and ladies and gentlemen, the chips are down—they are truly down. …

The reason why we find ourselves in a position of impotency is not because our only powerful potential enemy has sent men to invade our shores … but rather because of the traitorous actions of those who have been treated so well by this Nation. It has not been the less fortunate, or members of minority groups who have been traitorous to this Nation, but rather those who have had all the benefits that the wealthiest Nation on earth has had to offer … the finest homes, the finest college education and the finest jobs in government we can give.

This is glaringly true in the State Department. There the bright young men who are born with silver spoons in their mouths are the ones who have been most traitorous …

I have here in my hand a list of 205 … names that were made known to the Secretary of State as being members of the Communist Party and who nevertheless are still working in the State Department …

The impact of the Second World War

The New Deal had helped African Americans because it had helped poor Americans, and the Second World War had had three main effects. Northern African Americans, who had moved to the cities, were usually trained for the army in the South, where most training camps were; there, they witnessed for themselves the horrors of segregation. African Americans began to acquire a nationwide group consciousness. Second, African Americans who fought – and fought bravely – in the Second World War came back less willing to accept a second-class status. Third, the rising tide of prosperity that came after the war provided the economic backdrop that would be necessary for reform.

The Second World War had also seen specific legal progress for African Americans. In June 1941 FDR issued Executive Order 8802, creating the Fair Employment Practices Committee (FEPC). The federal government – now a major employer – would not hire any person based on their race, colour, creed or national origin. The FEPC was supposed to enforce the order to ban discriminatory hiring within the federal government and in corporations that received federal contracts. This was most corporations. In fact the FEPC did not work very effectively; FDR backed off from trying to make it work better because he was fighting enough, literal, battles already.

Meanwhile, in 1942 a group of civil rights advocates founded the Congress of Racial Equality (CORE) on the University of Chicago campus. The creation of CORE marked the beginning of a mass movement for civil rights. Early CORE membership was chiefly northern, and mostly white. With white support, returning African American veterans who had fought for American freedom (and witnessed Nazi prisoners of war with more freedom than they were allowed), and a rising tide of prosperity, African Americans expected improvement to come.

Campaigns for civil rights

The question of black rights and, more generally, how the South was going to align itself politically and fit into post-war economic and political development was a core question from 1945 onwards. One issue was that northern black people had often, when enlisted for military service, trained in the South, and experienced segregation there for the first time. This is why at least some of the opposition to southern segregation would come from northern towns. The Civil Rights Movement was ready to campaign. An example was the Journey of Reconciliation in 1947, when 16 CORE members travelled on buses around the South in violation of segregation laws to highlight that the Supreme Court's decision in *Morgan v Virginia* (see Figure 1.6) was largely being ignored. Most of the 16 were arrested, and the idea of **Freedom Rides** was born.

During Truman's time, however, there was little direct action campaigning – not of the sort that started in Eisenhower's presidency. Instead, black campaigners organised, consolidated and went to the courts (see Figure 1.6). Their visits to court were not random – the cases involved were selected for argument by civil rights campaigners expecting to win. This set the stage for future civil rights action.

Thematic link: democracy

The responses of the federal and state authorities

Truman's response was to be accommodating wherever he could. He used an Executive Order to establish the President's Committee on Civil Rights in 1946; the next year it produced a report called *To Secure these Rights*, which recommended improving civil rights laws, making lynching a federal crime (meaning it was not up to potentially segregationist states to decide whether to prosecute in lynching cases) and abolishing the poll taxes that some southern states used to prevent black people from voting. Truman tried and failed to get Congress to federalise lynching and, in response to *Morgan v Virginia*, to regulate interstate commerce. In 1948 he issued another Executive Order to integrate the armed forces, setting himself in further opposition to Congress. This sent a message about equality; it set a precedent for presidential intervention in issues of segregation, and was the first of a series of measures by which presidents took the lead. He did it, it has been suggested, not out of any great desire to move black Americans towards equality, but because he wished to emphasise the differences between the Democrats and the Republicans in the run-up to the election of 1948. He sought (and gained) the votes of northern African Americans. The liberal Supreme Court, most of them appointed by FDR, also began to roll back segregation. In the governments of the South, there was little enthusiasm for civil rights. Officials in South Carolina and Oklahoma ignored instructions to integrate education; the buses in Virginia, the Carolinas and Georgia remained segregated. Voters continued to be barred from voting by unfair means. Who was going to stop this? The Supreme Court could not enforce the laws it made; eventually, something was going to have to give.

3 June 1946: *Morgan v Virginia*	Bans segregation on interstate buses.
3 May 1948: *Shelley v Kraemer*	Bans selling a house to someone on condition that they could never sell it to a black person.
5 June 1950: *Henderson v United States*	Bans segregation in railroad dining cars.

Figure 1.6: Three Supreme Court cases affecting civil rights while Truman was president.

Practice essay questions

1. 'Harry Truman was motivated mostly by ideological concerns.' Assess the validity of this view.
2. To what extent do you agree that the Red Scare of the 1940s and 1950s was the invention of right-wing politicians?
3. 'African Americans in 1952 should have been optimistic about the future.' Assess the validity of this view.
4. With reference to Voices from the past: The Do Nothing Congress and Voices from the past: The Vandenberg Resolution, and your understanding of the historical context, which of these two sources is more valuable in explaining the relationship between Truman and Congress?

Taking it further

Do you agree that the American economy was so strong in 1945 that America's subsequent Superpower status was inevitable?

Further reading

For more on the causes of the Cold War you might read:

Norman Friedman, *Fifty-Year War: Conflict and Strategy in the Cold War*, Naval Institute Press; 2007. Friedman argues that Soviet strategy caused the Cold War.

George Kennan, 'The Sources of Soviet Conduct', *Foreign Affairs* magazine, 1947. A State Department analyst of the time, Kennan argued that Soviet ideology had caused the conflict. Kennan contributed this article anonymously. He also wrote the 'Long Telegram', an internal American government memorandum, which argued that the Soviets were seeking to create a closed, communist society based around total control of eastern Europe. He also argued (in two key phrases) that the Soviet government was 'Impervious to [the] logic of reason, and [it is] highly sensitive to logic of force', and that 'no one should underrate [the] importance of dogma in Soviet affairs'. He meant that the Soviet government would respond only to force and to communist (or Marxist) teaching. Whether true or not, this does seem to be the attitude that Truman consistently took in his dealings with the Soviets.

William A. Williams, *The Tragedy of American Diplomacy*, W.W. Norton; 1959. Williams argued that it was the overreaction of the Americans to legitimate Soviet concerns that caused the Cold War.

John Lewis Gaddis, *The Cold War*, Allen Lane; 2005. Gaddis argued that it was a combination of all these factors including Stalin's own paranoia that led him to disbelieve any reassurance from Truman.

Chapter summary

By the end of this chapter you should understand:

- Truman's role in changing the nature of the Democratic Party, maintaining the New Deal coalition and strengthening its support of civil rights
- Truman's role in forming American policy in the early Cold War, including the doctrine of containment, as a geopolitical, economic and ideological response
- Truman's role in maintaining the powerful presidency that he inherited from Roosevelt
- the role of Truman and others in promoting civil rights for African Americans.

End notes

1 http://www.newrepublic.com/article/politics/90685/turnip-day-in-washington
2 Schlesinger A. *The Imperial Presidency*. Mariner; 2004: 128.
3 http://avalon.law.yale.edu/20th_century/decad040.asp

2 Eisenhower: Tranquillity and Crisis 1952–1960

In this section, we will examine the ways in which President Dwight D. ('Ike') Eisenhower sought to change his country and the Republican Party, which he had newly joined. Eisenhower created – or perhaps did not hinder the development of – a booming and aspirational economy and society. He promoted a form of cold warfare that emphasised nuclear deterrence rather than actual fighting. We will also examine the very significant contributions to the Civil Rights Movement that took place during his presidency and which laid the groundwork for the more substantial changes that followed. We will look into:

- The presidency: Eisenhower's personality and the politics of 'dynamic conservatism', Nixon as vice president, the Republican Party and the end of McCarthyism.

- The growth of the American economy in the 1950s and the impact of the 'consumer society'.

- The USA and the Cold War: Superpower rivalry and conflict with the USSR, responses to developments in western and eastern Europe, reactions to the rise of communism in Asia, and responses to crises in the Middle East.

- African Americans in North and South: the emergence of the Civil Rights Movement, the policies and attitudes of the main political parties and the responses of the state and federal authorities.

Introduction: a reluctant president

Eisenhower, the Supreme Allied Commander (Europe) during the Second World War, became president out of duty. He had refused to allow himself to be nominated in 1948 by either party. By 1951 there was a 'Draft Ike' campaign, again with members from both political parties. When he had finally indicated that he was a Republican and allowed himself to be drafted, Eisenhower campaigned against communism, Korea and corruption. At the end of his presidency, the Cold War was more tense than ever, the Korean War was over but worse was building in Vietnam, and his powerful Chief of Staff Sherman Adams had been forced to resign because of corruption. Eisenhower's time in office featured the consolidation of the New Deal, the beginnings of the core Civil Rights Movement, diplomatic principles of deterrence against fellow Superpowers and the bullying of many of those nations without nuclear weapons. How should he be viewed? As the man who federalised the National Guard to uphold the Supreme Court's decision to desegregate education, or as the man who committed America to involvement in Vietnam? He is consistently ranked as one of America's top ten greatest presidents, perhaps because it is far easier to praise him for the former than to blame him for the latter.

Historians' initial reaction to Eisenhower was unfavourable. The first histories of his time were written in the light of the reforming Democratic presidents who succeeded and seemed to surpass him. Fred Greenstein, in *The Hidden-Hand Leadership Presidency: Eisenhower as Leader* (1982), began Eisenhower's rehabilitation, arguing that Ike's leadership style was indirect but effective. However, the modern view is that he did too little in terms of civil rights, social policy and economic management.

The 1950s seem now – and to an extent seemed at the time – a period of economic consolidation that led to a consumer boom and a change in American culture. The decade witnessed the birth of rock and roll and a new wave of movies and literature aimed at young people. It was the era of Arthur Miller's play *Death of a Salesman* and the highly popular TV show *I Love Lucy*. Prosperity seemed to have come to everyone, making the American Dream all the easier to live. The reality was, of course, more complex. Whatever the economic circumstances, it is important to remember as you work through this chapter that just because the president's name is in the title of the chapter, it doesn't mean that Eisenhower was responsible for the economic or cultural changes that took place on his watch.

The presidency

Eisenhower had made a very public show of reluctance to become president. His predecessor, Harry S. Truman, faced with a hostile Congress, had run foreign policy and attempted dramatic legislation at home, settling for minor gains. 'Poor Ike', Truman had said in his last days in office, thinking of Eisenhower's military background. 'He'll say, "Do this", or "Do that" and nothing will happen.' In fact Eisenhower well understood the power of persuasion and used it when necessary – although he was certainly prepared to threaten recalcitrant segregationist governors and non-nuclear foreign powers. Moreover, Eisenhower believed that the powers of the presidency had been extended too far by Roosevelt and

Truman – or at least he believed that they should not be extended further unless there was an emergency situation to deal with. A major effect of the criticisms of Senator Joseph McCarthy and others was that Eisenhower eventually defended the executive branch of government, which deals with daily administration of the state, by insisting on the **executive privilege** (from 1958) of secrecy, and that the executive should be freed from constant Congressional investigations and surveillance which, apart from anything else, made it inefficient.

Eisenhower had been 'drafted' for the presidency because professional politicians did not seem like the kind of people who should be running the country. He ran ahead of the rest of his party in the election and won in a landslide, while the Republicans only narrowly regained the House and the Senate. This gave Ike something of a mandate to impose himself upon Congress. By 1955 he faced divided government, as the **House of Representatives** and the Senate were recaptured by the Democrats (the former for 26 years, the latter for 40). Anything Eisenhower wanted to do to reconstruct the country would have to be acceptable to the Democrats. He also recognised that American politics had become systematised beyond his ability to control it. Eisenhower coined the term '**military-industrial complex**' to describe the situation, for which he was at least partly responsible, of a too-close relationship between the manufacturers of military hardware, the members of the executive responsible for ordering military equipment, and the members of Congress responsible for paying them, which created the total interdependence of politics and industry. The economy as a whole, Eisenhower warned, was now dependent on military expenditure. The reason why so much was being spent on military hardware was Eisenhower's own 'New Look', a policy designed to stimulate the economy by spending a vast amount building nuclear missiles rather than maintaining a large army, relying on deterrence for defence.

Eisenhower's personality and the politics of 'dynamic conservatism'

Eisenhower viewed the presidency as more than partisan and when he became president he did not automatically assume that his role was to implement Republican Party policies. Being president appealed to his sense of duty. He believed that the people wanted him to be president because they wanted him to look after the country, restore order and avoid war. Eisenhower was also an expert poker player, which perhaps explains his policy of brinkmanship – the deliberate raising of Cold War tension to see which side would blink first.

His policy position has been described as 'dynamic conservatism'. This essentially meant the government maintaining the New Deal legacy of looking after welfare, while providing whatever economic (or indeed social) stimulus was necessary. This was what the New Deal looked like when times were good. However, Eisenhower was not a slave to the New Deal – he believed in reducing spending, lowering taxes and trying to reduce the size of the **deficit**.

His policies included:

Figure 2.1: Eisenhower was a genial man, loved by the American people for his war record, his sense of responsibility and the fact that he was clearly a reluctant politician.

- Tax reduction.
- Creation of the Executive Department of Health, Education and Welfare.

- Exploitation of oil in the Gulf of Mexico to raise the revenue base.
- Supporting farmers through the 'soil bank', designed to prevent over-production.
- Building interstate highways.
- Establishing the National Aeronautics and Space Administration (NASA).
- Passing the Atomic Energy Act to encourage the peaceful use of nuclear power.
- Raising the minimum wage.

Eisenhower linked his policy ideas to the Cold War. He dressed up the interstate highway programme, which came in response to a slight economic downturn, in military clothes: interstates (motorways) would improve military transport. Nuclear power stations represented peaceful uses for nuclear material. In 1953 he offered to help the USSR to build them as well, to use up their nuclear stockpile. **NASA** was explicitly a Cold War creation, created in response to the successful launch of Sputnik, the first artificial satellite, by the USSR, so that America would not be behind in the space race for long.

Dynamic conservatism: how did Eisenhower's conservatism compare with that of previous conservative presidents?

When Eisenhower took office, he was the first Republican president to be elected since Harding, Coolidge and Hoover in the 1920s. Of those three, Warren Harding's reputation was sullied by scandal and Herbert Hoover's by the Great Depression, which dominated his presidency. Nevertheless, it is possible to trace some of the lines of Eisenhower's thought back to the 1920s. Like Warren Harding (1921–23), his view of presidential powers was conservative. Eisenhower thought his predecessors Franklin D. Roosevelt and Harry S. Truman had overreached their powers; Harding had felt similarly about Woodrow Wilson.

Harding's successor following his death in office in 1923 was Calvin Coolidge (1923–29). Coolidge believed that the federal government should promote private enterprise and then get out of the way – a **laissez-faire** policy. Eisenhower's dynamic conservatism was more active. Coolidge's own folksy charm, and the excellent economy, led to his election in 1924 in his own right. Eisenhower's people skills, and the excellent economy of the 1950s, led to his own re-election. The example of Herbert Hoover (1929–33), provided a warning: it was important for the federal government to do *something* during economic good times, lest bad times follow. Hoover's reputation had been destroyed by his inability to deal with the Depression.

Nixon as vice president

Richard M. Nixon was the first of a number of powerful vice presidents. In part this was a result of his somewhat difficult relationship with the president. Eisenhower had been a member of the Republican Party for only a few months prior to his nomination as its presidential candidate. Nixon had been a Republican all his life – and a relatively conservative Republican at that. Eisenhower was famously ambivalent about Nixon's talents, running for a second term in 1956 despite his heart attack in 1955 because he did not want Nixon to succeed him, and openly mooting the idea of running in 1956 with a Democrat as his running mate. Other Republicans were also wary of allowing Nixon to run. They had not enjoyed the prospect of a Nixon succession in 1955, when it was not yet known how serious the

ACTIVITY 2.1

Explain what Eisenhower was seeking to achieve with each of the policies listed.

ACTIVITY 2.2

Nixon knew that the Kitchen Debate would be broadcast around the world. How valuable is the debate for telling us about American attitudes during the Cold War?

president's heart attack had been. In 1960, when Nixon did run, Eisenhower (who was the first US president to be '**term-limited**' and barred from running for a third term in office) praised him for all the things he had done but, in an excruciating press conference conversation with *Time* magazine's Norman Mohr, was unable to provide an example.

What did Nixon do? Not much on a day-to-day basis, compared with vice presidents today, but he was the first modern vice president in that he functioned as a real deputy. He attended cabinet meetings, chairing them in Eisenhower's absence following his heart attack, and again when the president suffered a stroke in 1957. A former senator, Nixon helped to get the Civil Rights Act through the Senate. It was Nixon who travelled to the Far East in 1953 to assess the situation in Indochina, and Nixon who met Khrushchev and engaged with him in what has become known as the 'Kitchen Debate', at the American exhibition in Moscow. Nixon also carried out many of Eisenhower's party leadership functions, turning up at fundraising events for other candidates. This was a perfect arrangement between a president who was not entirely of his party and a vice president who desperately sought advancement, and who knew that he had to win friends, especially after his party had thought about selecting a new vice presidential candidate in 1956. By 1959, when it seemed that Nelson Rockefeller, Governor of New York might be in a position to challenge him for the Republican nomination in 1960, Nixon was able to claim the support of the majority of Republicans in the country and Rockefeller's challenge fizzled out.

The Kitchen Debate revealed the importance of gender in Cold War battles: the home, where American breadwinners supported housewives, was the place where American freedom was most apparent. This was a domestic counterpart to containment theory – the power of the Soviet Union would not endanger US national security if it could be contained within a clearly defined sphere of influence. Within the walls of the American home, the potentially dangerous social forces of the new age might be tamed.

The Republican Party

Eisenhower had opposed the isolationist wing of the Republican Party, led by Senator Robert A. Taft, in 1951. A year later, he defeated Taft in the Republican presidential primary election in New Hampshire – Eisenhower had not even been a presidential candidate at the time. Taft had tried to become Eisenhower's vice presidential running mate, but had failed, losing out to Nixon, a well-known anti-communist campaigner. Their election, and the subsequent appointment of John Foster Dulles as Secretary of State rather than the former Republican presidential candidate Thomas Dewey, who wanted the job, seemed to confirm that Eisenhower's presidency represented the effective end of Republican isolationism. Surely the great general and the face of anti-communism (Nixon's face was more acceptable than McCarthy's) would pursue a vigorous foreign policy.

Looking back, it is clear that Eisenhower presided over a time of electoral disaster for the Republican Party. Republicans would not control the House or Senate for more than 20 years after 1954. During this period, they would win the presidency only with Nixon in 1968 and 1972 – one a narrow defeat in the aftermath of an unpopular war and the death of the Democratic frontrunner, and the other a **landslide** against a Democratic Party unable to field a viable candidate of its own. Eisenhower intervened in the internal politics of the Party he had only recently joined, indulging those moderates who had persuaded him to run by opposing the Republican 'old guard' in Congress. In 1954, as the mid-term elections approached and it became clear that the Republicans were going to lose, Eisenhower blamed the conservatives and threatened to run as an independent in 1956 unless the Republican Party became more progressive.

The Republican Party's old guard was defeated in 1954. Eisenhower had proved unwilling to campaign until the very last minute; Nixon, by contrast, had criss-crossed the country supporting the lost cause. The defeat of McCarthyism (McCarthy was a Republican) in 1954 was accomplished with very little support from Eisenhower. In 1956, however, the Republicans re-nominated Eisenhower, despite his serious illnesses, perhaps from fear of having Nixon, whom they

Voices from the past

The Nixon–Khrushchev Kitchen Debate

Figure 2.2: The Kitchen Debate between Vice President Richard M. Nixon and Soviet leader Nikita Khrushchev, 1959.

Nixon: [Halting Khrushchev at model kitchen in model house]: "You had a very nice house in your exhibition in New York. My wife and I saw and enjoyed it very much. I want to show you this kitchen."

Khrushchev: [After Nixon called attention to a built-in panel-controlled washing machine]: "We have such things."

Nixon: "This is the newest model. This is the kind which is built in thousands of units for direct installation in the houses." He added that Americans were interested in making life easier for their women.

Mr. Khrushchev remarked that in the Soviet Union, they did not have "the capitalist attitude toward women."

Nixon: "I think that this attitude toward women is universal. What we want to do is make easier the life of our housewives." …

Nixon: "We have many different manufacturers and many different kinds of washing machines so that the housewives have a choice."

Khrushchev: [Noting Nixon gazing admiringly at young women modeling bathing suits and sports clothes]: "You are for the girls, too."

Nixon: [Indicating a floor sweeper that works by itself and other appliances]: "You don't need a wife."

Khrushchev chuckled.

Nixon: "We do not claim to astonish the Russian people. We hope to show our diversity and our right to choose. We do not wish to have decisions made at the top by government officials who say that all homes should be built in the same way. Would it not be better to compete in the relative merits of washing machines than in the strength of rockets? Is this the kind of competition you want?"[1]

disliked despite (or because of?) his hard work and obvious ambition, as their candidate: there was nobody else (Taft had died in 1954) who seemed to be a reasonable candidate for the presidency. In 1960 Nixon, who was politically more conservative than Eisenhower but still relatively moderate on everything except the Red Scare, ran with the progressive Senator Henry Cabot Lodge Jr as his running mate, seeing off a very unsuccessful challenge by Nelson Rockefeller, a liberal Republican, for the nomination. By 1964 reaction came in the shape of the ultra-conservative candidacy of Barry Goldwater, who had criticised Eisenhower severely for his acceptance of the New Deal. Nixon would be there to pick up the pieces and rebuild a Republican majority.

The end of McCarthyism

Joseph McCarthy rarely focused on actual threats, such as the USSR or China. In a world in which there were clear threats in Asia, and in which the government, Hollywood and various other organisations had been purged of anyone who might have had even the vaguest communist sympathies, he was not particularly relevant any more. McCarthy continued his crusade, trying to pick a fight with Eisenhower, whom he accused of doing too little to remove communists from the administration. He referred not to 20 years of treason (the Roosevelt and Truman presidencies) but to 21 years, including the Eisenhower administration in his accusations of treason. Eisenhower refused to give him the satisfaction of engaging with him. Meanwhile McCarthy's targets became wilder and wilder. After some pressure he dismissed J.B. Matthews, the staff officer of the Senate Subcommittee on Investigations, which McCarthy chaired, for an attack on communism among the Protestant clergy – an attack that appeared to have originated with McCarthy himself.

Figure 2.3: Joseph McCarthy was a leader of anti-communism in the US Senate.

In 1953–54 McCarthy held public hearings about communism in the army. They were televised, which was not to his advantage. He bullied, hectored and rambled. His victims began to fight back, challenging him actually to produce his lists of communists whom he claimed were working for various divisions of the army. It became clear that his attacks were ill-founded and ill-mannered, and he was criticised in print as being himself a barrier to effective anti-communist measures. The journalist Edward R. Murrow produced a series of documentaries critical of McCarthy for his *See It Now* series. Eventually, McCarthy's bubble was burst in 1954 when he laid into a blameless army lawyer in a televised hearing that revealed him as a bully and prompted the response, 'Have you no decency, sir?' Public opinion began to turn against McCarthy. By the end of 1954 he had been censured by the US Senate, and his crusade was over.

McCarthy, who had once been feared, was now shunned. On one occasion in 1956, when he was almost photographed sitting next to that other anti-communist campaigner, Vice President Nixon, at a campaign event in Wisconsin, an aide asked McCarthy to leave. He did so without demur but a journalist later spotted him weeping. He was dead from alcoholism within a year.

Thematic link: identity

The growth of the American economy in the 1950s and the impact of the 'consumer society'

From 1945 to 1960 the **Gross National Product** (GNP) of the USA doubled to $505 billion, thanks to a consumer spending boom. Although the welfare state established by the New Deal still needed funding, in the 1950s the good times were back. Price inflation was low and there was a 25% rise in real income from 1945 to 1960. Americans had been eager to spend their wartime savings once the good times returned: they bought American goods and the American companies that made those goods were able to export so much that they made a lot of money. In fact, America made more money than it spent, despite the fact that spending money was easy.

A family could get into their easily affordable automobile (by 1960, 90% of those who lived in the suburbs owned at least one car), drive on a well-maintained road and go anywhere they wanted – perhaps even using the federally funded interstate highway network that Eisenhower authorised in 1956. They might stay in a motel (a hotel for the motorist). They might go shopping in a mall – there were only eight in 1945, but 4000 by 1960. The middle classes lived in the suburbs, perhaps in one of the new Levittown homes built by the Long Island building contractor Arthur Levitt. Henry Kaiser, a Californian shipbuilding magnate, got in on the act on the West Coast. Between them they were constructing homes at the rate of 1.5 million a year at their peak. The poor were still poor, but less so; the welfare state worked well as a safety net and there was always the chance that hard work might enable even the very poorest to do better than their parents and live the American Dream. The ubiquity of television and new shows such as *I Love Lucy* meant that a vision of the contemporary lifestyle of the white middle classes was broadcast to the whole of America. The American 'economic miracle' meant that it became possible for Americans to believe that there were no limits to economic growth. The old scepticism about capitalism faded entirely. The economic pie was enlarged, so there seemed to be no need to fight over how it was shared out – everyone could be a winner.

So what did Americans buy? Whatever they could. They bought refrigerators, washing machines and televisions. They bought carpets, vacuum cleaners and encyclopaedias. Expensive goods could be bought on hire purchase. Women were encouraged to sell Tupperware to one another, holding Tupperware parties. Salesmen used their cars to visit people's homes or to tout their wares around businesses. It did not necessarily make them happy – the idea of the stressed white-collar worker and the corporate rat race comes from the 1950s.

The consumer society led to the invention of the teenager. Like older Americans, teenagers had money and advertisers recognised a distinct market for typical teenage phenomena – music, radios, distinctive (sometimes fast) food and clothing, and fads such as hula hoops, which appeared in 1958. The Beat

Generation of poets and novelists glorified the spontaneity, sexual adventurism, drug use and spirituality that would be more typical of the 1960s – examples include Allen Ginsberg (*Howl,* 1956) and Jack Kerouac (*On the Road,* 1957). Rock and roll – with singers such as Buddy Holly and Elvis Presley, and groups such as Bill Haley and the Comets – amalgamated white country and western music and black urban music, an offshoot of jazz, known as rhythm and blues. Music like this seemed dangerously subversive as it invited racial mixing and general disorder. In Hollywood, *The Wild One* (1951), starring Marlon Brando, and *Rebel Without a Cause* (1955), starring James Dean, were significant movies for the new generation. Dean's rebel had no particular reason for his actions – except that society deserved to be rebelled against. Like the general teenage rebellion of the 1950s, it would help to inspire the activism of the 1960s, when young people did indeed have multiple causes to focus on.

Many middle-class people reacted to the consumer boom by wanting more possessions, which drove the growth of the economy. The less well off reacted either by becoming aspirational or by becoming angry that prosperity was denied them. This applied to black people in the segregated South, who lived among the new restaurants, movie theatres and rock and roll clubs that they were not allowed to visit.

Advertising encouraged suburban dwellers to be aspirational, while hire purchase agreements, credit cards and shopping malls helped them to spend their money, and not just on domestic goods. They might eat out, perhaps at McDonald's, a company that was founded in 1940, became a burger restaurant in 1948 and became big in the 1950s. They might read comics, collect baseball memorabilia or enjoy *I Love Lucy*, the popular television comedy that began in 1951, and could be viewed in 13 000 000 American households: this number had trebled by 1959.

 Hidden voices

Arthur Miller

Arthur Miller's play *Death of a Salesman* is the story of Willy Loman, a salesman whose lack of success causes him considerable psychological pain. Nevertheless, towards the end of the play he laments the decisions made by his son Biff, who has reverted to a more traditional American way of making money: 'How can he find himself on a farm? Is that a life? A farmhand? In the beginning, when he was young, I thought, well, a young man, it's good for him to tramp around, take a lot of different jobs. But it's more than ten years now and he has yet to make thirty-five dollars a week!' Loman would rather be an unsuccessful participant in the consumer boom than a successful participant in old-style American productivity. Miller recognised that something was changing in American life, as happiness was becoming dependent upon material possessions.

Miller also wrote *The Crucible* (1953), which is about the Red Scare, and partly reflects Miller's own experiences after being called before the **House Un-American Activities Committee** (HUAC), and *A View from the Bridge* (1956), which is about corruption at the New York City docks.

The themes of the destruction of the typical family were also expressed in Eugene O'Neill's *A Long Day's Journey into Night* (1957), in which a home dissolves in full view of the audience; Tennessee Williams' *Streetcar Named Desire* (1947) and *Cat on a Hot Tin Roof* (1958), both claustrophobic plays about the pressure of family; and Edward Albee's *Who's Afraid of Virginia Woolf?* (1962), which outlines the breakdown of a marriage.

✓	✗
WASPs.	**Black people** – Levitt refused to sell to black people.
Whites from a non-WASP background – Poles, Italians and Jews.	**Poor people** – who moved to the cities, from which the suburbanites had come.
Petrochemical workers in Texas.	**Asians (Korean, Japanese, Chinese)** – many suburbs had restrictive covenants preventing sales to people of Asian origin. These covenants were illegal but that did not stop them being applied.
Defence workers in California.	
Retirees – attracted to the Sun Belt now that air-conditioning had been invented.	

Table 2.1: Who lived in the suburbs?

The consumer boom was a suburban phenomenon and was not universal. By 1962 a quarter of Americans were still living below the poverty line – but poverty no longer meant homelessness or hunger. Michael Harrington's book *The Other America: Poverty in the United States* (1962) brought this to the mainstream consciousness, as did popular musicals such as *West Side Story* (1957), which told the story of rival gangs in New York. Americans could also be aspirational about their personal lives, and self-help plans and psychotherapy became increasingly popular. Table 2.1 shows the kinds of people who lived in the suburbs.

If some Americans were beginning to rebel, for others clear visions of an idealised and peaceful America were springing up. One such vision was Disneyland, which opened in Anaheim, California, in 1955. Disneyland was a self-contained world of amusements and rides that conjured up dreams and pleasures that could be satisfied within the limits of Disneyland itself. There was nothing hedonistic – any desire that could not be fulfilled was repressed. Modern technology and organisation satisfied every conceivable wish.

 Thematic link: prosperity

Was there a liberal consensus in the 1950s?

The historian Geoffrey Hodgson maintained that the 1950s represented a period of (liberal) consensus that was later smashed apart by the conflict of the Civil Rights Movement in the 1960s and by disagreement over the Vietnam War. That remained the prevailing view among historians for many years. The liberal consensus might even have led to a new nationalism – a celebration of the corporation, economic abundance, consumerism and, according to Nixon, the quest for personal fulfilment. This new nationalism replaced the old, basically agrarian, sense of being 'American'.

ACTIVITY 2.3

Make mind maps of the ways in which the American economy and American culture developed over the 1950s. Identify overlaps between the two.

Figure 2.4: Walt Disney on the opening day of his theme park.

The idea of consensus – the assumption of increasing and virtually universal abundance, shared values and goals and belief in the end of conflict – reflected middle-class experience. The middle class was expanding in the following ways:

- Economically: 60% could afford a middle-class lifestyle. In 1956, white-collar workers outnumbered blue-collar workers for the first time.
- Educationally: 47% graduated from high school in 1945; by 1960 this figure was 63% and the number of college graduates doubled in the same period to 22%.
- Home ownership: 60% by 1960.
- During the 1950s over 14% of GNP was spent on leisure and entertainment.

These material advances transformed people's self-image, making them buy into the American Dream. The sociologist William Whyte called this the 'second great melting pot' – a process of socialisation that helped people transcend their class, creating an increasingly pervasive American bourgeoisie.

In Cold War terms, class, political and racial conflict could only harm the image of Americans abroad, undermining the idea of the USA as a global leader. The American media reinforced these conflicts, to the middle classes at least. By 1960 87% of Americans had a television. The airwaves were dominated by a very small

 Voices from the past

General Electric and People's Capitalism

This General Electric advertisement from 1956 exemplifies the consumer boom in America.

People's Capitalism – What Makes it Work for You?

Around the world, the term "capitalism" has been applied to economic systems which bear little resemblance to each other.

Our American brand of capitalism is distinctive and unusually successful because it is a 'people's capitalism'; *all* the people share in its responsibilities and benefits. As we see it, these are its distinguishing characteristics.

1. We in America believe in providing opportunities for each individual to develop himself to his maximum potential.

2. We in America believe in high volume, and prices within the economic reach of all – not low volume, and prices only a few can pay.

3. We in America believe in high wages, high productivity and high purchasing power. They must occur together. One without the others defeats its own ends, but together they spell dynamic growth and progress.

4. We in America believe in innovation and in scrapping the obsolete. By reinvesting earnings in research and in new production facilities, American business is creating more jobs, better products, and higher living standards for everyone.

5. We in America believe in consumer credit …

6. We in America believe in leisure for our people through a comparatively short and highly productive work week …

7. We in America believe in broad share ownership of American business …

8. And finally, we in America believe deeply in competition versus the cartel …

As we see it, the more the principles of America's distinctive brand of capitalism become known and understood, the more certain everyone can be of continued progress …

Progress Is Our Most Important Product
GENERAL ELECTRIC

number of network executives and advertisers. Whether they watched GE Theatre (hosted by a young actor named Ronald Reagan), the Pepsi Cola Playhouse, or the Camel News Caravan, Americans received the same anodyne message: America is middle class and white; women are homemakers; buy our product. Middle-class Americans seeing such constant affirmation of their own world on TV could easily conclude that this was the world in which virtually all Americans lived.

However, beneath this consensus there was still serious conflict. Many were poor. In the South, which considered the New Deal a final settlement, the legal rights of African Americans were severely restricted. Elsewhere, the New Deal was still contested. The notion of a liberal consensus was pervasive, compelling, but not entirely accurate.

Thematic link: identity

The USA and the Cold War

The major problem facing Eisenhower when he became president seemed to be the Korean War. He had promised to end it and indeed, within a few months it was over. Eisenhower was helped in this by the death of Soviet leader Joseph Stalin six weeks into his presidency. Soviet support for the Chinese and North Korea could no longer be relied upon. Eisenhower was also able to threaten the Chinese convincingly with the use of nuclear weapons. However, Eisenhower had two other major problems to confront. The first was the arms race with the Soviets, which was both threatening and terrifying. How many weapons should be built? Should they ever be used? The second was the Cold War. This was clearly now the new normal and would come to dominate United States' foreign policy. The various crises faced by Eisenhower, and the policies formed by both the USA and the USSR to control and contain these crises, marked the creation of a global strategy for dealing with localised international problems. There was no point in having separate strategies for foreign policy in different parts of the world; foreign policy was globalised. Even so, the particular location of incidents continued to matter. The main participants in the Cold War were far more likely to seek reconciliation over disputes in Europe and escalation in Asia. Figure 2.5 shows the main events of the period.

A major architect of Eisenhower's foreign policy was his Secretary of State, John Foster Dulles, who devised the New Look and the idea of **brinkmanship**. Dulles recognised that the USSR, no longer led by the unpredictable and ruthless Stalin, did not want war and might be induced to back down if a negotiation could be sufficiently threatening. He tried the same tactics with Mao's China, which he had not identified as the major threat it would later appear to be. The New Look was the other side of the same coin: American foreign policy would be strengthened by the acquisition of nuclear weapons. If brinkmanship was a game of poker, the New Look enabled America to up the stakes.

Key terms

brinkmanship: Dulles said of this strategy, 'The ability to get to the verge without getting into war is the necessary art. If you cannot master it, you inevitably get into war. If you are scared to go to the brink, you are lost.'

Superpower rivalry and conflict with the USSR

Among some in the USA there was a genuine hope that 1953 would bring something different in foreign policy. Truman had shown himself an antagonist of communists, especially Soviet communists. He had felt forced by the Red Scare to establish his anti-communist credentials and had a personal antipathy towards Stalin, because he had been forced to deal with the consequences of Stalin's meaningless promises at Yalta. By March 1953 both of the protagonists of this early Cold War drama were gone. Stalin was dead – left by his subordinates to die after suffering a stroke – and it was not clear who would replace him. Truman had also gone, replaced by Eisenhower, a pragmatic diplomat who had worked with the Soviets during the Second World War. The Korean War, which had been pointless and bloody, was over and the threat posed by China was not clear.

That said, there are some doubts about how well the USA was prepared to deal with the Soviet Union in the post-Stalin era. Stalin had become a well-understood adversary: he could not be trusted, was ruthless and unpredictable, and would clearly say one thing while believing another. This meant that nobody in America really knew what to make of the new Soviet leader, Nikita Khrushchev. By 1954, Khrushchev had emerged firmly as leader following an internal power battle during which nobody in the USA (or indeed in the USSR) really knew who was in

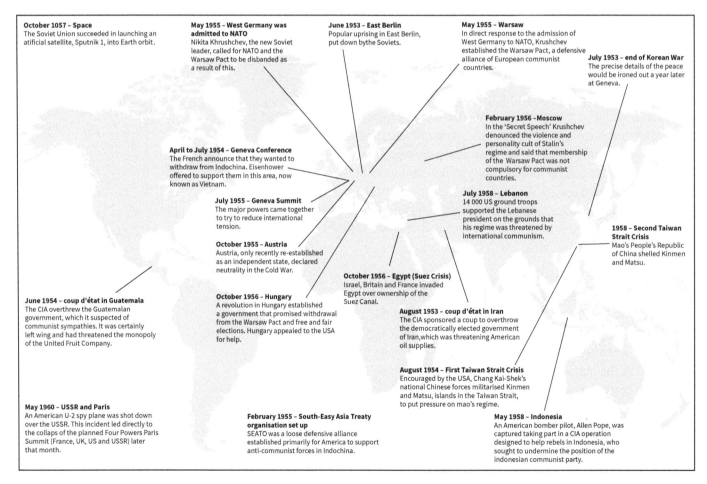

October 1057 – Space
The Soviet Union succeeded in launching an atificial satellite, Sputnik 1, into Earth orbit.

May 1955 – West Germany was admitted to NATO
Nikita Khrushchev, the new Soviet leader, called for NATO and the Warsaw Pact to be disbanded as a result of this.

June 1953 – East Berlin
Popular uprising in East Berlin, put down bythe Soviets.

May 1955 – Warsaw
In direct response to the admission of West Germany to NATO, Krushchev established the Warsaw Pact, a defensive alliance of European communist countries.

July 1953 – end of Korean War
The precise details of the peace would be ironed out a year later at Geneva.

February 1956 – Moscow
In the 'Secret Speech' Krushchev denounced the violence and personality cult of Stalin's regime and said that membership of the Warsaw Pact was not compulsory for communist countries.

April to July 1954 – Geneva Conference
The French announce that they wanted to withdraw from Indochina. Eisenhower offered to support them in this area, now known as Vietnam.

July 1955 – Geneva Summit
The major powers came together to try to reduce international tension.

July 1958 – Lebanon
14 000 US ground troops supported the Lebanese president on the grounds that his regime was threatened by international communism.

1958 – Second Taiwan Strait Crisis
Mao's People's Republic of China shelled Kinmen and Matsu.

October 1955 – Austria
Austria, only recently re-established as an independent state, declared neutrality in the Cold War.

October 1956 – Egypt (Suez Crisis)
Israel, Britain and France invaded Egypt over ownership of the Suez Canal.

June 1954 – coup d'état in Guatemala
The CIA overthrew the Guatemalan government, which it suspected of communist sympathies. It was certainly left wing and had threatened the monopoly of the United Fruit Company.

October 1956 – Hungary
A revolution in Hungary established a government that promised withdrawal from the Warsaw Pact and free and fair elections. Hungary appealed to the USA for help.

August 1953 – coup d'état in Iran
The CIA sponsored a coup to overthrow the democratically elected government of Iran, which was threatening American oil supplies.

August 1954 – First Taiwan Strait Crisis
Encouraged by the USA, Chang Kai-Shek's national Chinese forces militarised Kinmen and Matsu, islands in the Taiwan Strait, to put pressure on mao's regime.

May 1960 – USSR and Paris
An American U-2 spy plane was shot down over the USSR. This incident led directly to the collaps of the planned Four Powers Paris Summit (France, UK, US and USSR) later that month.

February 1955 – South-Easy Asia Treaty organisation set up
SEATO was a loose defensive alliance established primarily for America to support anti-communist forces in Indochina.

May 1958 – Indonesia
An American bomber pilot, Allen Pope, was captured taking part in a CIA operation designed to help rebels in Indonesia, who sought to undermine the position of the indonesian communist party.

Figure 2.5: Major events in the Cold War during Eisenhower's presidency.

charge. Khrushchev proposed 'peaceful co-existence'. Could his words of peace be trusted? Was Eisenhower himself so keen for peace that he might naively accept what Khrushchev said? Both sides made calculations and the policy that resulted was that neither could hope to destroy the other and that both sides – USA and USSR, West and East, capitalist and communist – should instead exist peacefully together. Khrushchev rejected his rival Georgy Malenkov's 'New Course', which opposed nuclear research as too dangerous. Instead he emphasised building up a strategic nuclear arsenal as a guarantee of good behaviour from the other side. This chimed perfectly well with Eisenhower and Dulles's New Look and led to a period during which the two sides could negotiate. Geneva, in neutral Switzerland, was a good place to do so. Mistrust still prevailed on both sides, however. This would come to the fore in 1960 and overshadow the presidency of Eisenhower's successor.

The Cold War was prosecuted through debate and technology. Television made it possible to transmit a message across the world and both sides did this well. This was the context of Nixon's Kitchen Debate. Khrushchev was very effective at getting his message across. In Moscow in 1956 he announced, 'We will bury you'. Khrushchev claimed to mean that the working classes would overthrow their own governments in Marxist revolutions, but the sound-bite, which had been translated by Khrushchev's own interpreter, appeared to threaten a nuclear strike. At the UN again in 1960, Khrushchev removed one of his shoes and banged it repeatedly on the desk in front of him, frustrated at references by Britain and the Philippines – both American allies – to the destruction of freedom in eastern Europe by Soviet action. This display played well at home in the USSR and resonated with other world leaders, potential Soviet allies, who were alarmed by American **imperialism**.

Meanwhile, the Soviet Union had scored a major victory in the space race. Sputnik I was the first satellite to be launched successfully. This was a blow to American pride and also to the war effort. The technology required for a satellite launch was the same as that required to build an intercontinental ballistic missile. Sputnik sparked renewed interest in the arms race. The '**missile gap**' – the difference in the number of missiles held by each side – formed an important part of the 1960 presidential election. A **U-2** plane piloted by Gary Powers had been attempting to photograph Soviet missiles when it was shot down in 1960, allowing Khrushchev to demonstrate his typical histrionics as he pretended not to know that the USA had been spying. The USA's response to the Soviet Union's success in the space race was initially unsuccessful. Rockets were lost to explosions in late 1957 and early 1958 and the Americans were falling behind in the race to put human beings into space.

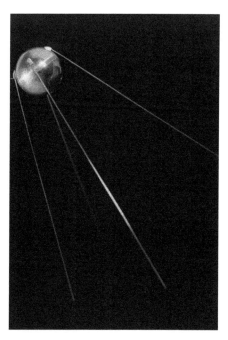

Figure 2.6: Sputnik I, the first manufactured object in space. News of its successful launch in October 1957 stunned Americans.

Khrushchev's visit to America in 1959 was an opportunity for personal diplomacy at Camp David, the US president's country retreat in Maryland, during which both Khrushchev and Eisenhower realised the limitations of their positions. It seemed both wanted peace and were in principle willing to compromise; it was just that there were very few issues on which compromise seemed possible. Neither was in sufficient control of his country to abandon the arms race. Moreover, Khrushchev, according to his memoirs, emerged so convinced that the USA was ahead of the USSR, the space race notwithstanding, that he resolved to use any means necessary to disrupt the normal pattern of international relations to force the USA onto the defensive.

ACTIVITY 2.4

1. List the ways in which Superpower rivalry developed in the 1950s.
2. Which do you think the most important issue was between the USA and the USSR, and why?

Figure 2.7: Fear of nuclear weapons became an important part of American culture. This image accompanied the article in *Life* magazine (1959) about newlyweds honeymooning in a bomb shelter, which was referred to in an essay by historian Elaine Tyler May in her 1988 book *Homeward Bound: American Families in the Cold War Era.*

 Thematic link: identity

Responses to developments in western and eastern Europe

Eisenhower's policy towards the USSR was largely dictated by events in Europe. His strengthening of West Germany by including it in NATO in 1955 was a recognition that the **Iron Curtain** was in place and would remain. It was equally a recognition that the Americans did not have the ability to support any form of uprising in East Berlin, such as the one that took place in 1953, which Eisenhower described as a 'show of courage' without taking any action to help. Some historians have suggested that if he had had American support at the time, the British Prime Minister Winston Churchill might have been able to persuade the Soviets, who were themselves consolidating following Stalin's death, to allow the reunification of Germany. As it was, West Berlin would henceforth be used as a base for western spies gathering whatever data they could about the East German government and its Soviet allies. This also marked the start of a concerted effort by the Americans to build up West Berlin to be a beacon of western values (or of capitalist excess, depending on your point of view). Later in 1953 Eisenhower and

Dulles both made it clear that nuclear weapons might be used should hostilities break out. Churchill was not impressed. He thought the rhetoric of Eisenhower and his Secretary of State put Britain at risk. The Austrian neutrality that emerged from 1955 was of no importance to American strategy. America had little need to smuggle spies across that particular border. Khrushchev retaliated to West Germany's inclusion in NATO by forming the Warsaw Pact, his own defensive alliance, so that he could use it as a bargaining chip to suggest the dismantling of both alliances. This was the context of the 1955 Geneva summit meeting, in which Eisenhower was able to create 'the spirit of Geneva', winning universal acclaim for the way in which he and Khrushchev had talked about peace. What did it matter if both sides were heavily armed, if their leaders could talk in a civilised way without any intention of using their weapons?

In 1956 it seemed as if Soviet attitudes were changing. Khrushchev had launched an extraordinary attack on the Stalinist system, denouncing Stalin in what we now recognise as very accurate terms, and appeared to suggest that communist countries could leave the Warsaw Pact. When Hungary tried to do just that in October 1956 the eyes of the world were on America, which did not intervene. Nor did America intervene in the Suez Crisis. There was no appetite for war.

Ike's only real decision was over Hungary. What could he do? America was supposed to be the leader of the democratic world and the democratic revolutionaries of Hungary were asking for help. Their popular movement had fought with the Soviet military in the capital, Budapest. After four days of street fighting, the Hungarians had created a multi-party government under democratic rule and attempted to leave the Warsaw Pact. Eisenhower, less than a month away from a presidential election, could do nothing. To 'assist' Hungary would mean an invasion, would endanger the situation in Germany and would involve rollback rather than containment. Besides, the Hungarian leader, Imre Nagy, was still a self-avowed communist. Eisenhower also recognised that whatever Khrushchev had said in a supposedly secret meeting at 2.00 a.m., Hungary was of vital strategic interest to the Soviet Union because it formed part of the central European bulwark against further German aggression. With all this in mind, the Truman Doctrine seemed to be satisfied. Invasion appeared unwise and posed geographical and political difficulties as Hungary was surrounded by communist or neutral states. So Eisenhower did nothing except voice his opposition as the Soviets rolled their tanks into Budapest, re-established communist control and executed Imre Nagy.

Reactions to the rise of communism in Asia

Eisenhower's Asian policy was focused on three areas: Korea, China and Indochina. With the benefit of hindsight we might be able to discern a clear policy of containment but the reality was somewhat murkier. In Korea, Eisenhower only sought an exit strategy to end an unpopular war. Korea is a narrow peninsula with mountainous and marshy ground and is much easier to defend than to attack. Neither side had a numerical or technological advantage because both had a massive military presence and the Americans did not want to use their nuclear weapons. Stalemate was the more or less inevitable consequence of the Korean War. The peace treaty that followed enabled the Americans to withdraw and reduce the size of their army, and allowed the Soviet Union to concentrate on its internal struggles and European borders.

It also allowed a renewed focus on China, where American policy deviated from containment. Dulles encouraged Chiang Kai-shek to threaten to reinvade the mainland. This caused the First Taiwan Strait Crisis, a year after the end of the Korean War, when the capitalist Republic of China (ROC, now called Taiwan) militarised the islands of Matsu and Kinmen (Quemoy) in the Taiwan Strait, which seemed an obvious prelude to a full-scale invasion of Mao's People's Republic of China (PRC). American doctrine had been that Mao could not win, then that he would not win, and by the 1950s the position was that he would be unable to hold on if put under sufficient pressure. There was serious discussion within the US government about using nuclear weapons to defend ROC positions on the islands in the Strait in 1954–55 and again in 1958 when Mao shelled the islands, at which point the US installed missile bases to defend them. The major result of the policy of brinkmanship in the East China Sea was the build-up of US military power on the borders of communist states, on behalf of the South Korean and ROC governments.

In Indochina the situation was different again. Southeast Asia had been part of the French Empire in the 19th century and then occupied by the Japanese during the Second World War. The French had taken the lead on post-war reconstruction of the area. It had not gone well and Truman had supported the French in their early efforts. Dean Acheson, Truman's Secretary of State, had seen the Vietnamese independence movement's leader, Hồ Chí Minh, as a communist rather than as a nationalist, and had interpreted the situation in Indochina in Cold War terms. This possibly mistaken assumption rapidly became a reality, as Hồ embraced whatever support he could find from China, the new communist powerhouse in the region. The French defeat at Dien Bien Phu in 1954 had confirmed that they had lost control of the north east of Indochina. It was clear that Vietnam, the northern part of which occupied that area, would have to be partitioned. The American role would be to protect the capitalist and supposedly democratic South Vietnam, and ensure that the free elections promised for 1956 would take place. Although the Viet Minh (Hồ Chí Minh's party, and the North Vietnamese government) had originally been American allies, the reality of the situation seemed very clear by 1954. North Vietnam has a long border with China and the spread of communism exemplified by North Vietnam would need to be contained. The North Vietnamese had a regular army of 250 000 soldiers and an irregular army of two million, which made them a force to be reckoned with. The Soviet Union, drawn into the idea of Indochina as a Cold War issue, and keen to obstruct French and American plans to attempt to reunify Vietnam, did not help matters. Recognising that domino theory applied, Eisenhower resolved to ensure that communism did not spread further, while attempting to avoid escalating the situation in Vietnam: this was a situation with which, for the moment, all sides could live. He resisted attempts (led by Nixon) to bomb the Viet Minh because he did not want to follow this up with a war on the ground. Instead he sent military advisers to South Vietnam to help the French – 300 at first but 1500 by the end of his presidency in 1961. Eisenhower prevented elections from being held in Vietnam in 1956 when it became clear that Hồ would win by a landslide across the country. This was a clear sign that resisting communism had become more important than allowing people a free and fair choice of government. Eisenhower also ordered an unsuccessful CIA intervention to try to prevent the further spread of communism in Indonesia in 1958; by now, containment had become the number one priority.

Figure 2.8: Map of China and the Korean and Indochinese peninsulas with the 1950s borders.

Response to crises in the Middle East

In 1953, in response to the Iranian government's enquiries into nationalising its own oil industry, a major supplier to the USA, Eisenhower authorised the CIA to launch a coup that enabled a military government to be created. This government ruled in the name of the Iranian Shah (king) and worked for American interests. This policy would unravel spectacularly in 1979, in a coup that dominated the final years of Jimmy Carter's presidency. In 1958, seeking to prevent the spread of communist influence into Lebanon, a small country with an important strategic location near the Suez Canal in the eastern Mediterranean, Eisenhower again intervened, this time with ground troops, to prevent the spread of communism. Oil, and the strategically important location of the Middle East, had turned it into an important Cold War battleground. The Arab world mattered intensely to the United States; ultimately, it mattered more than the country's Second World War allies.

ACTIVITY 2.5

Re-read the section headed The US and the Cold War.

- Do the ideas of brinkmanship and the New Look explain the whole of Eisenhower's foreign policy?

- What were the aims of Eisenhower's foreign policy?

- To what extent did Eisenhower meet his foreign policy aims?

When the major Middle Eastern crisis of Eisenhower's time arose, he was distracted by the Hungarian uprising and his own upcoming bid for re-election. The Egyptian leader, General Gamal Abdel Nasser, had declared himself neutral in the Cold War (thus beginning the 'non-aligned movement') and seized the British and French asset of the Suez Canal, a relic of their days as colonial powers and a major strategic link between Europe and Southeast Asia. Once again, what could Eisenhower do? He did not want to encourage countries to nationalise inter-oceanic canals – not while the Americans retained control of the canal in Panama. The Suez Canal, though, was vital to Britain and France, to the extent that Anthony Eden, the British Prime Minister, had been prepared to have Nasser assassinated even before he had actually seized it.

Dulles tried to persuade Nasser to moderate his decision, and then tried to persuade Britain and France not to take any action, while reassuring them that they were still American allies. His efforts failed. When Britain, France and Israel (which hoped to seize the West Bank) simply invaded Egypt while Dulles was in London trying to broker a solution, there were protests at the United Nations, led by the USSR. Eisenhower, who had advised against the invasion, was furious. It was clear that Eden, in particular, expected American support. As Vice President Nixon put it, how was the United States supposed to complain about the USSR invading Hungary to resist the actions of the government there if it did the same in Egypt? Again, nothing happened. Neither the USA nor the USSR was prepared to go to war in Europe or the Middle East. Eisenhower's administration had proven less supportive of Israel than Truman's had been and the Atlantic Alliance had been shaken. Relations with France, always the most awkward of American allies, did not really recover. Instead, France turned to West Germany, seeking European alliances.

Eisenhower had been worried that the Soviets might take advantage of the situation to attack Britain and France in the Middle East, perhaps with nuclear weapons. On 6 November 1956, the day of his re-election, he forced Eden into a ceasefire in return for helping to organise an emergency loan from the International Monetary Fund. Eisenhower had preserved peace but only after miscalculating how much Suez had mattered to his allies. Among the consequences of the Suez Crisis were the Eisenhower Doctrine of America, which provided economic and military aid to the Middle East, the Treaty of Rome, which led to the creation of the European Economic Community, and the rapid deconstruction of the empires of the UK and France. All of these had ramifications that resonated across the rest of the 20th century and beyond.

African Americans in North and South

The 1940s and early 1950s had been significant in the African-American experience for two reasons. First, second-generation members of northern African-American communities who had been trained for the military in southern training camps experienced the reality of life in the South. Neither segregation nor lynching was unknown in the North but in the South they were worse. The attitudes of southern whites helped to consolidate black identity. Second, the progress made under the Truman administration had been limited. The Supreme Court had made some important rulings but they were ignored. The federal government had begun to attack **segregation**, for example in the military, but this had not translated into any further benefits. Eisenhower's time in office saw a major change in American law, and the emergence of an important civil rights leader in Martin Luther King, but little actual change. The rising tide of prosperity in the 1950s was affecting African Americans too. This gave energy to the protest and meant that racial discrimination, rather than general poverty, became the most important issue for African-American communities.

The emergence of the Civil Rights Movement

The Civil Rights Movement existed before Eisenhower's time. In the 1940s, leaders including Asa Philip Randolph had secured concessions from President Roosevelt. The Supreme Court had made a series of rulings that found in favour of civil rights and active protests, such as sit-ins on buses, had begun. The nine Justices in the Supreme Court were mostly liberals. Eight had been appointed by Roosevelt and Truman and the ninth, Chief Justice Earl Warren, was a liberal Republican appointed by Eisenhower in 1953. Warren believed that the Court could and should use its power to protect individual liberties. The question of individual liberties that would clearly be coming to the Court soon was about segregation in schools.

The United States court system is complex and different courts in different areas often come up with different decisions. One role of the Supreme Court is to deal with those decisions, sometimes by determining that the actions or laws of a state or the federal government are banned under the US **Constitution**. In the 1940s and 1950s civil rights activists had carefully planned a rush of segregation cases, designed to give the Supreme Court the chance to make a final decision. Once the Court's decision is made, it is subject to the principle of ***stare decisis*** ('let the decision stand') and cannot be reversed, except by constitutional amendment or by a further decision of the Supreme Court. The Court had never reversed one of its own decisions.

Brown v Board

The case known as *Brown v Board of Education of Topeka, Kansas,* was the test case chosen by the Court. The case itself was of great importance to ten-year-old Linda Brown, who three years earlier had not been allowed to go to the school closest to her home. The school she was sent to, which was not as good and further away, was justified as 'separate but equal'. The District (lower) Court that had upheld Topeka's decision to segregate had specifically cited the case of *Plessy v Ferguson,* an 1896 Supreme Court case permitting segregation in railroad cars. By 1954, the case was about the whole legal basis for segregation. Specifically, could a state decide to provide 'separate but equal' facilities without violating the equal rights clause of the Fourteenth Amendment? The segregation of the South – in the use of buses, restaurants, water fountains – depended on the ruling.

Plessy said that it could. *Brown* said it could not. Chief Justice Warren, realising that the Court had a majority in favour of Linda Brown, ensured that the decision that came down was unanimous. All nine Justices voted to overturn *Plessy,* violating the principle of *stare decisis* by declaring that a decision of the Supreme Court had been incorrect. This is still the only time that this has happened.

ACTIVITY 2.6

1. Write a three-sentence précis of Klarman's Backlash Thesis.

2. Explain why it is called the 'Backlash Thesis'.

Figure 2.9: Rosa Parks, whose arrest in December 1955 generated a lot of publicity.

The Supreme Court had taken the most important step it could, throwing out segregation in education and ordering schools to integrate. By implication, the Supreme Court would throw out segregation in any other situation in which it occurred. In theory, segregation would melt away overnight – or at least by the next year. Warren's language in his ruling was explicit: 'To separate [Negro students] ... solely because of their race generates a feeling of inferiority as to their status in the community that may affect their hearts and minds in a way unlikely ever to be undone ... Any language in *Plessy v Ferguson* contrary to these findings is rejected ... We conclude that in the field of public education the doctrine of "separate but equal" has no place. Separate educational facilities are inherently unequal.'

Why did the Court make this ruling at this time? The fact that the justices were liberal is not in itself sufficient explanation, since New Deal Democrats were not all liberal when it came to race issues. Warren's language suggested that psychology had become important – the idea that a 'feeling of inferiority' was unacceptable was distinctly modern. There was also a reaction, after the Holocaust, against 'scientific' racism (the idea that there was a real scientific basis for the supremacy of one race above another). Finally, in the Cold War context, the obvious lack of freedom and liberty for so many inhabitants of the 'land of the free' was becoming an embarrassment.

Linda Brown went on to be a civil-rights campaigner in her own right. She was still fighting segregation in schools in Topeka in the 1990s.

Direct action protest

Segregation did not melt away; many state authorities simply ignored the Supreme Court's ruling. Civil-rights protestors began direct acts of protest, especially in the **Deep South**, where segregation was rife. In Montgomery, Alabama, in March 1955, a young woman called Claudette Colvin refused to give up her seat on the bus. It was her legal case that ultimately saw segregation on Montgomery's buses overturned. It was the quite deliberate and pre-planned actions of another woman, Rosa Parks, doing the same thing nine months later that became most famous. Rosa Parks also refused to give up her seat, in order to be arrested. Her arrest generated a boycott of Montgomery's buses, deliberately intending to hurt the bus companies – black dollars and white dollars, it turned out, were all green. The Montgomery bus boycott had two direct effects. It catapulted to national prominence one of the leaders of the local movement, the Revd Dr Martin Luther King, Jr, who formed the Southern Christian Leadership Conference (SCLC) with other leaders. It also inspired further protests by demonstrating the economic and moral vulnerability of segregation, the inability of even moderate segregationists to compromise, the resolute courage of many southern blacks, the political importance and emotional power of African-American religion, and the viability of nonviolent direct action.

Another good example of direct action came in Greensboro, North Carolina, in 1960. A series of sit-ins attracted 50 000 participants, of whom 3600 were jailed, mainly for disturbing the peace. The city demonstrated the capricious nature of segregation laws: blacks could buy toothpaste and underwear at Woolworth's but not a cup of coffee. The sit-ins led to the founding of the Student Nonviolent

Speak like a historian

Michael J. Klarman

Michael J. Klarman has made an influential argument about the Civil Rights Movement, known as the Backlash Thesis:

'In this view, *Brown* was indirectly responsible for the transformative civil rights legislation of the mid-1960s by setting in motion the following pattern of events. *Brown* crystallized southern resistance to racial change, which – from at least the time of Harry S. Truman's civil rights proposals in 1948 – had been scattered and episodic. The unification of southern racial intransigence, which became known as massive resistance, propelled politics in virtually every southern state several notches to the right on racial issues; *Brown* temporarily destroyed southern racial moderation. In this extremist political environment, men who were unswervingly committed to preservation of the racial status quo were catapulted into public office. These massive resistance politicians were both personally and politically predisposed to use whatever measures were necessary to maintain Jim Crow, including the brutal suppression of civil rights demonstrations. There followed nationally televised scenes of southern law enforcement officers using police dogs, high-pressure fire hoses, tear gas, and truncheons against peaceful, prayerful black demonstrators (often children), which converted millions of previously indifferent northern whites into enthusiastic proponents of civil rights legislation.'[2]

Coordinating Committee (SNCC), made up of black college students throughout the South and inspired by the long-time activist Ella Baker. Many leaders of the National Association for the Advancement of Colored People (NAACP, one of the oldest civil rights groups) and the SCLC were wary of the SNCC's confrontational style but King endorsed them.

Shortly after the end of Eisenhower's presidency, arrest would be the entire point of Freedom Rides, which were never all-black affairs, and part of the point of sit-ins and bus boycotts. This required organisation, but organisation often happened at a very low level – Freedom Rides came from university campuses, for example. Leaders might then emerge – for example, Martin Luther King, not one of the original leaders of the Movement, emerged from the Montgomery Bus Boycotts as a national figure. Much of the organisation occurred at the grassroots, in a piecemeal fashion. Sit-ins and boycotts spread around the country, with added publicity from the relatively new medium of television. They were at their most effective when they had a direct economic impact on businesses. When black people stopped riding the buses in Alabama, bus companies felt the pressure and many reversed their policies. In Greensboro, white store owners quickly realised that they would lose business if the protests continued. Sit-ins worked.

Thematic link: democracy

The SCLC campaign for voting rights

The first president of the Southern Christian Leadership Conference (SCLC), which was founded in 1957, was Dr Martin Luther King, Jr, who had come to prominence during the Montgomery bus boycott. Instructions were issued in his name about what speakers and participants in the SCLC should do when encouraging others to join their campaign. King made it clear that the SCLC was focused on delivering voting reform. He believed that if African Americans in the South voted in large numbers other social and economic opportunities would fall into place. The right to vote would bring increased wages, less police brutality, and justice, and improve the democratic accountability of elected officials in the South.

King's stated aim, in a memo of early 1958, was to double the number of African Americans voting in the South. He intended this to occur through voter registration and by persuading those already registered to turn out to vote, as well as struggling for the right to vote where it did not exist. This was to be done in conjunction with the legal work of the NAACP. The SCLC's campaign did indeed result in African Americans being given the right to vote in the South, after a long struggle.

The policies and attitudes of the main political parties

The Republican response to African-American pressure for civil rights was mixed. Eisenhower, as president, was broadly supportive. His Executive Order 10479 in 1953 ensured that there would be equal opportunities in employment on government contracts, while Executive Order 10590 in 1955 worked towards eliminating discrimination among federal employees. Eisenhower was willing to work towards civil rights but he was not willing to fight for law or practices to change in areas that were out of the remit of the federal government. Conservative Republicans were sometimes enthusiastic about civil rights for political reasons. Senator Robert A. Taft of Ohio had tried to drum up support for civil rights in 1946 as part of an attempt to re-engage the Republican Party with the African-American vote, which it had begun to lose as a result of the New Deal. In 1957, Nixon toyed with the idea of trying to push a Voting Rights Act through Congress in order to fragment the Democratic Party. He had already worked with Senate Majority Leader Lyndon Johnson in order to pass the first Civil Rights Act, which supported the *Brown* decision.

The Democratic Party was sorely tested by the Civil Rights Movement. The New Deal Coalition had depended on southern whites; now they prepared to leave the Party. In 1956, led by Senator Harry Byrd of Virginia, 101 mostly Democratic members of Congress signed a Southern Manifesto pledging 'massive resistance'. The *Brown* decision, they said, was a 'clear abuse of judicial power'. Half a million southerners joined **White Citizens' Councils** – new and short-lived institutions that were dedicated to blocking school integration and other civil rights measures. The **Ku Klux Klan** swelled to numbers not seen since the 1920s. By now the 'Klan' represented several disorganised racist movements, all linking themselves back to the well-known white-hooded secret societies of the 1860s and 1920s. They took actions such as placing burning crosses at black churches; by the 1960s members of organisations claiming affiliation with the Ku Klux Klan would be firebombing the churches themselves. Although Byrd and the influential Democratic senator

Lyndon B. Johnson were resolute in their support of civil rights, it seemed that this support might not be worth all that much.

The responses of the state and federal authorities

States found a variety of ways to wriggle out of compliance with *Brown*. West Virginia said that it would wait one more year. Mississippi abolished all its public schools. In 1957, the NAACP enrolled nine students at a school in the Arkansas state capital Little Rock, prompting Governor Orval Faubus to use the National Guard to enforce the segregation of the school. The mob then took over, taunting black students, shouting 'Go back to the jungle'. As vicious scenes were replayed on TV over the following fortnight, Eisenhower decided to send in 1000 federal troops and placed the state and National Guard under federal control. This was the first federal intervention in the South since 1877. The black students entered the school but met such strident protests and threats of violence that school officials removed them. As in other areas in the South, school officials in Little Rock decided to close the school for a time rather than carry out the desegregation order. Eisenhower, however, had placed the weight of the president's power as commander-in-chief squarely behind the Supreme Court's decision to end segregation. It may have been that he cared more about the Supreme Court than about civil rights – but that was not the point.

Eisenhower was accused by opponents of civil rights of using Hitlerite tactics by calling the army out against ordinary Americans. Eisenhower rebutted this, pointing out that his was a free government. Naturally, the opponents of civil rights were adamant that the freedom of individual states to decide on their own social orders was being infringed upon. The whole affair had worrying echoes of the conflict over slavery 100 years earlier, which had led to the American Civil War (1861–65). A large number of Americans – some 30% – disapproved of Eisenhower's actions.

ACTIVITY 2.7

Create a diagram to show the progress African Americans made towards civil rights during Eisenhower's presidency. Indicate any areas where their progress was dependent on events in Truman's presidency.

Practice essay questions

1. How far do you agree with the view that Eisenhower's foreign policy increased, rather than decreased, the possibility of nuclear confrontation with the USSR?
2. 'The greatest effect of the growing American economy of the 1950s was on American culture.' Assess the validity of this view.
3. 'Eisenhower's success owed very little to the rest of the Republican Party.' Do you agree with this?
4. 'Eisenhower's domestic policies were largely a response to the Cold War.' Explain why you agree or disagree with this view.

Taking it further

How much progress did Americans make in the 1950s towards living the American Dream?

Chapter summary

By the end of this chapter you should understand:

- Eisenhower's presidency as a continuation of his sense of duty to the nation, which he put above the Party he had only recently joined

- the progress of the Civil Rights Movement towards its apex in the 1960s, through a series of necessary steps that the president encouraged without directing

- the changes in fortunes of the Republican and Democratic parties during the 1950s

- Eisenhower's Cold War policies of containment and nuclear deterrence;

- the consumer boom, which changed Americans' views and expectations and made them on the whole more affluent.

End notes
1   http://everything2.com/title/The+Nixon-Khrushchev+%2522Kitchen+Debate%2522
2   *Journal of American History* 1994; 81(1): 82.

3 John F. Kennedy and the 'New Frontier', 1960–1963

In this section, we will examine the presidency of America's youngest president, John Fitzgerald Kennedy, whose reputation in death arguably exceeded his achievements in life. He won the presidency narrowly on a platform of progressive reform; more was achieved by his successor. In foreign policy he talked tough but achieved his greatest successes when refusing to go to war. He reluctantly set in motion some of the major achievements of the Civil Rights Movement. His death, after barely 1000 days as president, remains an iconic moment in American history. We will look into:

* The presidential election of 1960 and reasons for Kennedy's victory; the policies and personalities of the Kennedy administration; the ideas behind the 'New Frontier'.

* Challenges to American power: the legacy of crises over Berlin and relations with Khrushchev; the challenge of Castro's Cuba; deepening involvement in Vietnam.

* African Americans in the North and South: the rise of the Civil Rights Movement; the opponents of civil rights, including within the Democratic Party; Kennedy's policies in response to the pressures for change.

* The United States by 1963: its position as a world power; economic prosperity; the growing pressures for social change from women and young people.

Introduction: Kennedy and Camelot

The brief presidency of John F. Kennedy, which lasted just over 1000 days, was both exciting and disappointing. It was exciting because it brought glamour and hope to the presidency – a glamour that would not return for 20 years. It was exciting because Kennedy restored American pride in foreign policy; however, this concealed a major concession, as Kennedy allowed the Soviet Union free rein over East Berlin. It was exciting because Kennedy, as president, accepted his responsibility to take the Civil Rights Movement seriously, but disappointing because he did so very late and met with so little success. Kennedy's death enhanced, rather than created, a legacy of greatness. In any discussion of America's greatest presidents, his name comes up.

America's prosperity, which had suffered a slight hiccup towards the end of Eisenhower's presidency, continued to improve. The country's industrial output grew along with its balance of trade and increasing numbers of Americans shared in that prosperity. As ever, though, prosperity was not universal and certainly not as universal as America's cultural response might have made it appear. That cultural response was now exported around the world. Communications satellites and increasing television ownership among America's allies meant that American influence now spread across the world even more easily. There was a downside to this for those pushing the idea of American Exceptionalism, a downside to this, for now, when Americans excluded from mainstream political society were the objects of violence or arbitrary arrest, pictures were beamed across the world. In practice, this provided useful publicity for the Civil Rights Movement, helping to shape the strategy of leaders such as Martin Luther King, Jr.

Kennedy was not exactly the embodiment of the American Dream. His personal narrative was obvious enough – the son of a rich, influential man became president of the United States. Yet Kennedy seemed to stand for something more. To his contemporaries and his voters he seemed to represent a new vision and a new hope for America. As historians, we can be blinded by the glamour around him, by the weight of unfulfilled expectation caused by his untimely death, and by the myth of 'Camelot', which analysts immediately created to describe his time in office. We should remember that he only just won the 1960 election and that he was succeeded by two older and old-style politicians. Kennedy was the first president to have been born in the 20th century but his two successors (just 11 and four years older than him, respectively), although equally 20th-century by birth, had an older-style outlook.

The presidential election of 1960 and reasons for Kennedy's victory

The presidential election of 1960 was one of the closest in American history. The young Senator John F. Kennedy defeated Vice President Richard Nixon, the first sitting vice president to run for the presidency in a century and himself only marginally older than Kennedy. Nixon, a naturally bitter man, was further embittered by his defeat. For the rest of his life he was convinced (with some reason) that he had been denied the presidency by electoral fraud in Illinois, where Mayor Richard J. Daley of Chicago, a powerful Democratic Party figure, and the Mob were blamed, and Texas, where the Party leader was Kennedy's running mate, Senator Lyndon B. Johnson. Nixon lost the popular vote by only around 100 000 votes – 0.1% – and he lost those two states by 9000 and 46 000 votes respectively. Had he won them, they would have given him the presidency. Despite the closeness in the candidates' ages, the election felt like a generational struggle. Nixon had been around for a long time – leading the House Un-American Activities Committee, as Senator, and as vice president to Eisenhower. He represented White Anglo-Saxon Protestant America, and Kennedy (despite being very rich) seemed to represent immigrants, the poor, African Americans – the full New Deal coalition. The American people, upbeat after a decade of prosperity, elected the man who seemed to represent a glorious future. Kennedy's policies were new and forward-looking. Nixon's policies had been useful in the 1940s.

During the election campaign Kennedy criticised Eisenhower's administration (and by implication Vice President Nixon) for allowing America to have fewer nuclear missiles than the USSR. The 'missile gap' made Eisenhower's administration seem irresponsible. In fact, as Nixon well knew but could not say, the USA was ahead. The New Look had been successful but to admit that America was ahead in the missile gap might have led to calls to produce fewer missiles, which would have damaged the already slightly fragile economy. There had been a mini-slump in 1958–59 and while the age of prosperity was not dead, times were more difficult, which was never good news for the incumbent party at election time. Kennedy was able to blame the Republicans for the economy and for the decline in America's global standing, which he said had come from the missile gap and the fall of the friendly government of Fulgencio Batista in Cuba in 1959. Kennedy's 'New Frontier' would re-establish American prosperity and global pre-eminence. That his opponent was an experienced veteran of international diplomacy was irrelevant.

Kennedy's political machine was formidable. He defeated Hubert Humphrey, the Senator from Minnesota, for the Democratic nomination. As Humphrey said, 'You can't beat a million dollars.' Kennedy's campaign was well financed, primarily through the machinations of his father, Joseph (Joe). Joe Kennedy had always planned for his sons to be eligible for political high office. Jack, as he was known, was not his first choice; that had been Joe Jr, who had died in the Second World War. Now the full weight of the Kennedy fortune swung behind Jack, with his younger brother Robert (Bobby) as campaign manager and the youngest Kennedy, Edward (Teddy), responsible for campaigning in the West. The Kennedy machine recognised the importance of voter registration, especially among African-American and other poor communities. This helped Kennedy, as people who had not voted before turned out for him. The African-American vote in the North was becoming an important asset to the Democrats; meanwhile the Kennedy family had risen to prominence within the Democratic Party as the Catholic vote became more important. The Kennedy money also helped. Lyndon Johnson explained that he had swung the votes of Texas behind Kennedy's nomination for president by saying that he had thought about the Kennedys' influence and money and wanted them to be grateful to him. Johnson was an ambitious man and by supporting Kennedy he gave up his own chance for the presidency in 1961. Perhaps he expected Kennedy to lose, leaving Johnson in prime position to challenge Nixon in

Key terms

White Anglo-Saxon Protestant (WASP): a shorthand term with obvious racial overtones to describe Americans who were from particular white communities, in particular the Scots-Irish communities of the working-class North and South.

missile gap: the term used to describe the fact that one nation had more, more powerful or longer-range missiles than the other. For most of the Cold War, the Americans were ahead.

1964; or perhaps he expected Kennedy to pass the presidential nomination on to him in 1968.

As a Catholic – the first to stand for the presidency since Al Smith in 1928 – Kennedy would always be suspected of disloyalty by the WASP majority in America. Indeed, there were cartoons depicting Big John (the Pope, John XXIII) telling Little John (Kennedy) what to do. Kennedy addressed the issue head-on, declaring his loyalty to the United States and emphasising his record as a war hero (he had won the **Purple Heart** during the Second World War). His Catholicism appeared to cost him votes in the South but gain them in the urban North, although this was a continuation of the shifting politics of the New Deal coalition in the Democratic Party and was also exemplified by the increasing significance of the northern African-American vote.

The election is most famous for the debates between the presidential candidates. Tellingly, those who listened to them on the radio thought that Nixon had had the advantage, while those who watched them on the television thought Kennedy the winner. Nixon had a dreadful cold in one of the debates and a ghostly pallor. He also tended to sweat under pressure and refused to wear make-up. Kennedy, by contrast, looked youthful, vigorous and reassuring, which became the media narrative created afterwards. His narrow victory over Nixon came at a time when almost everyone agreed that had Eisenhower been allowed to run again, he would have done so and won.

Figure 3.1: Kennedy campaigned as a modern presidential candidate for a new era. This is one of his campaign posters.

 Voices from the past

The Kennedy–Nixon debates

This is an extract from Kennedy's closing statement in the fourth and final presidential debate between him and Nixon in 1960.

I run because I believe this year the United States has a great opportunity to make a move forward, to make a determination here at home and around the world, that it's going to reestablish itself as a vigorous society. My judgment is that the Republican Party has stood still here in the United States, and it's also stood still around the world. Uh - We're using about fifty per cent of our steel capacity today. We had a recession in fifty-eight. We had a recession in fifty-four. We're not moving ahead in education the way we should. We didn't make a judgment in fifty-seven and fifty-six and fifty-five and fifty-

four that outer space would be important. If we stand still here, if we appoint people to ambassadorships and positions in Washington who have a status quo outlook, who don't recognize that this is a revolutionary time, then the United States does not maintain its influence. And if we fail, the cause of freedom fails. I believe it incumbent upon the next president of the United States to get this country moving again, to get our economy moving ahead, to set before the American people its goals, its unfinished business … I believe in 1960 and sixty-one and two and three we have a rendezvous with destiny. And I believe it incumbent upon us to be the defenders of the United States and the defenders of freedom; and to do that, we must give this country leadership and we must get America moving again.[1]

The policies and personalities of the Kennedy administration

Figure 3.2: The Kennedy family.

John Fitzgerald Kennedy (JFK) was the oldest surviving son of Joseph and Rose Kennedy, who were leading members of the Massachusetts Catholic community. He was charismatic and an excellent public speaker. He had a knack for leadership that had been honed in wartime. He held press conferences, which were broadcast live, as part of his projection of confidence. Even the disastrous Bay of Pigs invasion of 1961 saw him emerge more popular, much to his surprise: his admission of responsibility went down well. He was chronically ill, prone to severe back pain and illness caused by Addison's Disease. He kept this secret from the general public. Also secret was his serial infidelity with a succession of women, including the famous actress Marilyn Monroe. His wife Jackie Kennedy was a style icon. Of a different generation from Mamie Eisenhower, who had preceded her as First Lady, she oversaw the updating of the decor and furniture of the White House, and acted as hostess in a series of well-publicised dinner parties at which the guests were American writers and artists. The First Family had been touched by tragedy. Jackie had suffered miscarriages while Jack was a senator and their new-born son Patrick died in 1963. All of this added to the popular view of the Kennedys as both glamorous and iconic, while also obviously human and in touch with ordinary people.

Jack Kennedy surrounded himself with an administration referred to by many, including Vice President Lyndon Johnson, as 'the brightest and the best'. Among them was his combative brother Robert. Even more liberal than Jack, Bobby had

ACTIVITY 3.1

With reference to the Kennedy–Nixon debates source and your understanding of the historical context, how valuable is this source in explaining why Kennedy won the election of 1960?

ACTIVITY 3.2

1. What problems did Kennedy identify in American society in 1960? Based on your reading of Chapters 1 and 2, how accurate was his diagnosis?
2. As you read through this chapter, consider how effective Kennedy's presidency was, judged by his own terms as set out in this speech.

ACTIVITY 3.3

Kennedy won the 1960 election by a very narrow margin.

1. Make a table with two columns headed 'Reasons for a Kennedy victory' and 'Reasons suggesting Nixon might have won'.
2. For each of the reasons in the first column, explain whether it was a *necessary* or a *sufficient* cause of victory.
3. For each of the reasons in the second column, explain why it did not ultimately lead to Nixon winning.
4. Use this information to explain what, precisely, enabled Kennedy to win.

been his formidable campaign manager and now became **Attorney General**. This was unusual, as he had no courtroom experience; instead, his legal experience had been in fighting organised crime. Bobby Kennedy came into regular conflict with the FBI chief, J. Edgar Hoover, and also initiated a 'blood feud' with the leader of the Teamsters Union, Jimmy Hoffa, who was well known to be behind financial and electoral corruption. Hoffa was jailed in 1964. The real significance of Bobby Kennedy was as his brother's closest adviser. He was known as the 'Number 2 in Washington' and had a role across the administration including in foreign policy, not the usual area for an Attorney General. Bobby's influence was often felt, for example, at the Executive Committee meetings surrounding the Cuban Missile Crisis in 1962.

The myth about Kennedy is that his **Cabinet** and close advisers lacked experience. This was not completely true. Dean Rusk, his second choice as Secretary of State, had been a former Assistant Secretary of State. McGeorge (Mac) Bundy had been a military intelligence officer and Harvard professor. He became National Security Adviser. Secretary of Labor Arthur Goldberg had been a union lawyer. They were the most qualified of Kennedy's appointments. The Secretary of Defense, Robert McNamara, had been the general manager at Ford, where he had helped to turn the major company around and make it more productive. Where Kennedy, and the 'wise men' who were his closest advisers – Bobby, Mac, McNamara, sometimes Rusk, and the speechwriter Theodore Sorenson – did lack experience was in dealing with other institutions, such as the military and Congress.

The ideas behind the New Frontier

Kennedy's domestic programme, the New Frontier, is summed up in Figure 3.3. Kennedy coined the term himself in his speech accepting the Democratic Party's nomination for president, in the following words: 'We stand today on the edge of a new frontier – the frontier of the 1960s, the frontier of unknown opportunities and perils, the frontier of unfilled hopes and unfilled threats. ... Beyond that frontier are uncharted areas of science and space, unsolved problems of peace and war, unconquered problems of ignorance and prejudice, unanswered questions of poverty and surplus.' A key question to consider when thinking about the New Frontier is what it was designed to do. Was it:

- Classic **progressive** legislation in the New Deal tradition (placing Kennedy in a line of Democratic presidents from Roosevelt to Johnson)?
- A series of attempts to restructure an economy in downturn, providing stability and trying to avert a repeat of the pattern of boom and bust that had followed the First World War?
- Aimed at improving America's image and standing abroad (America was a beacon of hope for the Free World, after all)?
- An attempt to preserve some form of Democratic coalition that could win elections, given the apparent loss of the 'Solid South' – the idea that the southern states were 'solid' in their support of the Democrats – because of the Democrats' support for civil rights?

Inspired by the Soviets' achievement in making Yuri Gagarin the first man in space in April 1961, two and a half months into his presidency, Kennedy challenged

NASA to put a man on the moon by the end of the decade. This would involve a single-minded focus and the diversion of vast resources. It also had the happy side effect of improving US missile technology. In his foreign policy Kennedy challenged communism aggressively. He was a reluctant champion of the Civil Rights Movement. In his economic and social policy, he was a Democrat in the progressive, New Deal tradition – or tried to be, at least.

On the face of it Kennedy's legislative record seems impressive. Around 60% of his suggested legislation passed. It was often watered down by Congress, reduced to its basics in order to secure votes: Kennedy's team lacked the experience to prevent this. Sometimes his policies were unsuccessful. He tried and failed to enact healthcare and to create a Department of Urban Affairs. Instead he managed to expand social security, pushing the pension age down to 62 and raising the level of unemployment benefits, and to address slum clearance and water pollution. He was also successful in passing an Omnibus Housing Bill in 1961, a classically progressive piece of legislation and New Deal-style stimulus. Equally progressive was his support of farmers – his Farmers Home Administration Act (1961) dealt with the age-old problem of mortgage foreclosures and falling farm prices.

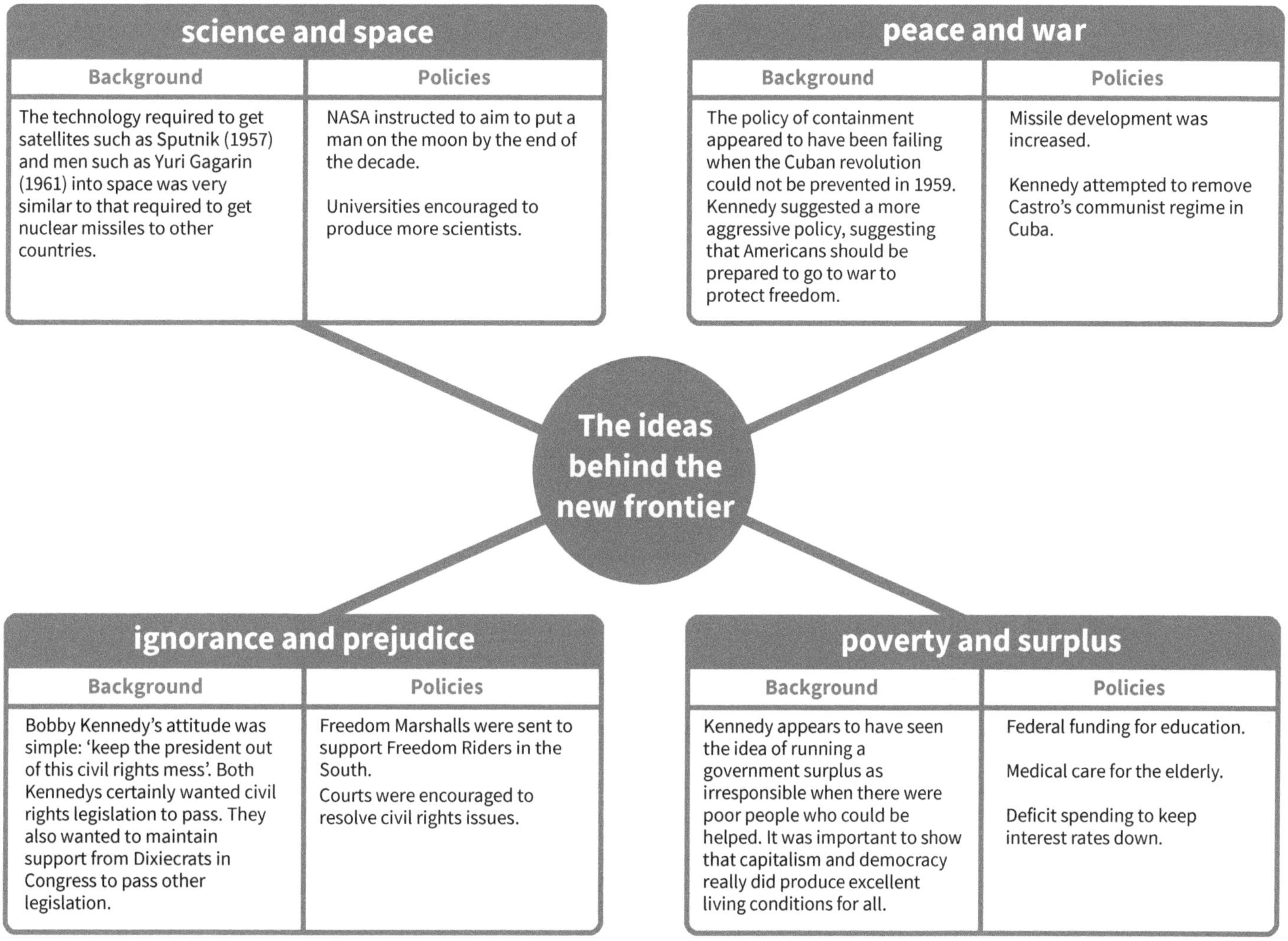

science and space

Background	Policies
The technology required to get satellites such as Sputnik (1957) and men such as Yuri Gagarin (1961) into space was very similar to that required to get nuclear missiles to other countries.	NASA instructed to aim to put a man on the moon by the end of the decade. Universities encouraged to produce more scientists.

peace and war

Background	Policies
The policy of containment appeared to have been failing when the Cuban revolution could not be prevented in 1959. Kennedy suggested a more aggressive policy, suggesting that Americans should be prepared to go to war to protect freedom.	Missile development was increased. Kennedy attempted to remove Castro's communist regime in Cuba.

The ideas behind the new frontier

ignorance and prejudice

Background	Policies
Bobby Kennedy's attitude was simple: 'keep the president out of this civil rights mess'. Both Kennedys certainly wanted civil rights legislation to pass. They also wanted to maintain support from Dixiecrats in Congress to pass other legislation.	Freedom Marshalls were sent to support Freedom Riders in the South. Courts were encouraged to resolve civil rights issues.

poverty and surplus

Background	Policies
Kennedy appears to have seen the idea of running a government surplus as irresponsible when there were poor people who could be helped. It was important to show that capitalism and democracy really did produce excellent living conditions for all.	Federal funding for education. Medical care for the elderly. Deficit spending to keep interest rates down.

Figure 3.3: The ideas behind the New Frontier.

ACTIVITY 3.4

Look at Figure 3.3. Create a single paragraph précis of the key ideas of the New Frontier.

The death of John F. Kennedy

One of the major aims of any history textbook is to introduce to its readers the idea that narratives of the past can be contested. That is, sometimes historians are not sure what is *true* and arguments can then arise about what actually happened.

The death of John F. Kennedy, by an assassin's bullet in Dallas on 22 November 1963 is an iconic moment in world history. The dramatic tragedy of the moment – the young, charismatic president killed in his motorcade next to his wife – helped to consolidate the Kennedy myth that was already growing around him. Sensible historical analysis of his achievements should not be clouded by the manner of his death.

So what happened? Lee Harvey Oswald, an ex-marine with apparent communist sympathies, concealed himself in the Texas School Book Depository in Dallas, Texas, where he could be guaranteed a good view of the presidential motorcade as it passed. Oswald shot at the motorcade, hitting the Governor of Texas, John Connally, and hitting Kennedy twice. Kennedy was pronounced dead at a local hospital. In fact his wounds had been instantly fatal. Oswald was himself shot two days later by Jack Ruby, a nightclub owner who said he wished to spare Jackie Kennedy from having to attend Oswald's trial.

So far, so clear. Conspiracy theories grew up overnight. Oswald had fired two shots, one of which had hit both Kennedy and Connally – except that Connally believed that he had been hit by a separate bullet and an indistinct recording appeared to suggest that three shots, not two, had been fired. Perhaps there had been another gunman, firing from a different angle – perhaps concealed from view by a nearby grassy knoll? And why had Jack Ruby killed Oswald? Perhaps because Oswald would shortly reveal that he had been put up to the assassination by the Soviets, the Cubans or the CIA. And wasn't it a coincidence that Kennedy had been shot in Texas, the home state of the new president, Lyndon B. Johnson?

Johnson himself believed that there might have been a wider conspiracy, aimed at him as well. This had been the case when Abraham Lincoln was killed in 1865 and a plot against Vice President Andrew Johnson failed. Lyndon Johnson set up the Warren Commission, under Chief Justice Earl Warren, to investigate the assassination. The Commission's conclusion was that both Oswald and Ruby had acted alone.

Then again, the government would say that, wouldn't it? The problem with conspiracy theories is that they never go away; denial only makes them stronger. The conspiracy theories about Kennedy's death remain to this day. We will not list any more here: you will be able to find them easily enough on the Internet.

Challenges to American power

During the election campaign that saw him arrive at the presidency, Kennedy claimed that American power had been diminished in Khrushchev's time. His inaugural address, the most famous part of which appears in Voices from the past: JFK's inaugural address, was entirely based on foreign policy and was interpreted by many as an expression that the logical consequence of American Exceptionalism was that Americans should accept leadership of the free world,

Figure 3.4: Lee Harvey Oswald (centre), the assassin of President Kennedy, was arrested at the Texas Theatre around an hour after the assassination.

which might involve a call to arms. In other words, freedom might be worth fighting for.

Any challenge to American power would come, it was clear, in one of five forms. It might involve Cuba – Kennedy made a reference to the recent communist revolution there in his speech and had campaigned on the issue. It might involve nuclear weapons, where Kennedy believed there was a 'missile gap' between the USA and the USSR. It might involve Indochina, where American interests would be particularly threatened if China decided to become involved, although China seemed to have been contained. It might involve the unpredictable leader of the USSR, Nikita Khrushchev, doing something unexpected in the wake of the U-2 incident, over which he was still smarting. Finally, there might be another demonstration of American technological backwardness in the space race. Kennedy knew that the Soviet plans for putting a man into space were more advanced than those of NASA.

Kennedy's response was characteristic. He threatened war, but set up the Peace Corps, which was designed to enable young Americans to go abroad, especially to developing countries, to provide aid and promote friendship – a means of recruiting allies. He enhanced and renewed weapons testing, fulfilling his campaign pledge to close the missile gap, even though the gap was in his favour. All this made Khrushchev believe that Kennedy was willing to talk about war rather than commit to it. Khrushchev resolved to see how far Kennedy could be pushed.

Thematic link: identity

The legacy of crises over Berlin and relations with Khrushchev

When he heard that Kennedy, rather than his old sparring partner Richard Nixon, had won the presidential election, Khrushchev wrote to the new president hoping that US-Soviet relations might return to how they were in the time of FDR – that is, before the Cold War. Kennedy, once installed as president, suggested that they meet, believing that he and Khrushchev might be able to work out their differences. The summit, when it came, was in neutral Vienna, the capital of Austria, in June 1961. Although the two leaders discussed the situations in Indochina and Cuba, their major focus was Berlin, as it would have been at the Paris summit between Khrushchev and Eisenhower had that summit not been disrupted by the U-2 incident.

The USSR had come under pressure from the East German authorities to close the border between East and West Berlin. There were a number of reasons for doing this. Western spies used their freedom of access to and from the East with impunity. Eastern residents were moving west, attracted by the opulent lifestyle that the Americans and West Germans had ensured was on display in West Berlin, as part of their propaganda campaign against communism. This was resulting in a 'brain drain', as many of the most able East German citizens were moving west. Khrushchev wanted to test Kennedy's resolve. He feared that acceding to

Voices from the past

JFK's inaugural address

This is the end of JFK's **inaugural address** of 20 January 1961. After setting out his agenda (freedom, liberty) he finished with this …

Now the trumpet summons us again – not as a call to bear arms, though arms we need – not as a call to battle, though embattled we are – but a call to bear the burden of a long twilight struggle, year in and year out, "rejoicing in hope, patient in tribulation" – a struggle against the common enemies of man: **tyranny**, poverty, disease, and war itself.

Can we forge against these enemies a grand and global alliance, North and South, East and West, that can assure a more fruitful life for all mankind? Will you join in that historic effort?

In the long history of the world, only a few generations have been granted the role of defending freedom in its hour of maximum danger. I do not shrink from this responsibility – I welcome it. I do not believe that any of us would exchange places with any other people or any other generation. The energy, the faith, the devotion which we bring to this endeavour will light our country and all who serve it – and the glow from that fire can truly light the world.

And so, my fellow Americans: ask not what your country can do for you – ask what you can do for your country.

My fellow citizens of the world: ask not what America will do for you, but what together we can do for the freedom of man.

Finally, whether you are citizens of America or citizens of the world, ask of us the same high standards of strength and sacrifice which we ask of you. With a good conscience our only sure reward, with history the final judge of our deeds, let us go forth to lead the land we love, asking His blessing and His help, but knowing that here on earth God's work must truly be our own.

Figure 3.5: JFK delivers his inaugural address.

ACTIVITY 3.5

Kennedy's inaugural address is usually regarded as a fine example of American rhetoric. Which features in particular make it so? You should think about the content and style of what he says. You might want to look up the full text and a video of the speech online.

East German requests to close the border would raise tensions with the West, but wanted to know how much Kennedy really cared. He found that Kennedy, who thought that he was trying to be reasonable, was equivocal in his support for West Berlin; he had conceded the idea that the division of Berlin might be permanent, which is what Khrushchev had wanted for the whole of East Germany. Kennedy also, against all advice, engaged Khrushchev in an ideological rather than a practical debate. Khrushchev's normal approach to such debates was to abandon logic and repeat communist positions as forcefully as he could.

In the weeks after the Vienna summit, Kennedy came to feel that Khrushchev had been rough on him, while Khrushchev came to believe that Kennedy was weak and could be bullied. In early August 1961, Secretary of State Rusk and his French and British equivalents, meeting in Paris, decided that any action taken by the USSR in Berlin would be defensive and it was not worth risking a war. Khrushchev's intelligence operation was excellent and he knew about their conclusion. Within a week, a barbed-wire fence was erected in Berlin, during the night of 12 to 13 August 1961. Over the next few months it became a solid wall. Two months later, on 22 October, the US Chief of Mission in West Berlin, Allen Lightner, was stopped in his car at Checkpoint Charlie, the border between the American and Soviet zones inside Berlin. This violated the agreement made at Potsdam that all allied forces could move freely across Berlin. By 27 October the situation had degenerated and tanks faced each other across Checkpoint Charlie and at the Brandenburg Gate, the iconic central point of Berlin that was just behind the wall. Rusk told the American commander not to risk war over the Berlin Wall; meanwhile, Kennedy and Khrushchev brokered a solution that saw the tanks retreating in turn, a few metres at a time. A wall, Kennedy said, 'is a hell of a lot better than a war'. West Berlin became increasingly a focal point of the Cold War. Kennedy expressed his solidarity in 1963 by saying that he was proud to be a Berliner; their precarious situation was representative of that of the whole world.

Why did Khrushchev build the wall and why did Kennedy let him? The answer to the second question is very easy indeed: Kennedy had no real choice. To have gone to war over the wall would have risked the very existence of America's allies in Western Europe. If Eisenhower, in 1956, had feared that the Suez Crisis could lead to a nuclear stand-off, how much more dangerous must this have appeared? So what was Khrushchev up to? All the suggested answers were broadly true:

- Educated East Germans were going west and not coming back. They were attracted by the better living standards that were maintained (at great cost to West Germany and ultimately to the USA) in West Berlin. That the migrants were largely educated caused a 'brain drain' and damaged the East German economy. Even without that factor, the population of East Germany had declined by 10% over the 1950s.
- East Berlin was a major point at which western spies crept behind the Iron Curtain.
- The East German government had long wanted to build a wall to keep its citizens in.

Ultimately, though, Khrushchev's calculation seems to have been twofold. First, the Berlin Crisis and associated rhetoric had become extreme, apparently risking nuclear conflict. At least a wall would prevent any further unpredictable increases in tension. Second, he wanted to put Kennedy onto the defensive – just as he had tried to do with Eisenhower.

The challenge of Castro's Cuba

The revolution in Cuba in 1959 had been a serious blow to American business and prestige. Cuba had been a valuable trading partner and that advantage had been lost as the socialist revolutionary government led by Fidel Castro nationalised American industry and businesses on the island. Other Latin American republics

Figure 3.6: The stand-off at Checkpoint Charlie, 27 October 1961.

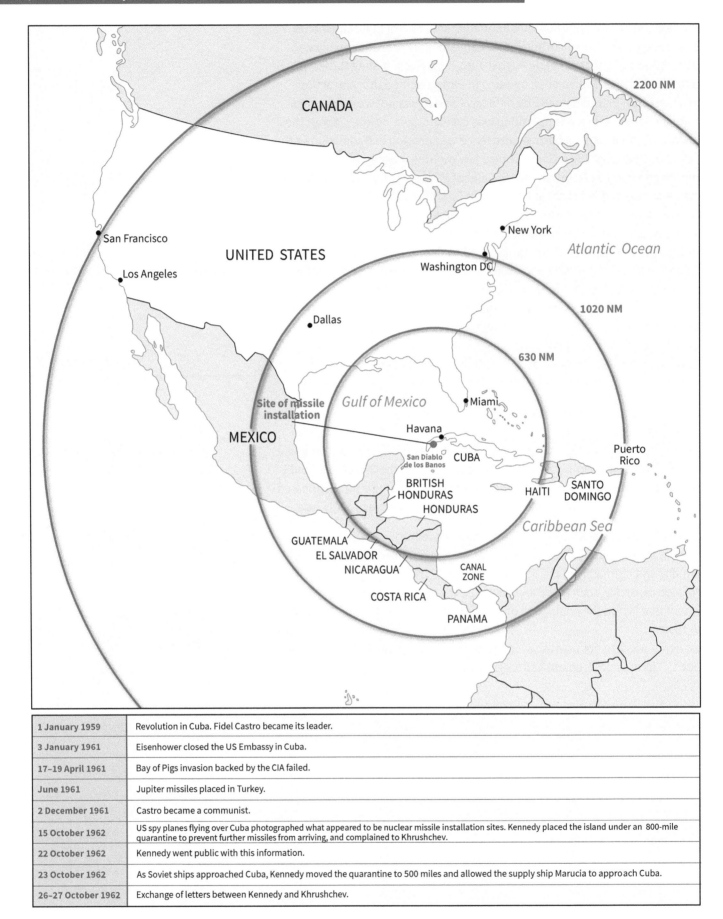

1 January 1959	Revolution in Cuba. Fidel Castro became its leader.
3 January 1961	Eisenhower closed the US Embassy in Cuba.
17–19 April 1961	Bay of Pigs invasion backed by the CIA failed.
June 1961	Jupiter missiles placed in Turkey.
2 December 1961	Castro became a communist.
15 October 1962	US spy planes flying over Cuba photographed what appeared to be nuclear missile installation sites. Kennedy placed the island under an 800-mile quarantine to prevent further missiles from arriving, and complained to Khrushchev.
22 October 1962	Kennedy went public with this information.
23 October 1962	As Soviet ships approached Cuba, Kennedy moved the quarantine to 500 miles and allowed the supply ship Marucia to approach Cuba.
26–27 October 1962	Exchange of letters between Kennedy and Khrushchev.

Figure 3.7: Map of the Cuban Missile Crisis and timeline of the events.

were threatening to follow suit. American trade embargoes on Cuba had led to Castro seeking to trade with other powers, and the Soviet Union had been only too pleased to receive and pay for Cuban sugar. President Eisenhower had prepared a plan for a counter-revolutionary invasion of Cuba, intending it to be inherited by Nixon. In the event, it was inherited by Kennedy, who at Nixon's insistence had known nothing about it.

The plan was a dubious one. It involved the CIA training 1200 Cuban exiles who had left the country after the revolution to return to the country and regain control of the government. The plan relied on a popular uprising in support of the rebels as they moved through Cuba. Kennedy changed the landing point to the Bay of Pigs, which was closer to the capital than the original intended landing point of Trinidad, an area thought more likely to attract popular support for the rebels as they closed in on Havana. The invasion was an utter failure. There was no popular uprising and the fiction that America had nothing to do with it was barely worth maintaining. Kennedy looked a fool. Castro, fearing for his regime's stability, declared himself a **Marxist-Leninist** at the end of the year in return for greater access to Soviet goods and trade.

A timeline of the Cuban Missile Crisis, as the events of October 1962 became known, is set out in Figure 3.7. The events of the 13 days in October are reasonably well known, as least on the American side, as we have transcripts of the Executive Committee (ExComm) meetings that Kennedy convened to deal with it. The immediate problem was caused when American U-2 spy planes noticed that missile launch sites were being prepared in Cuba. They were not yet ready and Kennedy needed to act fast to prevent their becoming established. It was not clear what the range would be of any missiles that the Soviet Union (the only potential source of missiles) might place there. In the best case, the missiles might only reach Florida; in the worst case they would be able to reach almost every major city in the United States. To public opinion, and a president who had campaigned on the missile gap, this would not be acceptable.

The ExComm transcripts and tapes reveal that Kennedy argued against a full-on invasion to maintain the American sphere of influence, on the grounds that the Soviets would take this as a green light for their own invasion of Berlin. Instead, Kennedy proposed a quarantine of Cuba. As Soviet ships steamed towards the island, Khrushchev indicated that he would reject American demands to stay away. Kennedy instructed Adlai Stevenson, his ambassador to the United Nations, to raise the issue but the Soviet ambassador to the UN refused to admit what was going on. The Americans raised their defence status but the Soviets made no moves at all and their ships came to a halt outside the eventual 500-mile quarantine zone. Stalemate had been reached and Kennedy and Khrushchev exchanged letters. Khrushchev offered to remove the missiles from Cuba in exchange for the removal of American missiles from Turkey (where they were in range of Moscow). Khrushchev sent a second letter asking for this to be done publicly. Bobby Kennedy, who had been meeting the Soviet ambassador, advised that Khrushchev's offer was genuine, and Jack Kennedy agreed to remove the missiles – but in secret. Kennedy appeared to have had the better of the deal – to have won. The major consequences of the Cuban Missile Crisis were the establishment of a telephone hotline between Washington and Moscow that

Speak like a historian

John Lewis Gaddis on the Soviet and Cuban views of 1962

Historians have long debated Khrushchev's motivation in putting missiles on Cuba. Was he seeking revenge for the American missiles in Turkey and Italy? Was he seeking to protect his communist ally from further invasions? Was it revenge for Kennedy making it known that the Americans had closed the missile gap because they had more long-range missiles than the Soviets? The historian John Lewis Gaddis, who has had access to Soviet archives, says this:

Historians assumed, for many years, that it was [Kennedy's revelation that the Soviets were behind in the arms race] that drove Khrushchev into a desperate attempt to recover by sending intermediate- and medium-range missiles, which he did have in abundance, to Cuba in 1962. 'Why not throw a hedgehog at Uncle Sam's pants?' he asked in April, noting that it would take a decade for the Soviet Union to equal American long-range missile capabilities. It is clear now, though, that this was not Khrushchev's principal reason for acting as he did, which suggests how easily historians can jump to premature conclusions. More significantly, the Cuban missile crisis also shows how badly great powers can miscalculate when tensions are high and the stakes are great …

Khrushchev intended his missile deployment chiefly as an effort, improbable as this might seem, to spread revolution throughout Latin America. He and his advisers had been surprised, and then excited, and finally exhilarated when a Marxist-Leninist insurgency seized power in Cuba on its own, without all the pushing and prodding the Soviets had had to do to install communist regimes in Eastern Europe. …

As Castro saw it [the Bay of Pigs] invasion reflected counter-revolutionary resolve in Washington, and it would surely be repeated, the next time with much greater force. 'The fate of Cuba and the maintenance of Soviet prestige in that part of the world preoccupied me,' Khrushchev recalled. 'We had to think up some way of confronting America with more than words.'[2]

allowed direct contact between the two leaders, the Nuclear Test Ban Treaty of 1963 and the eventual fall from power of Khrushchev in 1964.

It could have been worse. Castro had urged a pre-emptive nuclear strike on the USA. A US destroyer had fired on a Soviet submarine, one of whose officers had refused to agree to launch its nuclear missiles. Protocol demanded that all the available officers agree before a missile could be launched. Both sides sent aircraft armed with nuclear missiles airborne. Neither Kennedy nor Khrushchev wanted nuclear war but it could have been started nevertheless.

Deepening involvement in Vietnam

Meanwhile, in Indochina, Laos and South Vietnam seemed to be falling to communists. These represented, for Kennedy, vital military interests in South East Asia. At Vienna, Kennedy and Khrushchev had agreed to the neutralisation of Laos, as they were keen to avoid actual conflict between the USA and the USSR. Meanwhile the Americans began to put pressure on the South Vietnamese government of Ngô Đình Diệm and stepped up military aid. By the end of 1963, there were 16 000 American military advisers in South Vietnam and 7000 other personnel (around 500 had died that year), but Diem had been assassinated by right-wing forces who felt that he had not done enough to stop the spread of communism. Kennedy had co-operated with the coup that led to his murder, around three weeks before he himself was assassinated. America's position seemed to be neither one thing nor the other. They were definitely involved but in insufficient numbers to achieve their objectives of neutralising the communist insurgency in South Vietnam, which was backed by Hồ Chí Minh in North Vietnam. Kennedy viewed his role as trying to persuade the South Vietnamese to do what was necessary; meanwhile American involvement deepened to the point where withdrawal would seem like a defeat. The rest of the story is well known: Kennedy died and the war in Vietnam was a disaster. Whether Kennedy, alive, might have improved matters is one of the great counterfactual arguments.

So what had actually happened in Vietnam? The South Vietnamese army had been losing a war against North Vietnamese guerrilla forces. The American and French advisers who were with them were also suffering casualties. What seemed sensible tactics to Hồ (why take on the Americans in open battle?) were interpreted by Kennedy as terrorism. His response had been insufficient. He had tried to create what he termed 'strategic hamlets', where South Vietnamese villagers were protected in a single location (or perhaps, from their point of view, confined) to make it easier for the South Vietnamese army. The Viet Cong opposition (the name given to North Vietnamese supporters fighting in South Vietnam) was not as unpopular as the Americans suggested. The Viet Cong were often received warmly by the South Vietnamese, and sometimes even welcomed into strategic hamlets. Meanwhile Kennedy tried using American helicopters and special forces to support the South Vietnamese in the jungle, but they were not well-suited to the terrain and were not much use.

ACTIVITY 3.6

What do you think were the major consequences of the Cuban Missile Crisis? Justify your answers.

'Kennedy's calmness was the main reason why the Cuban Missile Crisis of 1962 was resolved.' Explain why you agree or disagree with this view.

Voices from the past

Arthur Schlesinger, Jr on the Cuban Missile Crisis

As well as being a prize-winning historian, the author of this extract, Arthur Schlesinger, was an adviser to Kennedy and an admirer of the president. He had not been a member of ExComm but had helped UN ambassador Stevenson during the Cuban Missile Crisis. Here he discusses Kennedy's decision to exclude Congress from the decision-making process during the Cuban Missile Crisis.

… The missile crisis seems an emergency so acute in its nature and so peculiar in its structure that it did in fact require unilateral executive action.

Yet this very acuteness and peculiarity disabled Kennedy's action in October 1962 as a precedent for future Presidents in situations less acute and less peculiar. For the missile crisis was unique in the postwar years in that it *really* combined all those pressures of threat, secrecy and time that the foreign policy establishment had claimed as characteristic of decisions in the nuclear age. Where the threat was less grave, the need for secrecy less urgent, the time for debate less restricted – i.e. in all other cases – the argument for independent and unilateral presidential action was notably less compelling.

Alas, Kennedy's action, which should have been celebrated as an exception, was instead enshrined as a rule … The very brilliance of Kennedy's performance appeared to vindicate the idea that the President must take unto himself the final judgments of war and peace. The missile crisis, I believe, was superbly handled, and could not have been handled so well in any other way. But one of its legacies was the imperial conception of the Presidency that brought the republic so low in Vietnam.[3]

The American contribution was ineffective in the defence of South Vietnam. Diem, though, was hated. One reason why Kennedy acted to remove him was that Vietnam had captured the international imagination and could no longer be ignored. In June 1963 a South Vietnamese monk, Thích Quảng Đức, committed suicide by burning himself alive. As he died he called for Diem to respect religious freedom. The iconic photograph of his death, by the Associated Press journalist Malcolm Browne, inspired other monks to do the same thing. South Vietnam was out of control and the world was watching. Diem's assassination had not been an explicit part of Kennedy's plan – he wanted his removal – but it could hardly have been much of a surprise that the leaders of the coup that overthrew him made absolutely certain that he would not be coming back.

Kennedy also needed somewhere in the world where he could look decisive and credible, especially after deriding the Eisenhower–Nixon administration as weak during the election cycle. He had been humiliated over Berlin and in the Vienna summit and at the Bay of Pigs, but the Cuban Missile Crisis had improved his, and America's profile. In 1961, Lyndon Johnson, visiting Vietnam, had compared Diem to Churchill, before privately admitting that he had to build Diem up because the Americans had no alternatives. By 1963, Kennedy thought that he might have found an alternative but Diem's removal was a final throw of the dice. He had tried every means at his disposal to prevent Viet Cong incursions ('attempts to reunify the country'). One of the great 'what-ifs' of American history is what Kennedy would have done in Vietnam if he had not died. It is difficult to see the general course of events being much different. By 1963 America had either to fight a ground war in Vietnam or abandon South Vietnam to communism.

African Americans in North and South

The lives of African Americans continued to be less easy and less economically fulfilled than the lives of people of other races. In the North, many African Americans lived in the cities, where they had moved when the original, white, inhabitants had moved to the new suburbs. They had begun to vote Democrat in the 1930s and now formed a reliable voting block behind the Party, bringing Kennedy himself to the White House in the close election of 1960. In the South, segregation continued and the Ku Klux Klan was coming back. Meanwhile, the Civil Rights Movement, which had grown during Eisenhower's presidency, now reached an impressive peak in the South. There, African Americans were rarely allowed to vote for anybody. What should the priority of African Americans in the South be? Votes, respect or economic opportunity? Martin Luther King, the most prominent black leader in the South, maintained and encouraged an emphasis on votes. In the North, but also in the South, a 'black freedom' movement was also beginning to form, looking beyond the narrow focus of campaigning for and passing a Voting Rights Act.

The rise of the Civil Rights Movement

In December 1960 the Supreme Court, in the case of *Boynton v Virginia*, had banned segregation on buses and in waiting rooms and restaurants serving interstate bus passengers. This was largely ignored by southern states, which led to the Freedom Rides that began in May 1961. On Freedom Rides, civil rights campaigners rode on the buses in mixed groups, with the aim of being arrested. This was a form of non-violent protest often undertaken by young people and students and fed directly into the later student experience of protest. Freedom Rides prompted white opposition and the arrests generated legal cases. This added to the economic pressure of the sit-ins and boycotts that had begun in Eisenhower's time and meant that the South was seething with protest by the end of 1961.

In 1962, the student James Meredith had attempted to enrol at the University of Mississippi. While he genuinely wanted to study there, he was also an activist seeking to provoke a confrontation. He got one. The NAACP helped to manage the legal situation, supporting Meredith in the judicial challenge – which confirmed that he had the right to be enrolled, but the governor of Mississippi turned up in person to turn him away. When federal troops came to help Meredith to register, there was a riot.

In 1963 Martin Luther King's SCLC attempted to force the issue. Realising that international television gave them priceless propaganda, they tried to provoke white people into committing various sorts of atrocities that could be photographed. The protests in the USA were becoming internationally embarrassing. As the SCLC strategist Bayard Rustin put it, 'Protest becomes an effective tactic to the degree that it elicits brutality and oppression from the power structure'. This did not always work. In Albany, Georgia, there was a famous example of how non-violent direct action could backfire. The Chief of Police there, Laurie Pritchett, avoided making a martyr out of King and treated protestors with courtesy, while also being savage towards white supremacists. He made African Americans appear as irresponsible law-breakers.

There was a parallel protest in Birmingham, Alabama, which became known as 'Bombingham' because of the strength of racist feeling. The SCLC had selected Birmingham for a protest because the white community was divided between two governments, and also because of the Chief of Police, Eugene 'Bull' Connor. Connor had refused to investigate half a dozen bombs in black areas of the city and had been responsible for attacks on sit-ins and Freedom Riders. Now he obligingly called out the dogs against peaceful protestors. King was jailed. President Kennedy was moved to say, 'The Civil Rights movement should thank God for Bull Connor. He's helped them more than Abraham Lincoln.' From his cell King wrote in response to a statement of concern from white southern religious leaders: the letter became famous around the world. King made it clear that the whole point of direct action was to force the authorities into negotiation – he spoke of 'dramatising' the civil rights issues of the South.

King and other civil rights leaders came to three main realisations throughout this period. The first was that they could easily manipulate the media. The second was that they had to pick their battles – Laurie Pritchett's refusal to engage with King's preferred narrative of white law enforcement violently oppressing peaceful protestors had shown that. The third was that the focus of the Civil Rights Movement had to be votes. Only by taking a full part in the civic life of their states and municipalities would African Americans in the South hit their opponents where it hurt, in the ballot box. Table 3.1 shows the major civil rights groups of the 1960s.

 Thematic link: American Dream

The NAACP called for a campaign to be 'Free by '63' – a reference to the 100th anniversary of the Emancipation Proclamation. Leaders, including Martin Luther

King, continued to agitate for the president to become involved, but Kennedy feared being dragged into an apparently insoluble situation, preferring to wait for the courts to take effective action. His brother Bobby took the lead, meeting the novelist James Baldwin in New York on 24 May. The meeting seemed inconclusive, and Baldwin left disappointed, but Kennedy had become convinced of the seriousness of the situation and the need for presidential action, and he began to spur his brother on. Meanwhile the NAACP, CORE, SNCC and SCLC came together to call for a march on Washington in August 1963. Although the different groups did not initially agree about what they wanted the march to achieve – whether it was a gesture of support for the Civil Rights Act the president had been promoting, or a more generalised protest against black economic exclusion – they did agree to march together. Bussed in to the sound of the protest songs such as 'We Shall Overcome', which characterised the sit ins and other peaceful protests, 250 000 people turned up in Washington to listen to a platform of singers and speakers, including Bob Dylan, a young singer of protest songs, and Martin Luther King, who gave a speech in which he consistently repeated the refrain, 'I have a dream', describing a future world in which segregation, especially in education, did not exist.

Group	Leader(s)	Founded	Aims	Major events
Black Panthers	Huey Newton Bobby Seale	1966, Oakland, California	Protection from police brutality. Becomes a Marxist revolutionary group.	Considered by the FBI to be the biggest threat to national security
Congress of Racial Equality (CORE)	James Peck Bayard Rustin	1942, Chicago, Illinois	Non-violent resistance to segregation	Freedom Rides (1961) March on Washington (1963) Freedom Summer (1964)
National Association for the Advancement of Colored People (NAACP)	Thurgood Marshall Rosa Parks	1909, Baltimore, Maryland	Legal challenges to segregation	*Brown v Board* (1954) Montgomery Bus Boycott (1955–56) Little Rock (1957) March on Washington
Nation of Islam (NoI)	Elijah Muhammad Louis Farrakhan Malcolm X	1930, Detroit, Michigan	Black power Equal rights Violent response to white violence	Assassination of Malcolm X (1965)
Organization of Afro-American Unity (OAAU)	Malcolm X	1964, New York, New York	Heightening the political consciousness of black Americans Pan-Africanism	Freedom Summer
Southern National Leadership Conference (SCLC)	Martin Luther King, Jr Bayard Rustin Ella Baker	1957, Atlanta, Georgia	Non-violent direct action against segregation	Birmingham Campaign (1963) March on Washington March from Selma (1965)
Student Non-violent Coordinating Committee (SNCC)	Ella Baker Stokely Carmichael (1966)	1960, Raleigh, North Carolina	Direct action protests, voter registration Peaceful (before 1966) Black Power (after 1966)	Sit-ins (1960) Freedom Rides March on Washington Freedom Summer

Table 3.1: The major civil rights groups of the 1960s.

ACTIVITY 3.7

How useful is this leaflet for a historian studying the reasons why so many people marched on Washington in August 1963?

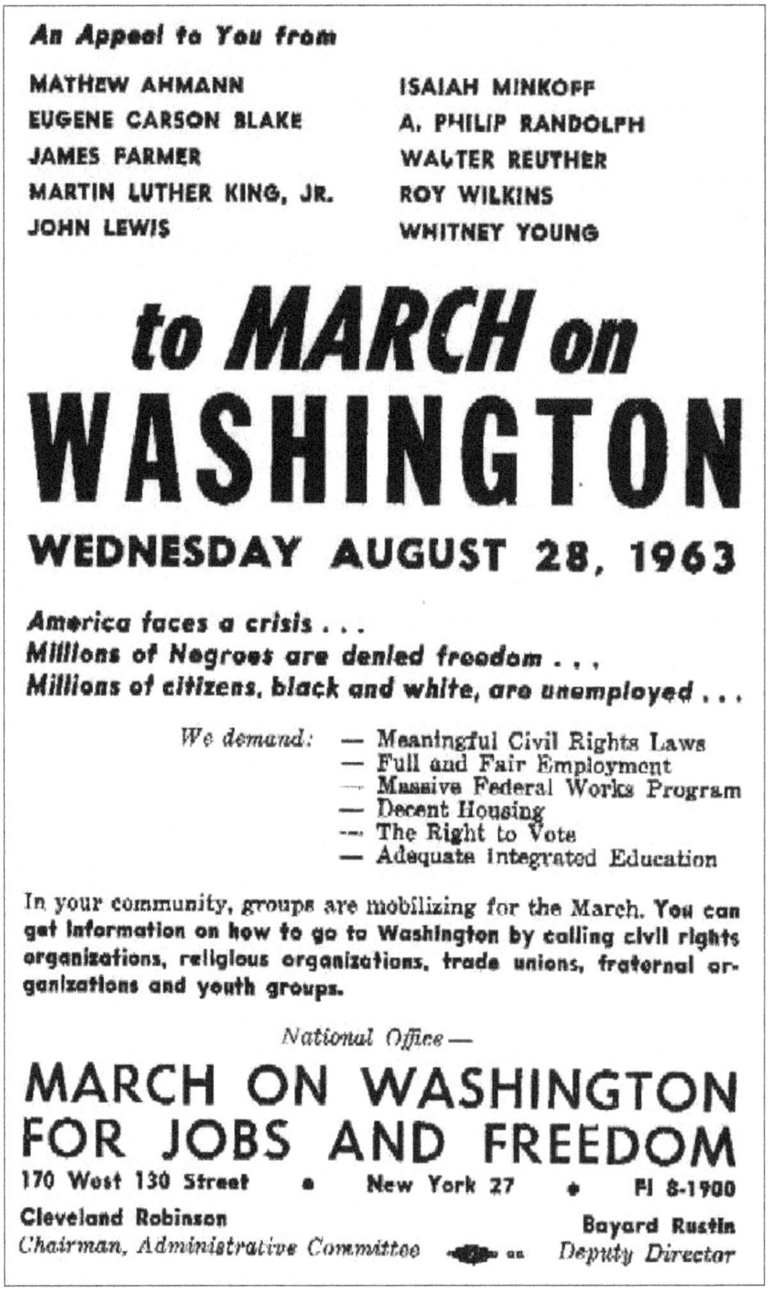

An Appeal to You from

MATHEW AHMANN   ISAIAH MINKOFF
EUGENE CARSON BLAKE   A. PHILIP RANDOLPH
JAMES FARMER   WALTER REUTHER
MARTIN LUTHER KING, JR. ROY WILKINS
JOHN LEWIS   WHITNEY YOUNG

to MARCH on WASHINGTON

WEDNESDAY AUGUST 28, 1963

America faces a crisis . . .
Millions of Negroes are denied freedom . . .
Millions of citizens, black and white, are unemployed . . .

We demand:
— Meaningful Civil Rights Laws
— Full and Fair Employment
— Massive Federal Works Program
— Decent Housing
— The Right to Vote
— Adequate Integrated Education

In your community, groups are mobilizing for the March. You can get information on how to go to Washington by calling civil rights organizations, religious organizations, trade unions, fraternal organizations and youth groups.

National Office —

MARCH ON WASHINGTON FOR JOBS AND FREEDOM

170 West 130 Street   ●   New York 27   ●   FI 8-1900

Cleveland Robinson
Chairman, Administrative Committee

Bayard Rustin
Deputy Director

Figure 3.8: This leaflet advertised the March on Washington for Jobs and Freedom, 1963.

The opponents of civil rights, including within the Democratic Party

White opposition to civil rights had been violent and intensive. In May 1961, a bus had been burned in Anniston, Alabama, in response to the Freedom Rides. This led to riots, arrests and general tension. A mob was waiting for the Freedom Riders on their arrival in Birmingham; Connor had been complicit in its formation. On 21 May a mob besieged King and the Freedom Riders in a church in Montgomery, Alabama. In September Herbert Lee, a voting registration activist, was killed in Mississippi. In November, students were arrested in Albany, Alabama, for walking in white areas. The next month King was arrested there for walking on a white sidewalk.

Alabama and Mississippi were the two most obvious focuses of white protest. In Mississippi it was not just the actions of Governor Barnett in opposing James Meredith in his attempt to enrol at university and the murder of Herbert Lee. There were bombings and shootings – such as that of Corporal Roman Ducksworth was shot by a Mississippi police officer in April 1962. State governments cut off food supplies in retaliation for voter registration drives. These state governments were all Democratic. This was another sign that the attitude of southern Democrats was utterly incompatible with the liberal democratic politics of their northern president, who found himself in a fix. Should he take action to repair the situation, and risk party unity? It would be Johnson, rather than Kennedy, whose actions would lead directly to long-established Democrats, elected officials and voters alike, leaving the party.

Kennedy's policies in response to the pressures for change

Kennedy's commitment to civil rights came under scrutiny at the time, as well as since. He had certainly started well, by speaking personally to King's wife Coretta and having Bobby arrange King's release from jail in Atlanta during his election campaign, when Eisenhower and Nixon had been silent. Was this a genuine concern that injustice was being done, or naked political calculation that he needed the African-American vote to win? Early in his time in office, he issued an Executive Order calling for any company that held federal contracts to take **'affirmative action'** to move towards equality in hiring. This built on the work of Truman and Eisenhower in using Executive Orders. In 1961, as the Berlin Crisis escalated and the Freedom Rides continued, Kennedy was keenly aware of the problems he faced trying to enforce America's will abroad, when he could quite clearly not enforce his will at home. In September, Kennedy's executive agency, the Interstate Commerce Commission, outlawed discrimination in seating on long-distance buses. In 1962 he finally came good on his campaign promise to establish a Committee on Equal Employment Opportunity, which was headed up by Johnson, an enthusiastic supporter of civil rights. Kennedy appointed African Americans to positions of influence where he could – for example making Thurgood Marshall, the NAACP's lawyer, a circuit judge. He also put a number of segregationists into the courts in the South.

King accused Kennedy of accepting only token progress. Kennedy urged King to prioritise voting rights and to trust the courts to do the rest; he was vindicated in the Meredith case and in a similar situation in Alabama in 1963. The crisis in Birmingham in 1963 appears to have changed Kennedy's mind, along with the report Bobby Kennedy brought back from his meeting in New York with James Baldwin. The violence against African Americans that was endemic to parts of the South was not going away. Although the laws were eventually enforced, Southern governments took little notice of court decisions that established precedents. There were simply too many ways to prevent black people from voting, using economic intimidation, political exclusion or plain violence. In the summer of 1963, Kennedy sent a civil rights bill to Congress, heedless of the effect on the Democratic Party, or perhaps realising that the parts of the South that opposed

Key terms

affirmative action: a deliberate decision, usually by a government contractor or an educational establishment, to give priority to under-represented workers – in an American context often African Americans.

civil rights were already irreconcilable. At least some of those who marched on Washington in the stifling summer heat of August 1963 did so in support of this bill. Kennedy did not live to see it passed.

The United States by 1963

What was American identity in 1963? America was prosperous and free. It stood as the leader of the free world, in opposition to the forces of communism wherever they were. The country was united in mourning for its slain president, whose courage and heroism were magnified by death, and whose errors were glossed over. There was considerable resentment among the protectors of President Kennedy's legacy – the survivors of Camelot – that his great programmes would now have to be taken up by Lyndon Johnson, who appeared rougher and uncultivated. In fact, Johnson would bury his personal distaste for the Kennedy family, supporting Bobby's campaign for the Senate, and would push through civil rights and progressive economic legislation with greater skill than Kennedy had ever shown.

For many Americans, the path to prosperity was clear. There were very few white Americans left for whom there was not at least hope of advancement, and while the very poorest might not be able to access the American Dream of life, liberty and the pursuit of happiness, they were at least unlikely to starve. African Americans, however, did not yet share in that dream. The 1950s had established that it was very difficult to be both American and communist; now African Americans fought for the right to be both fully American and black. Some African Americans were beginning to change their minds about this, preferring to identify with the Nation of Islam, or in opposition to white people. This seemed to Americans in 1963 to be the most urgent problem to be dealt with.

 Thematic link: American Dream

In 1945, America was a newly-minted Superpower, earning its position through its economic might, a war won with (almost) no damage to its homeland and the exhaustion of other, competing countries. Under Truman's stewardship its economy had been successfully transformed and its military had become a major employer and driver of technological change. By 1963, one unpopular war later, it led the free world in an undeclared but very apparent conflict. Its economy continued to boom. The three presidents of this era had been a politician, a general and a low-ranking officer during the Second World War. With Kennedy, especially, there was a sense of the baton being passed on down the generations.

The position of the United States as a world power

By 1963, the United States was one of two nuclear-armed superpowers and three nuclear powers in the world (the other was the UK). American power was founded not merely on nuclear weapons but also on a strong economy. American military production was unparalleled; even when Soviet technology ran ahead, as it had in the production of thermonuclear weapons and rockets, American production meant that the USA held the strategic lead.

Americans saw themselves as leaders of the free world and guarantors of freedom. Their opponents in this were domestic communists, although by 1963 the Red Scare at home had blown over. The Cold War was clearly set to stay and the Soviets were the enemy. That enmity had nearly caused a nuclear exchange that, it was widely believed, might have destroyed much of the world. The logic of Eisenhower's policy of the New Look was deterrence, and deterrence, it seemed, worked – nobody wanted to risk a nuclear conflagration. The Cuban Missile Crisis, the most dangerous single period of the entire Cold War, had only really been possible in the early 1960s; a few years later, both the USA and USSR had so many long-range missiles that it made little difference where in the world they were. Nevertheless, the Americans retained their position as the dominant power in the western hemisphere while perhaps also conceding the Soviets' position in the East.

At the time of Kennedy's death the world was a safer place than it had been a year earlier. The Moscow-Washington hotline and the Test Ban Treaty saw to that; the arms race appeared to have reached an end point, or at least the realisation that things could not continue as they had before. America's position, however, was perhaps a little less secure. Kennedy had been forced to concede that there was little he could do to prevent the Soviets from taking whatever action they liked in East Berlin. In Indochina all America's agreements and posturing could do little to prevent the deterioration of the situation that would shortly engulf America's army and society alike. Meanwhile Kennedy had set the Apollo mission in motion, encouraging NASA to aim to put an American on the Moon, in an attempt to reverse the damage caused to American prestige by earlier Soviet successes in being first to put a satellite (Sputnik, 1957) and a man (Yuri Gagarin, 1961) into space.

There was a major, unanswered question: did there have to be a Cold War? Throughout his campaign and his presidency, Kennedy's rhetoric emphasised the position of the USA as the leader of the free world (implying the existence of a non-free world). The engagement of the Soviet Union and the USA in an ideological and geopolitical Cold War seemed to be an unalterable reality of world politics when, in fact, it was really very new. For the majority of the lifetime of any member of either government, the Cold War had not existed. Yet by 1963 the Cold War was a major part of American culture. Children practised bomb drills at school – hiding under their desks was intended to provide a distraction rather than protection from a thermonuclear blast. American culture emphasised capitalist expenditure and conspicuous consumption. American heroes were rugged individualists reminiscent of the cowboy age, whether the star of the Westerns, John Wayne or, by 1966, James T. Kirk, Captain of the Starship Enterprise. The Cold War, and America's role in it, had become a normalised part of American identity. The Cuban Missile Crisis was extremely serious; it provoked genuine fear around the world (as well as in the White House, and perhaps also in the Kremlin) that nuclear annihilation was imminent. The reaction to this was not to abandon the Cold War as too dangerous but to make it into a more stable status quo.

The arms race and the logic of deterrence

The arms race is the name given to the process in which the USA and the USSR each attempted to have more, and better, nuclear weapons than the other. In technological terms the initial atomic fission bombs of the 1940s gave way in the early 1950s to two-stage thermonuclear devices, which used a small fission trigger to control a fusion (hydrogen) bomb. H-bombs produce a far greater yield than A-bombs. This in turn makes delivery easier. The need for a higher-yield bomb is in reality the need for a less cumbersome delivery system. The bombs dropped in Japan in 1945 needed the USAAF's largest bomber to drop them; by the 1950s nuclear warheads could be put on missiles with varying ranges. By the middle of the 1960s, both sides had intercontinental ballistic missiles (ICBMs) that could travel halfway round the world's surface in half an hour. Both sides positioned them in well-defended launch sites, often carved into mountainsides, and on submarines that patrolled the oceans.

The best way to deal with an A-bomb was clearly to shoot down the bomber carrying it; the best way to deal with short- and medium-range missiles was to prevent their being placed within range; and the best way to deal with a missile that is within range, including an ICBM, is to prevent its being launched. Shooting missiles down is very difficult.

The logic of all this was deterrence. If both sides had nuclear weapons – and it was obvious by the 1960s that both sides had so many nuclear weapons that they could destroy each other – then the situation of 'mutually assured destruction' (MAD) would apply. Any country thinking it was being fired upon would have half an hour to respond by firing back. So the arms race came to be about having so many nuclear weapons that nobody could ever fire them.

 Thematic link: identity

Economic prosperity

Kennedy recognised that the major challenge he faced economically was inflation. He tried to deal with it using persuasion and managed, for example, to bring steel prices down in 1962. He supported farmers in the usual way, with price controls and help to prevent mortgage foreclosures. He also worked to keep inflation down and create a mild stimulus (mild because Congress watered his proposals down). Kennedy was content to create a budget deficit in order to stimulate recovery, and the strategy worked: during his thousand days GDP expanded by 5% a year on average, while unemployment went down and production rose by 15%.

America's economic prosperity was remarkable in 1963. The consumer society was flourishing. America's ability to make goods for its people was matched by people's ability to pay for them, and the economy kept on growing. There had been a wobble in 1958–59, and a failure to recover thereafter, but in Kennedy's time the economy had re-established its upward trajectory. It would continue to grow throughout the 1960s. That it was reliant on low oil prices was perhaps apparent; that oil prices would not remain low was not. The economic prosperity of the USA was also reliant on the ongoing war. The military-industrial complex, as Eisenhower had called it, provided a massive stimulus to American production. At some point, however, it would have to slow down, as America had more nuclear missiles than it could possibly use.

Economic prosperity was widely dispersed but not shared by everyone. The poor were less poor, but they were still there, and many of the poor were black. In the South African Americans were excluded by segregation and racist governments. In the North they were excluded, as they were largely urban dwellers in a suburban world. The inner cities were inhabited by black people but owned by white people. Their political leadership was still white, although this was slowly beginning to change. Across America, African Americans as a class were excluded from the economic prosperity that benefited so many white people, included those from previously excluded groups.

Thematic link: prosperity

The growing pressures for social change from women and young people

The protests of the Civil Rights Movement had inspired others to protest too. Women like Rosa Parks had been important in the Civil Rights Movement. Now a women's movement was beginning in its own right. In 1963 the feminist Betty Friedan published *The Feminine Mystique*, which criticised the tendency of people in society to refer to women not in their own right but as someone else's wife or mother. Friedan drew on 20th-century science, culture and psychology to argue that women should also realise their potential as human beings. In the Kitchen Debate Nixon had let slip his expectation that women should be grateful for all the new labour-saving devices in their homes. The family, with the mother playing a traditional child-rearing role, represented the new aspirational suburban lifestyle where a nuclear family would live in a family house with a family car, going on family vacations. Increased access to higher education and job opportunities meant that it was harder to persuade women to remain in the home. The shrillness

Voices from the past

John F. Kennedy

Extract from President Kennedy's State of the Union address to Congress, 14 January 1963:

America has enjoyed 22 months of uninterrupted economic recovery. But recovery is not enough. If we are to prevail in the long run, we must expand the long-run strength of our economy. We must move along the path to a higher rate of growth and full employment.

For this would mean tens of billions of dollars more each year in production, profits, wages, and public revenues. It would mean an end to the persistent slack which has kept our unemployment at or above 5 per cent for 61 out of the past 62 months – and an end to the growing pressures for such restrictive measures as the 35-hour week, which alone could increase hourly labor costs by as much as 14 per cent, start a new wage-price spiral of inflation, and undercut our efforts to compete with other nations.

To achieve these greater gains, one step, above all, is essential – the enactment this year of a substantial reduction and revision in Federal income taxes ...[4]

with which the message of domesticity was proclaimed by some was a response to how far women had come towards attaining a measure of equality. In the New Deal era many women had worked out of sheer necessity. Now, many of the one third of women who worked did so in order to finance greater participation in the consumer society.

Young women found themselves liberated in the 1960s. The greater availability and reliability of birth control measures helped to cause this, and went hand-in-hand with a change in sexual morality. The greater mobility of the automobile age, and the greater opportunities for young people to mix afforded by universities, created more opportunities for women to be women without the pressure of early motherhood. The change was not enough. Women found themselves relatively excluded from the job market, unable to reach the highest levels in many professions and paid less than men for doing the same jobs. The women's movement would grow during the 1960s, fighting for women's participation in politics and the labour market, and for the right of women across the USA to abort unwanted pregnancies.

The idea of the teenager was essentially invented in the 1950s. The consumer society provided many opportunities for young people to enjoy themselves – at the movies, through music, and through an independent social life facilitated by cars. Universities helped this, too. As young people came together, they found themselves at odds with the expectations of their elders and attracted by the liberal ideas of the Civil Rights Movement – at least, some of them did. Some of the activities and pastimes young people enjoyed included:

- Music – rock and roll stars included Elvis Presley and Bill Haley and the Comets (as early as 1954). By the 1970s this involved disco dancing to the Bee Gees.
- Crazes such as hula hoops (1958).
- Movies – especially drive-ins – that featured film stars such as Marilyn Monroe (d. 1962) and James Dean (d. 1955).
- Sexual freedom facilitated by a decline in traditional morality on the one hand and increased availability of means of contraception including the contraceptive pill (early 1960s).
- Fast-food restaurants such as McDonalds (which began to make it big in the mid-1950s).

Extracts from interviews with Earl Tupper, the inventor of Tupperware, which became a major consumer product in the 1950s.

What a time we would have if we had plenty of money. Our life almost depends upon money ... In nearly all of the dramas of life money takes an important part.

Of course if we could only become millionaires we would assume a very important air, we would travel extensively, talk of the wonderful paintings we had seen and visit 'ye shop' and buy old broken spinning wheels, rag rugs, etc.

What a life for sports. Midnight golf, go fox hunting, entertain the Prince of Wales, etc. We would go South with the smart set and spend plenty of time getting a nice tan. With money we would soften some picture producer's heart and get him to star us in a screen hit ...

A person must have a wonderful never-failing faith in himself in order to succeed. No matter how many times his best efforts seem to fail.[5]

The youth movement did not yet exist separately – it would take the escalation of the Vietnam War before that happened.

The older generation – some of it, anyway – looked on all of this with bemusement and occasional intolerance. Such hedonism, made possible by economic prosperity and peace (or at least, the absence of any conventional war) had been unknown to those who were young during the Depression or either of the two world wars. To some older Americans it must have seemed that their children wanted to have their cake and eat it: a college education *and* rock and roll music? Domestic appliances *and* an independent identity as a woman? It was not just older Americans who felt excluded. Over the later 1960s and 1970s two new kinds of American identity would emerge: a liberal, hippy America and a conservative **middle America**.

 Thematic link: identity

 Practice essay questions

1. Assess the validity of the view that Kennedy's presidency was largely ineffective, except for his solution to the Cuban Missile Crisis of 1962.
2. How far do you agree that the pressures for change in American society had become very urgent by 1963?
3. 'Kennedy's importance in the development of the Cold War was not a product of his tough talk, but of his intelligent and calm responses under pressure.' To what extent do you agree with this statement?
4. With reference to Voices from the past: The Kennedy–Nixon debates, Voices from the past: JFK's inaugural address and Voices from the past: Extract from President Kennedy's State of the Union address, how valuable are these sources in explaining why Kennedy was such a well-loved president?

 Taking it further

Should Americans in 1963 have been less optimistic than they were about the future?

ACTIVITY 3.8

Read the earlier section headed The United States by 1963. Highlight anything that might have made Americans optimistic, and anything that might have made them pessimistic.

How far had the American Dream been achieved by 1963?

Chapter summary

By the end of this chapter, you should understand:

- arguments about Kennedy's success, or otherwise, in his domestic policy, which was based on a programme of progressive reform
- the way in which the USA and the USSR adjusted to a situation in which the Cold War seemed to be a permanent feature of international relations, and the way in which they avoided actually going to war
- the way in which the tactics of the Civil Rights Movement evolved in the early 1960s, and the role of Kennedy as a reluctant key player in this
- the optimism Americans felt about the future in 1963.

End notes

1 http://www.debates.org/index.php?page=october-21-1960-debate-transcript
2 Gaddis JL. *The Cold War*. Allen Lane; 2005.
3 Schlesinger A. *The Imperial Presidency*. Mariner; 2004: 176.
4 Source: http://www.presidency.ucsb.edu/ws/?pid=9138 (section 2)
5 http://www.pbs.org/wgbh/americanexperience/features/primary-resources/tupperware-success/

The four presidents of the USA from 1963 to 1980 presided over a tumultuous time in American history. The booming economy of the 1960s gave way to a decline in growth, economic shock and high inflation. American self-confidence was shaken by a disastrous war and by the recognition that if America was the leader of the free world, it was possible that the free world did not want to be led. The French, for example, were willing to accept nuclear protection without providing unquestioning support. Yet all was not bad. The position of African Americans improved, if not as rapidly as it might have done. Economic trouble did not lead to collapse. No hostile powers were waiting to invade.

Two of these four presidents, Lyndon B. Johnson (LBJ) and Richard M. Nixon, have claims to be among the greatest visionaries ever to hold their office. Johnson's social reforms have become a controversial part of the American society that they changed. Nixon's foreign policy would ultimately help to end the Cold War and undermine the economic basis of communism. These two presidencies both ended in failure, disappointment and even disgrace, and the two that followed them were low-key and ineffective. In the 1980s it would become clear that the American Dream had not died; it had been dormant. America came to the end of its long night, and was ready for the dawning of a new era. The problems it faced in the 1960s and 1970s had not been so serious after all.

That was the conservative perspective. For liberals, the 1960s and 1970s were a period of liberation and immense advances. The small-state politics and high military spending of the 1980s were unwelcome policies rooted in the new conservatism that had arisen in response to a religious revival and decades of liberal policy-making, and which would dominate Republican Party politics for decades to come.

President Johnson identified the prosperity that Truman, Eisenhower and Kennedy had built (or, if you prefer, that had built up during their presidencies) as something that should not be squandered. It should be used, instead, to transform American society, building something lasting in terms of education and the elimination of poverty. Arguably, Johnson then squandered it on preserving America's international identity as a superpower, leader of the free world and the protector of capitalism. His successor Nixon would face genuine economic challenges, as the Arab world woke up to its dominance of the global oil supply and the influence it could exert on (and money it could extract from) the West. Nixon would also face the challenge of extricating America from the war in Vietnam and rebalancing global politics to America's advantage. Neither of these processes would bring him down; instead, he brought disgrace upon himself and his office.

Johnson and Nixon were both, in their way, exceptionally unpleasant men as well as visionaries. Johnson was unfaithful, foul-mouthed and domineering, and Nixon was a liar who put himself, as president, above the law. Their successors, Gerald Ford and Jimmy Carter, were apparently genial men who were simply not qualified to be president. They might even have done more damage to American prestige than their predecessors.

And yet, America was not severely damaged. The economy held up – in this crash of the late 1960s nobody was reduced to the grinding poverty of the 1920s. If civil rights did not make much more progress after 1968, they didn't slip back too much either. America was still the leader of the free world in 1980; it still had a serious claim to moral superiority over the Soviet Union. It had also undergone a series of religious and cultural revivals that would shape its politics, and the course of international relations, for decades to come.

4 The Johnson Presidency, 1963–1969

In this section, we will examine the great successes and failures of Johnson's presidency. By 1965 he presided over a booming economy. His Democratic Party seemed to hold an impregnable electoral coalition; his mastery of the political process had enabled him to push through a progressive liberal agenda; and he had ensured that he shared some of the credit for the advances in civil rights that had been the new focus of protests. By 1968, Johnson and America were locked into an unsuccessful war in Vietnam that was harming the economy and had wrecked his legacy. Both Johnson and the Democrats had become the focus of the mood of protest. We will look into:

- Johnson as president: personality and policies; his pursuit of the 'Great Society'; the impact of the Kennedy legacy; economic developments.
- Maintaining American world power: escalation of the war in Vietnam; relations between the USA and its Western allies.
- African Americans in North and South: developments in the Civil Rights Movement; Johnson's role in passing civil rights legislation; the impact of change, including urban riots.
- Social divisions and protest movements: education and youth; feminism; radicalisation of African Americans; anti-war movements; the role of the media.

Introduction: the master of the Senate, as president

Johnson's presidency was the last great creative liberal presidency of the 20th century. Coming to power to serve just over a year of Kennedy's term, he was re-elected in 1964 on a platform of prosperity and peace. In the White House he proved himself immediately able to continue the mastery of Congress he had displayed as Senate Majority Leader in the later 1950s. In 1968, he no longer seemed a great president. The economy showed signs of strain due to expensive social reforms and (much more) expensive foreign wars, and American over-reliance on the automobile impaired its ability to recover. Johnson's social reforms were grinding to a halt. Civil rights had not stopped racial strife, his war was a failure and his army was no longer the unstoppable force it had once been; soon it would be viewed by some as a disgrace. The students who chanted his name in 1968 did not do so out of support, and he was prevented by his own protection detail from leaving the White House. This experienced politician had lost control of his administration, his Party, Congress and the country. What had gone wrong? The American economy remained fundamentally sound, despite the expensive, failing war. The Vietnam War could be seen as a necessary experiment, almost designed to demonstrate to the mighty Superpower the point at which it began to over-reach itself. Had the USA not failed there, it would have failed somewhere else. In any case, it was hardly Johnson's fault (was it?) that he inherited a war started by his two immediate predecessors. Culturally, the USA went from strength to strength during Johnson's presidency. Socially, real progress was made in terms of civil rights; if Johnson was at times reluctant, he nevertheless presided over the effective end of segregation in the South. Educational reforms meant that there was genuine social mobility through education in Johnson's time, when college education became usual rather than an expression of privilege. American culture continued its global march, its movies and music now enhanced by a tradition of protest. Perhaps the greatest achievement of Johnson's presidency was one inspired by Kennedy and celebrated by Nixon: the bulk of NASA's work was done during Johnson's time in office and ended in the landing of men on the moon in 1969.

Johnson's presidency marked the end of unbridled American confidence, but only temporarily. It marked the end of America's exceptional economic growth, but America remained the pre-eminent economy in the world. It marked the end of the American assumption that all that was required to win a war was for the American army to turn up in force (the Korean War was generally glossed over in American discourse). It marked the end of Democratic dominance of the South. It also marked the last time that serious misbehaviour (in this case sexual) in the White House was not reported. However, it was Johnson's successor whose behaviour would be so egregious that the press corps could not ignore it.

Johnson as president

Johnson came to power in tragic circumstances, which he then leveraged expertly. He had been a leader of the liberal wing of the Democratic Party and by 1960 was its most experienced Congressional manager. As vice president he had assumed the overview of the Kennedy administration's space and civil rights policies – the former because it was a project that might fail, in which case Kennedy wanted to be shielded from it, and the latter to shield Kennedy from the political damage that might be caused by the project's success. Johnson was happy: both civil rights and the space race were priorities for him. But after many years as a senator dominating everything and everyone, he watched in frustration from the White House in which Johnson had an office as bill after bill proposed by the Kennedy administration was watered down in Congress, or narrowly failed when more experienced management might have seen it through as he, on the sidelines, did nothing. On 22 November 1963, he got his chance.

Johnson's personality and policies

It was difficult to get the better of Lyndon B. Johnson. Physically imposing, he was used to getting his own way. As Senate Majority Leader he had developed 'the Treatment' as a means of winning political arguments, by standing over people and blinding them with statistics and arguments, which involved cajoling them, flattering them and, if necessary, shouting at them. He made it his business to know everything about everyone he dealt with. As a Congressional leader this had made him very powerful indeed. He knew which buttons to press to get particular colleagues to see things his way. As president, he retained this ability. Gone were the days of legislation that narrowly failed to pass. Johnson, in his first couple of years, was once again the master of the Senate – and also of the House.

In his dealings with his own executive, he liked there to be consensus, which according to the historian, presidential observer and Kennedy confidant Arthur Schlesinger stifled debate and was often choreographed. According to George Reedy, Johnson's press secretary from 1964–65, this particularly characterised his National Security Council meetings.

What of his personal life? He was, no less than Kennedy, a womaniser and on occasion a drunkard. His wife, Lady Bird, accepted this. He was also rude, with a habit of walking around naked in company and of using the toilet – with the door open – while conducting meetings, and had a mouth every bit as foul as his successor Richard Nixon. He was a passionate supporter of progressive legislation, a bully, a boor, a sophisticated manipulator of other politicians: a complicated man.

Johnson's domestic policy achievements, collectively known as the **Great Society**, are listed in Table 4.1.

Johnson's pursuit of the Great Society

For Lyndon Johnson, the Great Society was the logical conclusion of the New Deal. The New Deal had been formed in a time of economic hardship, to rescue the country. It had been successful in this but whether it had succeeded further was questionable. The economy had certainly been repaired but it was the Second World War that had guaranteed the return of prosperity. The Great Society was something different. The economy was booming, so there was no need for repair. Johnson wanted both to guarantee the boom would continue and to share the dividends of America's wealth, remodelling the society around him.

Key term

Great Society: the label first applied in May 1964 to LBJ's radically liberal domestic policies.

Year	Legislation	What it provided
1964	Twenty-fourth **Amendment**	Banned poll tax in federal elections
	Civil Rights Act	Banned discrimination in public accommodation and employment
	Urban Mass Transportation Act	Provided financial aid for urban mass transit systems
	Economic Opportunity Act	Authorised the Job Corps and VISTA (domestic Peace Corps); established the Office for Economic Opportunity
	Wilderness Preservation Act	Barred commercial use of 9.1 million acres of national forest
1965	Elementary and Secondary School Act	Provided $1.3 billion in aid to schools
	Medicare	Provided medical care for the elderly
	Voting Rights Act	Prohibited literacy tests and other voting restrictions, reinforcing the provisions of the Twenty-fourth Amendment
	Omnibus Housing Act	Created Department of Housing and Urban Development; provided rent supplements to low-income families
	National Endowment for the Arts	Provided federal assistance to the arts
	Water Quality Act and the Air Quality Act	Required states to establish and enforce water quality standards
	Immigration reform laws	Repealed 1920s immigration restriction, fundamentally altering the countries of origin of new immigrants in favour of Latin Americans
	Higher Education Act	Provided federal scholarships for university and college education
	Highway Beautification Act	Controlled billboards along interstates and encouraged scenic roadside development
1966	National Traffic and Motor Vehicle Safety Act and the Highway Safety Act	Set federal safety standards
	Model Cities	Rehabilitated slums

Table 4.1: Legislation of the Great Society.

In this respect what Johnson did was unprecedented. He was paying for the implementation of the American Dream – or for his version of it. His Economic Opportunity Act was a billion-dollar stimulus passed in 1964, which also set up a Job Corps, a domestic equivalent to the Peace Corps, and the Office for Economic Opportunity. Johnson drew on all the best traditions of American political and social thought. He preserved the wilderness and beautified the highways because he thought that Americans should be able to live in a country with beautiful surroundings, and because he thought that journeys on the interstate should be more than merely functional: they should be beautiful. The Highway Beautification Act even paid to hide the junkyards that had sprung up along

ACTIVITY 4.1

Examine Table 4.1.

Create a mind map to illustrate Johnson's Great Society legislation.

interstates (a long road was an obvious place to put a junkyard). He followed Franklin Roosevelt in producing legislation to allow federal patronage of the arts. If America was going to be exceptional, it would beautiful and if would have its own culture. Johnson wanted to invest in the unnecessary, luxurious things in life on behalf of his nation.

He also wanted to eliminate poverty. He did not accept that poverty was a necessary part of modern economic systems and, in 1964, he declared war on it. It was unacceptable that any Americans should live below the poverty line. He sought to create jobs through targeted federal stimulus and tax cuts. With American business booming, he had the money to do so. Another, connected, preoccupation of Johnson's was the rising age profile of Americans. As life expectancy went up, the more retired people there were, the higher the pension bill was and the higher their medical bills were. Medical care was becoming a problem for the elderly of America. Johnson brought back Truman's Medicare bill and had it passed. At first he was careful to ensure that it did not provide primary access to doctors, but only paid for hospital stays and the like. In Congress he was able to get the bill amended so that it was comprehensive, and **Medicaid** was created to provide medical care for those under the retirement age but too poor to purchase medical services. Two of the next three Democratic presidents would attempt to reform the same system, with different degrees of success. Johnson also passed federal laws about education at every stage from kindergarten to college, ensuring minimum standards and access.

It seemed clear to many that this was a time of liberal consensus. Where had this idea come from? The Cold War had created a form of consensus in American society, which the Red Scare of the 1950s had tested. The historians of the time, such as Louis Hartz, had begun to argue that America had been born liberal. In the early and mid-1950s there had been a decline in liberal activism, with no real attempts to identify and address new social problems. Identifying social problems (the most obvious being civil rights) might lead to conflict, perhaps to class conflict, and that might allow communism in. The liberal consensus was characterised by three assumptions:

- America was in a cycle of increasing prosperity.
- Americans had shared values and goals.
- American exceptionalism rested on pragmatic avoidance of class conflict, which would harm the image of America abroad.

If America could look like this, then Americans would have a legitimate claim to global leadership. In global terms, Johnson saw liberalism as a way to defeat communism, which shared these assumptions about what a perfect society might look like but had very different means of getting there. The Great Society was Johnson's way of achieving this goal. He saw the Great Society also as completing Lincoln's work – as part of the Civil Rights Movement – because so many African Americans were poor. He struggled to convince civil rights leaders such as Martin Luther King, Jr, of this.

Finally – civil rights had to be dealt with (see the section headed African Americans in North and South). In doing so, Johnson said that he would lose the South for the Democratic Party for at least a generation. Was the Great Society about more than a liberal politician trying to implement his policies? Was it also about a Democratic Party leader, who had been a Party leader long before assuming the presidency, trying to rebuild a coalition for his Party to retain power? Did Johnson think it unlikely that the Democrats would lose the South as a result of his actions – and want to appear bold and statesmanlike, above Party politics? The Democrats (when Johnson ran again, in the 1968 election) would, after all, be compensated by votes gained in the North, meaning that the presidency would then fall to the candidate who could win the West and Midwest.

 Thematic link: American Dream

Further reading

The Great Society played a role in the changing perception of what 'liberal' meant. There are two issues here:

* **Welfare:** the title of Gareth Davies's book *From Opportunity to Entitlement: The Transformation and Decline of Great Society Liberalism* (Kansas University Press; 1996) captures one perspective on what happened in these years: 'big government' support for people ceased to be seen as something that aided an entrepreneurial individualistic society and became one in which certain sectors of society (the shiftless, the work-shy and so forth) developed a sense of entitlement. This was about a shift from a conception of government as a helping hand for everyone (although in fact social security was discriminatory in racial and gender

ACTIVITY 4.2

Prepare a short presentation arguing that Johnson's motivation for launching the Great Society programme was one of the following:

* Creating a situation whereby the liberal consensus would be a permanent feature of American society.
* Integrating the New Deal into American life so thoroughly that it could never be unpicked.
* Achieving as many liberal goals as he could because he knew that a revival of Republican conservatism was inevitable.
* Fulfilling the legacy and honouring the memory of John F. Kennedy.

 Voices from the past

Johnson on the Great Society

Extracts from Lyndon B. Johnson's 'Great Society' Speech, May 1964, delivered at the Universities of Ohio and Michigan.

The Great Society rests on abundance and liberty for all. It demands an end to poverty and racial injustice, to which we are totally committed in our time. But that is just the beginning.

The Great Society is a place where every child can find knowledge to enrich his mind and to enlarge his talents. It is a place where leisure is a welcome chance to build and reflect, not a feared cause of boredom and restlessness. It is a place where the city of man serves not only the needs of the body and the demands of commerce but the desire for beauty and the hunger for community.

It is a place where man can renew contact with nature. It is a place which honors creation for its own sake and for what

it adds to the understanding of the race. It is a place where men are more concerned with the quality of their goals than the quantity of their goods.

But most of all, the Great Society is not a safe harbor, a resting place, a final objective, a finished work. It is a challenge constantly renewed, beckoning us toward a destiny where the meaning of our lives matches the marvellous products of our labor …

Today, eight million adult Americans … have not finished five years of school. Nearly 20 million have not finished eight years of school. Nearly 54 million – more than one quarter of all America – have not even finished high school.

Each year more than 100,000 high school graduates with proved ability do not enter college because they cannot afford it. And if we cannot educate today's youth, what will we do in 1970 when elementary school enrollment will be five million greater than 1960?

ACTIVITY 4.3

How valuable is Johnson's speech as a source of evidence about the reasons why he advocated the Great Society?

terms) to one in which 'welfare' (which became a dirty word) went to 'special interests' and 'minorities'.

- **Multiculturalism:** the Great Society also seemed to be divisive in a cultural sense, by promoting groups and interests that seemed to challenge the mainstream liberal consensus that had been so confidently promoted among the American middle classes just a decade before.

 Thematic link: identity

The impact of the Kennedy legacy

Johnson knew that he owed his position to Kennedy and that Kennedy's legacy could be useful to him. In his first few months in office he achieved what Kennedy could not, passing much of Kennedy's stalled legislation in his name, including an $11 billion tax cut. It helped that the dead president was beyond criticism. It also helped that the economy was booming and the Republican opposition was in disarray. Essentially, Kennedy's death had removed the biggest single obstacle to good government, which was that nobody in Kennedy's team had been able to impose his or her will on Congress. Johnson had been doing that for his entire career. Johnson sold the Great Society as the logical successor to Kennedy's New Frontier, which had been beset by failure and Congressional attempts to water down his policies. In fact, it was an extension of his political hero FDR's New Deal.

Johnson followed the tradition of most of his predecessors as accidental presidents in retaining the Cabinet he inherited. Unlike in Truman's time, many of them stayed with him for some time. He brought in some of his own staff but he lacked the close confidant that Bobby had been for Jack – Johnson's relationship with the Attorney General was the most difficult among the Cabinet, for understandable reasons, and Bobby Kennedy resigned to run for the Senate shortly after the Civil Rights Act was passed. Johnson also inherited Kennedy's foreign policy and foreign policy team. He did not have anyone around him to counsel him into any diplomatic way out of the unpleasant situation in which America found itself in Indochina, except Dean Rusk, whom the Kennedy brothers had felt to be a weak link in their administration. Nevertheless, an excellent economy, a dead president whose name could be invoked in any appeal to the public, a divided opposition, and a clear plan about the future all seemed promising for Johnson's administration. It was not.

Figure 4.1: Johnson is sworn in as president aboard the presidential plane, Air Force One. Jackie Kennedy is at his side.

ACTIVITY 4.4

What can we learn about life in 1960s New York from Schama's recollections?

Economic developments

Johnson inherited an excellent economy but the economy he bequeathed to Nixon was teetering on the brink of disaster. Part of the reason for this was structural, part cyclical and part was Johnson's fault. One structural problem was American over-reliance on oil. The military used oil, manufacturing industries used oil for power and raw materials, and in this consumer society everyone used gasoline to move themselves and their goods around. Whole communities were growing up in the southern **Sun Belt**, where air conditioning and cars were vital to maintaining the standard of living that Americans expected. The cyclical problem underlined a further structural problem. Since the 1940s, the American economy had benefitted from exporting goods and raw materials that other countries either did not make or could not process efficiently enough. During the 1960s, European countries and Japan recovered their pre-war positions. America entered the decade a net exporter of textiles, steel and household goods (such as washing machines). By 1969, America was a net importer of all these goods. Instead, America began to export construction machinery – the kind of machinery that refined steel and made washing machines.

The net effect of this change was that by 1969 the American balance of trade had reverted to a more normal position, but American economic planning (now, under the Great Society, quite obviously the domain of the federal government and therefore of Johnson) had at its heart the dangerous assumption that the good times would continue. To be fair to Johnson, one reading of the Great Society is that he was attempting to spend money while times were good in order to cushion the blow should times become worse. He spent on infrastructure and job creation, and also on education. The cumulative effect of the rising prosperity enjoyed by

Speak like a historian

Simon Schama's experience of New York City

The historian Simon Schama first spent time in America in 1964. This is his account, written shortly after the 2008 election, of what he experienced in New York City.

We thought we knew America, but what we actually knew was Malamud, Bellow, Baldwin, which was something else entirely. Beyond the elegant museums on 5th and the tonier stretches of Park and Madison, where, if we played our cards right and affected an Oxbridge accent, we'd be sure to run into Holly Golightly, New York seemed lurid and jumpy. As the thermometer climbed into the nineties, sidewalkers slowed to a gasping shuffle as they made their way to or from Grand Central, dripping into their poplin. The city was gamely trying to put on its welcome face as a World's Fair opened on Flushing Meadows. **Modernist** pavilions, steel and pine, celebrated the achievements of General Electric or the dawning of the jet age. Much of it was free. Investigate The Charms of Norway, and a braided blonde would greet you hospitably proffering brisling on rye. Takk, Solveig. In the Ford Pavilion the brand-new, dangerously sexy Mustang was being unveiled by peppy young men in blazers. But out in swelterland, NY, the Long Island Expressway was a parking lot and drivers were aggravating their ulcers, leaning on their horns, and getting testy with the kids.[1]

ACTIVITY 4.5

1. List the reasons why the American economy faltered in the late 1960s.

2. What, in your view, was the biggest single reason why the American economy faltered in the late 1960s? Justify your answer.

Compare your answers to question 2, which is a very tough question, to the answers of others in your class.

Americans, and the federal support given through New Deal and Great Society programmes, meant that even in a downturn there was no danger of the sort of collapse that had begun in 1929.

The economy had boomed during the 1960s and now the boom was slowing down. Johnson was spending a lot of money although he knew that doing so was endangering the Great Society by diverting vital funds. And so it proved. The Great Society at least brought something with it in terms of investment and stimulus. The Vietnam War, on the other hand, was hugely expensive and, in economic terms, pointless. The effect was doubly bad as war spending took funds away from the positive programmes of the Great Society. Even a victory would hardly have managed to make the Vietnam War profitable (it was difficult to see how Americans would profit from infrastructure investment and increased trade). Victory did not come. Rising fuel costs did not help; the American economy relied to a disproportionate extent on oil, both because fuel was needed to power manufacturing and move goods around, and because automobile manufacture was such an important part of the economy. The higher the price of gas, the less affordable were the cars on which so much of the American economy depended.

 Thematic link: prosperity

Maintaining American world power

Kennedy's challenge to Americans had been clear – the country was to assume world leadership. Kennedy himself had, ultimately, done this, and avoided nuclear war in so doing. Even with the more predictable Leonid Brezhnev installed as leader of the USSR from 1964, Johnson faced a number of challenges in maintaining America's power. In 1964 China exploded a nuclear weapon, becoming the fourth nuclear power and providing Johnson with a headache. It was perfectly clear that Mao Zedong, the Chinese leader, was not under the control of the Soviets; it was equally clear that China had ambitions of her own. Johnson did not know – no American politicians knew until much later – how utterly desperate Sino-Soviet relations were becoming, and assumed that he might now be facing two nuclear-armed communist powers who were willing to work together, perhaps over Indochina.

In Czechoslovakia in 1968 Johnson faced a further challenge to America's aspirations to promote freedom. The new Czechoslovakian leader, Alexander Dubček, initiated a programme of reform. In the USSR Brezhnev attempted to negotiate and then sent in the Soviet army to reverse Dubček's reforms. This was known as the Prague Spring. Brezhnev promulgated the Brezhnev Doctrine, which held that the USSR could and would intervene in the affairs of communist countries to keep them communist. This seemed like a shot across America's bows. In fact it was not far different from the Truman Doctrine, which had prompted Johnson to send 30 000 troops to prop up the regime in the Dominican Republic in April 1965. This seemed like a further confirmation that the Cold War was here to stay and that Soviet power would not be challenged in eastern Europe.

Escalation of the war in Vietnam

The eastern part of the Indochinese peninsula had been French before the Second World War, and it was the French who gained control of it after that conflict. In 1946 the communist nationalist Hồ Chí Minh launched an immediate war of independence. This ended in 1954 with the partition of Vietnam, the crescent-shaped country on the east of the peninsula, between a socialist country in the north and a capitalist (and in theory democratic) country in the south. The French were unable to protect the new southern republic and asked the Americans for help. Eisenhower had sent military advisers to provide that help, fearing that if any country in Indochina were allowed to be communist, domino theory would prevail and the other countries around it would become communist too.

When Kennedy died there were well over 10 000 American 'military advisers' in Vietnam. These military advisers had been sent into Vietnam since Eisenhower's time to provide advice and assistance to the South Vietnamese, but by the time their numbers reached five figures it was difficult to pretend that they were not there to run the war themselves. The reasonably American-friendly South Vietnamese leader Ngô Đình Diệm had been assassinated, with Kennedy's agreement and maybe on his initiative. American unease was beginning to stir: pictures of the protests against Diệm, including an iconic image of a monk burning himself to death, had been published. The American worldview, which suggested that communists such as Hồ Chí Minh, the leader of North Vietnam, were bad and their opponents were good, was breaking down. There were only two sides, or poles, in a **bipolar** world. In truth, Hồ was far more a nationalist than he was a communist. His ideology brought welcome support from the Chinese, and was genuinely held, but he cared more about reuniting Vietnam than about any world revolution. Meanwhile, to American eyes, the democratic capitalists (they were in truth neither) of the south were arguing among themselves.

 Key terms

polarity: in international relations, the identification of particular groups of countries that are aligned. During the early Cold War, most American politicians saw the world as bipolar, meaning that countries were either democratic, capitalist, individualistic and free; or socialist, communist and non-free.

The Americans had been conducting covert operations against the North Vietnamese for some time, but why did Johnson choose to escalate the war, and why in 1965? There were three major reasons. The first was that he did not realise quite how difficult the Vietnam War would be. If anything he saw it as a 'police action' like the Korean War, in which defeat was unlikely. Besides, the USA had learned the lessons of Korea – hadn't it? Containment worked. Second, he had an excuse, and Congressional legitimacy for whatever action he wished to take – 'continuing authority to take all necessary measures' – following the Gulf of Tonkin incident (see Figure 4.2) in 1964. This took the form of a Joint Resolution of Congress, the Southeast Asia Resolution – although it is usually referred to now as the Gulf of Tonkin Resolution. Third, the Great Society was mostly in place and he viewed civil rights legislation as done, and so he was free to concentrate on what he thought would be a short war. Johnson's official justification, a combination of his first two reasons, was 'national security'.

Johnson had campaigned on a message of peace, but this was relative: Senator Barry Goldwater had suggested dropping nuclear weapons on the forests of North Vietnam to destroy enemy troops' hiding places. Johnson was a 'dove' and Goldwater a 'hawk' – terms that came into widespread use during the Vietnam War to describe advocates of peace and of aggression respectively. Johnson may well have seen the role of the USA as peacekeeping; he certainly said he did, and the war always remained at least in theory a Vietnamese civil war. There was also the issue of the value of American promises. JFK had promised in his inaugural speech to uphold free peoples across the world but Johnson can hardly have felt bound by this by 1965. Whatever Johnson's reasoning, by March 1965 there were 100 000 American soldiers in Vietnam, and by 1968 that had gone up to 500 000. The cost of the war was $30 billion per annum, which was around 6% of America's GNP. The most significant events of the Vietnam War during Johnson's time in office are shown in Table 4.2. In his memoirs Secretary of Defense Robert McNamara said that the administration had been confident in its ability to solve every problem, but now found itself in a situation where national pride was costing human lives. Johnson and his team could see no ways out. By 1968 there were protests against the war, protests against the draft, protests against Johnson ('Hey, hey, LBJ, how many kids did you kill today?'). Out of ideas, Johnson decided not to run again for the White House.

On 2 August 1964 the USS Maddox engaged with North Vietnamese torpedo boats in the Gulf of Tonkin off the coast of North Vietnam. There were ten North Vietnamese casualties and no US casualties. On 4 August the US Navy claimed that the Maddox had been involved in a further confrontation. The incidents were taken as an example of unprovoked North Vietnamese aggression. Johnson was able to ask for, and receive, Congressional approval for him to do essentially whatever he liked in response.

There were suggestions during the Vietnam War itself that all was not quite as it seemed with the Gulf of Tonkin incident. There is conflicting evidence about whether the Maddox was fired upon, as it claimed, or fired first on 2 August. If the Maddox had initiated the fire fight, then faulty sonar was one possible reason an 'attack' might have been registered. It has also been suggested that the National Security Agency faked the evidence. As for the second incident two days later –

there is no independent evidence that the Maddox had been firing at anything at all. In an unguarded moment in 1965 Johnson openly wondered whether they might have been shooting at whales rather than submarines.

Figure 4.2: The Gulf of Tonkin, August 1964.

So, after the war was escalated with the Gulf of Tonkin Resolution, what went wrong? Johnson, who had consulted widely over his decision to go into Vietnam, seems to have had a strategy of provoking the north and then rapidly overwhelming it. The North Vietnamese, however, were equal to his strategy. Their attack on the US base at Pleiku in February 1965 caused Johnson to launch Operation Rolling Thunder in March of that year. Johnson appears to have been trying to take out the North Vietnamese quickly by flattening their industrial production and morale through bombing, and then sending an elite force of marines to mop up the leadership. This failed because the North Vietnamese distributed their industrial production around the country and were not demoralised. Johnson rapidly escalated troop levels, indicating that he sought a more conventional military solution.

By the middle of 1965, Operation Rolling Thunder, the bombing campaign against the north, was being dictated by Washington. Targets were selected with not just military but political objectives in mind: give in, Johnson was saying, and

1964	September: Gulf of Tonkin incident.
1965	February: Eight American servicemen were killed in a North Vietnamese attack on their base at Pleiku, in South Vietnam. March: Operation Rolling Thunder, the bombing campaign and military invasion of Vietnam, began in response to deteriorating South Vietnamese morale, as 3500 US marines, supported by air strikes, landed in the north. December: There were over 180 000 US military personnel in Vietnam.
1967	November: General Westmoreland, the US commander, predicted victory within a year.
1968	January: After two years of stalemate, North Vietnamese forces launched an overwhelmingly successful attack, the Tet Offensive. This was a coordinated attack across South Vietnam. May: As public opinion at home turned against him, Johnson asked for peace talks. There were now around half a million US troops in Vietnam.

Table 4.2: Timeline of the Vietnam War to 1968.

we will stop bombing. Bombing was sometimes halted to seek peace. The North Vietnamese response was usually simple enough. Ever since 1956 their position had been that free elections in South Vietnam would be acceptable, because they knew that free elections would lead to a unified, national government of Vietnam under the Communist Party. Johnson could not, would not, allow this. So the fighting continued. Meanwhile the North Vietnamese continued to resist American incursions in the north and to harass American and South Vietnamese positions in the south. No ground was gained throughout 1966. Small gains were made in 1967 – enough for General Westmoreland, the US commander, to predict victory.

Meanwhile, people were dying. Significantly for Johnson, Americans were dying in large numbers. They were now mostly conscripts and, given how easy it could be for those with money to avoid the draft, they were mostly poor. They were not well trained, certainly not well enough to operate in the jungle. Helped by the sight of money draining away from the Great Society and towards the war, and by the growing protests at home, Johnson had realised by the end of 1967 that the war had to be finished. This was the context of Westmoreland's prediction of victory.

The North Vietnamese knew all this too, and in January 1968 they launched the Tet Offensive. The Viet Cong presence in South Vietnam had long been significant and American troops had not been very good at figuring out where, or who, they were. To the ill-trained American troops, Vietnamese villagers and Viet Cong guerrillas were hard to tell apart. Now they erupted, in a coordinated way, across three-quarters of the country. Only (only!) 6000 US and allied troops were killed – as against nearly 60 000 communists and at least 10 000 civilians. But it took nearly a month to regain Saigon, the South Vietnamese capital. The US Embassy had been breached and four of its staff killed. Although the Viet Cong and North Vietnamese militarily lost the Tet Offensive definitively – by March they had nothing to show except the 60 000 casualties – the effect on the Americans was even worse. Psychologically, it was devastating. All the promises of victory – and all the deaths (most families in America knew someone who had died) – had come to nothing. The only way to win this war against the North Vietnamese, who had been assumed by the Americans to be poor combatants because they were communists living in the jungle (and there was an overtone of racism here, too), was now, clearly, to launch an all-out invasion in the style of the Second World War. But Johnson was no Roosevelt and the North Vietnamese were no Nazis: they were trying to invade a country many of whose citizens actually wanted to be invaded. In this context Johnson began to seek peace and announced that he would not stand for re-election.

Relations between the USA and its western allies

The USA's relations with its western allies were shaken during Johnson's presidency, at least partly because of the Vietnam War. In 1966 the French asked all NATO troops to leave French soil (including, Johnson is supposed to have asked, those buried under it as a result of the First and Second World Wars?). This was partly connected to the Vietnam War, from which the French, the former colonial masters of Vietnam, wished to distance themselves. It was partly connected to the recent French acquisition of nuclear weapons, which gave them the self-confidence to do without NATO (i.e. American) troops for protection. Finally, it was connected to the personality of Charles de Gaulle, the French president. He was a patriot, certainly, but also a difficult ally. De Gaulle had long resented what he saw as a special relationship between the UK and the USA; in 1958 Eisenhower had rebuffed his efforts for closer relations in the aftermath of a crisis over Algeria that had nearly ripped France apart. The USA also found itself almost alone over Vietnam, supported only by Australian troops. Even its most reliable European ally, Britain, failed to send troops to support it. A document that was accidentally released showed that Prime Minister Harold Wilson feared that Britain would be portrayed as America's stooge. Canada, its friendly neighbour, proved willing to host a large number of American **draft-dodgers**.

The United States retained its position at the forefront of the Organization of American States, the alliance set up under Truman to attempt to promote

ACTIVITY 4.6

Produce a mind map to show the reasons for Johnson's escalation of the Vietnam War.

 Voices from the past

Lyndon Johnson

Lyndon Johnson was interviewed in 1971 by historian Doris Kearns.

I knew from the start that I was bound to be crucified either way I moved. If I left the woman I really loved – the Great Society – in order to get involved with that bitch of a war on the other side of the world, then I would lose everything at home. All my programs. All my hopes to feed the hungry and shelter the homeless … But if I left that war and let the communists take over South Vietnam, then I would be seen as a coward and my nation would be seen as an appeaser and we would

both find it impossible to accomplish anything for anybody anywhere in the entire globe. Everything I knew about history told me if I got out of Viet Nam and let Hồ Chí Minh run through the streets of Saigon, then I'd be doing exactly what Chamberlain did in World War II. I'd be giving a big fat reward to aggression. And I knew that … [there] would be in this country an endless national debate – that would shatter my presidency, kill my administration, damage our democracy. I knew that Harry Truman and Dean Acheson had lost their effectiveness from the day that the communists took over in China.

democracy throughout the Americas. The death in 1967 of Che Guevara, attempting to foment unrest in Bolivia, removed one major irritant – Guevara had been spreading ideas of revolution, and knowledge of guerrilla tactics, across Latin America. There were nine coups in Latin America in the 1960s, including one in 1965–66 that prompted Johnson to send troops to the Dominican Republic to restore order and protect the government, threatened by what Johnson saw as a communist revolution. Across the Atlantic, Johnson gave covert support to Israel during the Six-Day War against Syria and Egypt in 1967. He remained willing to take steps to promote the interests of America's capitalist and democratic allies.

 Thematic link: identity

African Americans in North and South

Johnson's presidency looked like heralding a new dawn for African Americans. In some ways it did, but in other ways more problems arose. In the South the final push against segregation and the denial of voting rights was underway. Around 7.5 million African Americans lived in the North, generally in the cities, and generally apart from white people. 'Urban' was becoming synonymous with 'black' in American political discourse. The problems faced by African Americans in the North were the problems faced by the inhabitants of distressed and underresourced cities, controlled by white landlords and often inhabited by black populations who had taken the place of white people who had moved to the suburbs. By 1966 Martin Luther King, Jr, the great leader of southern protest, was marching through suburban Chicago trying to shame the white population there into caring more about the plight of black people in Chicago's urban centre.

Developments in the Civil Rights Movement

The lynching that became known as the Mississippi Burning occurred during the passing of the Civil Rights Act. In June 1964, three civil rights workers were killed by members of the Ku Klux Klan, the local police and the sheriff's office in Philadelphia, Mississippi. The three had been organising voter registration and setting up a 'Freedom School', a temporary school for African Americans. The FBI took over a month to find the bodies. The state government then refused to accept a prosecution for murder, so the federal authorities had to prosecute for civil rights violations. The resulting sentences were derisory. Eventually, in 2005, one man (in his 80s) was convicted of the manslaughter of James Chaney, Andrew Goodman and Mickey Schwerner.

The lesson of the so-called Freedom Summer of 1964 in Mississippi was that legislation was needed. Even when it passed, attitudes in that part of Mississippi did not change. To Mississippians the civil rights activists descending upon their state in the summer of that election year felt like an invasion. The picture was the same the next year in Alabama. The four-day march from Selma to Montgomery, the capital of Alabama, in March 1965, was the setting for the murder of two civil rights volunteers – as in Mississippi, the victims were both black and white. As the marchers reached Montgomery, the Confederate flag could be seen flying from the state capitol building. The local sheriff in Selma had used electric cattle prods on the protestors. The Voting Rights Act of 1965 was passed in response to the events in Montgomery.

The marches from Selma to Montgomery provide a useful microcosm of the Civil Rights Movement. They were designed to protest against African Americans' exclusion from the right to vote. They were an uneasy collaboration between the Student Non-violent Coordinating Committee, which had local organisation and contacts, and Martin Luther King's Southern Christian Leadership Conference, which brought publicity, national organisation and, through King, contact with President Johnson. The first march, on 7 March, became known as Bloody Sunday after Alabama's state troopers gassed and beat local protestors. The second march, two days later, attracted national attention from the start and was attended by many protestors from out of state. The state troopers stood aside but a wary King obeyed a court order not to march. That evening James Reeb, a white minister from Boston, was killed by opponents of the march. In the face of national and international outrage, President Johnson went to Congress to push for the passage of the Voting Rights Act, declaring that Selma represented a pivotal point in history. On 21 March, the march to Montgomery finally went ahead, with federal troops protecting the marchers whom Governor George Wallace – like Johnson, a Democrat – refused to protect. The key elements of these marches were:

- SCLC's insistence on the deliberate provocation of violent reaction from white authorities.
- SCLC's focus on voting rights above all else.
- Support from external, multi-racial, protestors.
- Media coverage undermining America's position as the 'land of the free' and international standing.

 Voices from the past

James Baldwin

The African-American author James Baldwin, who had negotiated with Bobby Kennedy in 1963, wrote this letter from Harlem, which is part of Manhattan, New York City.

Now I am perfectly aware that there are other slums in which white men are fighting for their lives, and mainly losing. I know that blood is also flowing through those streets and that the human damage there is incalculable. People are continually pointing out to me the wretchedness of white people in order to console me for the wretchedness of blacks. But an itemized account of the American failure does not console me and it should not console anyone else.

… All other slum dwellers, when the bank account permits it, can move out of the slum and vanish altogether from the eye of persecution. No Negro in this country has ever made that much money and it will be a long time before any Negro does. The Negroes in Harlem, who have no money, spend what they have on such gimcracks as they are sold. These include "wider" TV screens, more "faithful" hi-fi sets, more "powerful" cars, all of which, of course, are obsolete long before they are paid for. Anyone who has ever struggled with poverty knows how extremely expensive it is to be poor; and if one is a member of a captive population, economically speaking, one's feet have simply been placed on the treadmill forever. One is victimized, economically, in a thousand ways – rent, for example, or car insurance. Go shopping one day in Harlem – for anything – and compare Harlem prices and quality with those downtown.[2]

ACTIVITY 4.7

How valuable is Baldwin's account of conditions in Harlem, New York City, as a source of evidence about the lives of African Americans in the northern United States in the 1960s?

- Reluctant intervention by a sympathetic president.
- There were murders associated with each march. An African-American protestor, Jamie Lee, died following an assault by a police officer. His death sparked the first march. Reeb died after the second and Viola Liuzzo, a civil rights organiser, was murdered shortly after the third.

Figure 4.3: Malcolm X's only public meeting with Martin Luther King, 26 March 1964.

Martin Luther King and Malcolm X

The two most famous civil rights leaders of their day did not see eye to eye. There was mutual respect for their shared aim of achieving racial equality but there were several differences between them. Martin Luther King was a Christian preacher who practised and preached non-violence and believed that a combination of economic action, voting reform and protest would produce integration. X was a Muslim who believed that relations between white and black people had broken down irretrievably in America and that only a violent black response could prevent further white violence. He advocated 'the ballot or the bullet'. X was, obviously, a pseudonym: the Nation of Islam's practice was for adherents to abandon their 'slave name', which in his case was Malcolm Little. X left the Nation of Islam for its refusal to cooperate with other civil rights groups: members of the group murdered him a year later.

The civil rights legislation of 1964–65, with appropriate federal support, did the job for African Americans in the South, whose civil rights were now protected. However, white attitudes were not improved and African Americans remained overwhelmingly poor. There were other developments – a bomb in Mississippi in 1966 that killed a local NAACP leader; James Meredith's march against fear later that year in Tennessee and Mississippi, which ended in his being shot; and the Southern Nonviolent Coordinating Committee elected Stokely Carmichael as its leader, dropping its commitment to non-violence. King, meanwhile, had switched his focus to the North and to workers' rights. It was while he was further north (not the Deep South, his previous focus) in April 1968 to lend support to striking sanitation workers that King, the major advocate of nonviolent civil rights protest, was assassinated. His death triggered outbursts of violence across the country.

Johnson's role in passing civil rights legislation

Johnson had to use his full range of persuasive powers to have civil rights legislation passed. The Twenty-fourth Amendment was passed largely on the basis that it was Kennedy's legislation (which it was). This removed one tactic white governments in the South had used to disenfranchise African Americans, which was to claim that they had failed to pay the non-existent poll tax and therefore could not vote. Predictably, more was needed, and that would come in the Civil Rights Act, which had also been Kennedy's project. Johnson was helped by his address to Congress following his accession to the presidency in which he called the Civil Rights Act the most fitting tribute they could possibly pay to Kennedy. He was also helped by his threats to use an arcane procedural motion called a 'discharge petition' to embarrass the powerful chairman of the **House Rules Committee**, Howard Smith, a Dixiecrat from Virginia. Normally if the chairman of the House Rules Committee wanted to block a bill, he could. In the Senate, Johnson encouraged his replacement as Majority Leader, Mike Mansfield, to adopt similar tactics to keep the bill away from James Eastland of Mississippi, the chairman of the Senate Judiciary Committee. This was important because Johnson had encouraged abnormal tactics in both chambers of Congress. His status as a former Congressional manager helped him to do this.

The violence in Selma and Montgomery in 1965 led to Johnson's decision that the calls of Martin Luther King and Malcolm X for voting reform should be heeded. He ensured that he gained the support of the Republican leader in the Senate, realising that he would need Republican votes to pass the bill. Johnson also made it clear that he – having just been re-elected in a landslide – wanted the bill to be passed. It was passed: a bill, Johnson said, that was part of a fight comparable to the American Revolution and that was about neither states' rights nor voting rights, but human rights. The Voting Rights Act and other civil rights legislation are summarised in Table 4.3.

Date	Legislation	Effect
23 January 1964	Twenty-fourth Amendment (adopted)	Prohibits using failure to pay poll tax as a reason to deny the right to vote.
2 July 1964	Civil Rights Act	Outlaws discrimination based on race, colour, religion or sex. Bans segregation.
6 August 1965	Voting Rights Act	Allows voting rights across the United States and introduces special measures for certain states thought unlikely to comply.

Table 4.3: Civil Rights legislation 1964–65.

The impact of change, including urban riots

African Americans in the North were allowed to vote. They were not very often formally segregated, except that they often had no choice but to live in black neighbourhoods with few white people around. Sometimes this was because African Americans were still poor, and so lived in the cheapest housing; sometimes it was because the laws preventing restrictive covenants on suburban housing – that is, the laws preventing individuals or house builders from simply refusing to sell houses to black people – were ignored. In the North the problems were racism, economic exclusion and exploitation by unscrupulous white landlords. The two main consequences of this were a rise in prominence of violent African-American groups (see the section headed The radicalisation of African Americans) and serious urban disturbances with a racial character.

There had been rent strikes in Harlem in 1963. The economic issues that underlay this were in no way ameliorated by the legislation of 1964–65. King's message of non-violent protest did not work in urban areas where black people and white people did not, generally, come into close daily contact. The riots began in Watts, Los Angeles, in 1965, when 34 people died and massive damage was done. During Johnson's second term there were riots in 100 cities, including Detroit, where 43 died, and half a billion dollars of damage was caused. Paratroopers and the National Guard were sent in to stop the rioting. The 12th Street riot in Detroit in 1967 was covered extensively in the national press. Johnson set up a Commission of Inquiry that led to a federal Open Housing Act (see Table 4.3) but it did not work. The slum clearance measures that Johnson wanted to implement were watered down and nothing changed the fact that the inner cities were the cheapest and therefore most accessible places to live. There was no way forcibly to integrate a white suburb, so African-American communities in the North remained largely intact in worse houses and with worse jobs. Elsewhere, the riots had begun to worry white people. The political reaction to this was to complete the fragmentation of the Democratic Party. Johnson had predicted that his passage of civil rights legislation would lose the South for a generation, fracturing his coalition. The former Governor of Alabama, George Wallace, ran as an American Independent in 1968 and won Georgia, Alabama, Mississippi, Louisiana and Arkansas, taking sufficient votes from the Democrats in the rest of the South that only Texas remained in the Democratic fold.

Open Housing Acts
Open Housing Acts had been passed at state level for several years – and in California one had been overturned in 1964 by Proposition 14. The supporters of Proposition 14 in California (including Ronald Reagan) argued that the anti-segregation statute of an Open Housing Act was a violation of a seller's right to sell to whom he chose and thus struck at the core of the transactional property-based conception of individual liberty. This was a matter of individual property rights.

Table 4.4: Open Housing Acts.

Speak like a historian

Stephen Halpern on Title VI

Title VI of the Civil Rights Act of 1964 is that part of the legislation that allows the Federal Government to cut off federal funds from any state or municipality that refuses to desegregate schools: in other words, this is the part of the legislation that sought to prevent a repeat of the events of Little Rock in 1957.

Viewed in the context of the history of southern race relations and of segregated public education, or in comparison with subsequent administrations, the Johnson administration enforced Title VI in a uniquely active and energetic way.

Yet the enforcement of Title VI during the Johnson years was limited in scope to the South, to elementary and secondary schools, and to a large extent to non-urban districts with small minority populations. Consequently, Johnson's 'active' enforcement of Title VI did not affect most of the major metropolitan centers of the South, where the overwhelming proportion of southern blacks attended public schools, nor did it affect segregated schools in the North. This ... highlights the central impact that enforcement priorities can have.[3]

Social divisions and protest movements

During Johnson's presidency any notion that there was a liberal consensus in America – indeed, any notion of a united America – was lost. By the end of his time in office there was a deeply embedded conflict between what Richard Nixon called the '**silent majority**' and vocal, sometimes violent protestors – in fact, the conflict was so deeply embedded that it must have been there before. The later 1960s were a perfect time for protest for a number of reasons:

- The economy was sound but turning down – this was enough to provoke protest without placing people under so much economic stress that they did not have time to protest.
- There was a large younger generation – the **Baby Boomers** – that was educated and available for protest.
- Communications technology meant that local protests could quickly become global through the medium of television.
- There were clear focuses for protest, including an unpopular war.

Education and youth

For a number of reasons, Americans' participation in education increased after the Second World War. The rising tide of prosperity cut the need for young people to go out to work. Johnson's Great Society programme sought to guarantee elementary and secondary education for the very poorest in recognition that the job of providing it was almost done. It was also important to get students to go to universities. Nuclear missiles did not build themselves and the space race needed rocket scientists. Increasingly, the kinds of jobs American industry needed to be done involved higher levels of education. The neutrality of the curricula and

ACTIVITY 4.8

Account for Johnson's failure fully to enforce Title VI of the Civil Rights Act.

research programmes of universities and colleges was arguably adversely affected by the drive to attract corporate sponsorship; it was difficult to be a disinterested rocket scientist whose funding depended on corporations with government contracts.

There was a competing rationale for expanding education in America, and that was the elimination of poverty. Then, as now, learning was seen as a tool of social mobility. Desegregation of schools became important in this, although progress was slow. Johnson did not entirely have the stomach for that particular fight: besides, in the North whole areas were segregated, and in the South it was hard to unpick the effects of choice (on both sides of the racial divide) and public busing of children across town to attend schools that were not near their homes, which meant that previously integrated schools could begin to self-segregate.

University attendance was also becoming a positive lifestyle choice for the children of the middle classes. By 1970 there were 2500 colleges in America and 40% of young Americans attended them. College cost money but there was money to spend. If the local college did not suit, transport options were now good enough that Americans could go to colleges across the country. This created concentrations of young people in institutions run by an older generation used to austerity and war. In the late 1950s this became known as the 'Beat Generation', with authors such as Allan Ginsberg at its cultural heart. By the middle of the 1960s a hippie counterculture had developed. This was not just an American phenomenon. There were student protests across the western world in 1968 – in France, they nearly brought down the government.

Student movements also became associated with drugs. Cannabis use was rife on student campuses, as was the use of LSD, a powerful hallucinogen also known as 'acid'. The jazz music of the 1920s had become a form of up-tempo blues – rock and roll. To drugs and rock and roll was added sex. The influence of the women's movement, a general decline in religious feeling among the young and greater access to contraception combined to create a generation of young people who were keen and able to protest politically from the universities and colleges of America. A further benefit of this was that enrolment on a university course meant protection from the draft, and thus from the Vietnam War.

Feminism

The role of women in American society was a burning issue in the 1960s. In the Kitchen Debate in 1959 Nixon had measured the progress of a society by how much technological help women enjoyed at home: domestic appliances were key. Betty Friedan and other feminists disagreed and began to push for women to be valued as people in their own right, rather than only as someone's mother, wife or daughter. Legally, this was true, but in practice women's rights had a long way to go. As late as 1970 women often had difficulty obtaining credit without a man's signature. Female politicians were the exception rather than the norm – there were two female Senators in the 1960s, one of whom, Margaret Chase Smith of Maine, made a spectacularly unsuccessful attempt to gain the Republican presidential nomination in 1964. She had originally come to national prominence after taking on her late husband's old House seat. As a senator she had supported issues relating to women serving in the military but had never particularly sought leadership in the women's movement. Her most notable contribution to the cause of women seeking to enter politics was the observation that, given that women generally ran the home, they could certainly run Congress.

The National Organization for Women ('What do we want?' 'Equal rights!' 'When do we want them?' 'NOW!') was formed in 1966 by activists including Betty Friedan, the author of *The Feminine Mystique*. Feminism as a political movement had been a long time coming. Why did it come in the 1960s? Figure 4.4 gives some suggested reasons. Betty Friedan provides an interesting example of the kind of person who became a radical feminist. In her youth she had been a Marxist and she remained left-leaning. She was a journalist who had lost a job in the 1950s because she was pregnant. She was an alumna of the University of California, Berkeley, the centre of the **Free Speech Movement** and other student/academic protests. Friedan was a psychologist by training, familiar with the work of Freud (who suggests, among other things, that many women wish they were men). It is possible to see all of this in her feminism. 'Is this all?' Friedan had asked in her famous book *The Feminine Mystique*. The National Organization for Women (NOW – the 'for' in the name, rather than 'of', is significant) sought to remove legislative barriers to women working and living on equal terms with men.

Friedan contrasted this with the more dramatic tactics advocated by leaders such as Gloria Steinem, another left-leaning journalist. Steinem had come to prominence in 1963–64 when she exposed the working conditions among Playboy Bunnies – the name given to waitresses at the Playboy Clubs, who were expected to wear tight-fighting and revealing uniforms complete with a tail like that of a rabbit. She continued to campaign throughout Johnson's presidency, eventually publishing an article entitled 'After black power … women's liberation' in 1969. Steinem also campaigned against the Vietnam War. Other radical feminists of the time occupied male-only bars (a clear echo of the tactics of the Civil Rights Movement) and picketed shows such as Miss America (Atlantic City, 1968) that they believed degraded women. Although no bras were actually burned at that particular protest, contrary to the myth that arose, the feminist protestors gained headlines with crude placards suggesting that the women in the beauty pageant were prostituting themselves. The event, led by Robin Morgan, a journalist, veteran of the civil rights and anti-war movements and founder of New York Radical Women, was a far cry from NOW's attempts to secure equal pay and access to the best jobs. Like so much of the protest of 1968 it seems to have alienated middle America – including its women.

Two other notable events concerning the development of feminism happened in 1968:

- Valerie Solanas, a writer who had studied psychology, attempted to kill the artist Andy Warhol, who had assumed that the play Solanas had given him to produce represented a police trap as it was so pornographic. The murder attempt and her subsequent trial gave publicity to her 1967 work *The SCUM Manifesto*, which calls for the elimination of men on its first page. This was truly radical feminism!

- The death of Martin Luther King, Jr, elevated his wife Coretta Scott King to effective leadership of the Civil Rights Movement. She immediately expanded its platform to include women's rights.

By the end of the 1960s, feminism was a force both on the ground and in Congress, where the inter-racial nature of the movement became apparent when Shirley Chisholm, a Democrat representing a district of New York, emerged as a leader of women's rights. Chisholm said that she felt she had faced far more discrimination over her gender than over her race. She had been an educator and New York state politician before entering Congress. She had also been a member of the League of Women Voters, which had been around for as long as women had had the vote and specifically excluded men from membership. A remarkable woman, Chisholm would later gain greater fame when running for the presidential nomination in 1972. She visited George Wallace, the segregationist former Governor of Alabama, who had been seriously wounded in an assassination attempt while he was also running for president, because in her view it was the right thing to do. Meanwhile, what was becoming known as the second wave of feminism (the first wave was in the 1920s) was moving in three different but broadly linked directions. First, reproductive rights – a euphemism for the right to use contraception and, ultimately, to have an abortion – were coming to a head. Steinem, who had had an abortion in her teens, was speaking out about it, and the pressure group the American Civil Liberties Union was steering legal cases towards the Supreme Court. Second, discussions about women's sexuality were becoming common; books and leaflets were published with varying degrees of academic rigour, often directly taking on Freud. One of these was Germaine Greer's *The Female Eunuch* (1970), published in London but popular in America. Third, issues about women's lifestyles were becoming more prominent as women worked out how to 'have it all'. All of these became clearer in the 1970s.

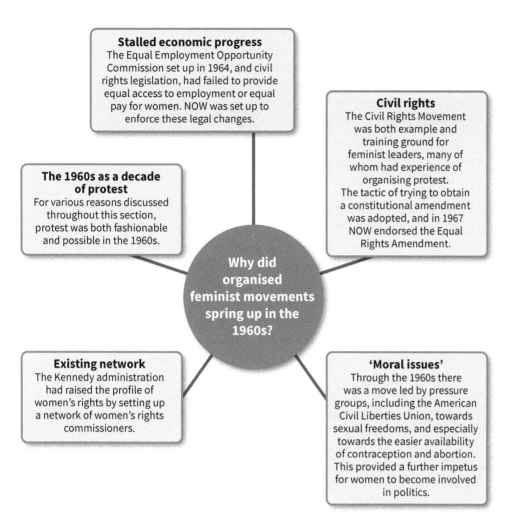

Stalled economic progress
The Equal Employment Opportunity Commission set up in 1964, and civil rights legislation, had failed to provide equal access to employment or equal pay for women. NOW was set up to enforce these legal changes.

Civil rights
The Civil Rights Movement was both example and training ground for feminist leaders, many of whom had experience of organising protest. The tactic of trying to obtain a constitutional amendment was adopted, and in 1967 NOW endorsed the Equal Rights Amendment.

The 1960s as a decade of protest
For various reasons discussed throughout this section, protest was both fashionable and possible in the 1960s.

Why did organised feminist movements spring up in the 1960s?

Existing network
The Kennedy administration had raised the profile of women's rights by setting up a network of women's rights commissioners.

'Moral issues'
Through the 1960s there was a move led by pressure groups, including the American Civil Liberties Union, towards sexual freedoms, and especially towards the easier availability of contraception and abortion. This provided a further impetus for women to become involved in politics.

Figure 4.4: Feminist movements in the 1960s.

Radicalisation of African Americans

The late 1960s was not the time when African Americans became radicalised, but it was the time when radicalised, violent African-American leaders became more noticeable than peacemakers such as King. The reasons for the Black Revolt, as it became known, were clear enough. In the North, black unemployment was twice the national average and black poverty twice as bad. Schools were worse, housing was worse and there was little money in the affected communities to make things better. The radical Nation of Islam, under Elijah Muhammad, had splintered. Malcolm X left to form the Organization of Afro-American Unity and brought even greater publicity to the idea that white and black people had fundamentally different needs and goals. In the wake of his death and the riots that began in 1965 other groups were formed, such as the Blank Panthers in Oakland, California (1966). The idea of **Black Power** recalled Marcus Garvey's call in the 1920s for racial consciousness and pride. Black Power wanted black businesses, homes, schools, politics – and even guerrilla warfare.

The Vietnam War provided further impetus towards radicalising African Americans. The war needed people to fight and this meant young people. People with money and power (white people, on the whole) were able to avoid the draft – by moving to Canada, by going to university (like Bill Clinton), or by pulling some strings to ensure a safer deployment at home (like George W. Bush). Poor people could not avoid the draft. Martin Luther King damaged his previously cordial relations with Johnson by criticising the irony that Americans who were denied freedom at home were expected to fight for it abroad. Muhammad Ali, the boxing champion and member of the Nation of Islam who had abandoned his original 'slave name' of Cassius Clay, achieved iconic status when he burnt his draft card, explaining that he had no quarrel with the Viet Cong, unlike with the white men around him who subjected him to frequent racial abuse.

How did this radicalisation express itself? In a sense, African-American radicalism encompasses all that is examined in the section on 'African Americans in North and South'. King's continued insistence on non-violence was just as radical as Malcolm X's separatism; they each paid for their views with their lives. What really happened was the development of a sense of racial self-consciousness around African Americans empowering themselves through their own efforts. Stokely Carmichael publicised the phrase 'Black Power' following his arrest while marching with Martin Luther King in support of James Meredith, who had been shot in 1966. Carmichael intended the phrase to provide a focus for all those frustrated that civil rights were coming slowly. Later that year he voted to exclude white people from the SNCC, believing that the next phase in attaining black rights should involve black people's efforts – black agency. He also dropped the group's commitment to non-violence.

Carmichael was extremely influential. Although based in the South, his message was heard by those in the North seeking leadership following the death of Malcolm X. His message went with the riots against poor living conditions in northern cities, which were generally segregated by sheer economics, in that black people lived in poor areas because they were poor. Separation, African-American agency and Black Power all worked well together. It would be difficult to argue that Carmichael caused the urban riots of the late 1960s but he does seem to have expressed many of the ideas and much of the anger underlying them.

The Black Panthers were another radical African-American party. They are an interesting example not only of radical tactics but also of the reasons why more traditional civil rights groups were unable to provide the solutions needed. The Black Panthers were formed in Oakland, California, in 1966, in response to fairly typical urban conditions for African Americans. Oakland was a growing town – California was a growing state – and many of the members of the Black Panthers had moved to escape discrimination elsewhere, only to find economic opportunities closed to them because of the colour of their skin. They might have had the vote but it did them little good. A particular bone of contention was the attitude of the police force (99% white) to African-American populations. Bobby Seale and Huey Newton founded the Panthers to 'police the police'. They followed police cars around, with openly displayed weapons, watching for instances of police brutality and threatening legal action should they be challenged (they were doing nothing illegal unless they actually pointed the weapon at someone). When legislators tried to change the law, Seale disrupted the legislative session.

Figure 4.5: Stokely Carmichael, the leader of the Student Nonviolent Coordinating Committee from 1966–67, who viewed non-violence as a tactic that was sometimes effective rather than as a firm principle; he would later become a separatist.

The Panthers' demands were summarised in the Ten Point Program of 1967. The Panthers wanted freedom, full employment for black people, the end of exploitation by capitalists, housing, education, an end to the draft (the draft tended to catch the poor, who were often black), an end to POLICE BRUTALITY (their capital letters), the release of black prisoners, trial of black defendants by all-black juries and finally: 'We want land, bread, housing, education, clothing, justice and peace'. What they achieved was the special attention of the FBI, who deemed them very dangerous, and the imprisonment of Huey Newton from 1968 to 1971 for manslaughter; his conviction was overturned on appeal. The 'Free Huey' campaign that sprang up provided extremely valuable publicity. At the 1968 summer Olympic Games, held in Mexico City, two American medallists gave the Black Power salute during the American anthem. This was a reminder, in a tremendously difficult year for America, that the racial problem had not been solved. It was a reminder seen by the entire world.

Anti-war movements

It was not just black draftees who burnt their draft cards. The white establishment did not stand fully behind the Vietnam War. **Doves** in Congress, including Bobby Kennedy, opposed it. Perhaps more than anything else, the anti-war movements highlighted the differences between Americans during the Vietnam War. To dodge the draft seemed baffling to many in the older generation. To protest against the war seemed downright unpatriotic.

By 1968 youth culture in America was synonymous with opposition to the Vietnam War. A point that was not lost on young Americans was that the draft affected them but not their parents. They were less ready than their parents' generation had been to embark upon a far-off war, especially when, as with Vietnam, the causes of the war seemed murky, the reward uncertain and the opportunities for glory and pride far distant. The protest movements of the 1960s were virtually all youth movements at heart – if not in leadership, then in their activists. Young people had time, ideas – and ideals. A 20-year-old could risk – or encourage – arrest in the cause of civil rights far more easily than a 40-year-old with a family to support.

It was not just students. Some of the earliest opposition to the war had come from the faculty of the University of Michigan, who held teach-ins within a month of the start of Operation Rolling Thunder, modelled on seminars they had held about the Civil Rights Movement, and focusing on the morality of the war. Their students, organised as Students for a Democratic Society (SDS), called for a march on Washington to protest against the war – around 20 000 marched in April 1965. By 1967 conscientious objection was becoming fashionable at universities across the country. Objectors bombarded Secretary of Defense Robert S. McNamara with advice about what else those opposed to violence might do as a form of national service that did not advance the war effort. McNamara received 10 000 letters in June 1967 alone.

Protestors did not all have the same motives. Some wanted to protest against spending money on a war between far-off peoples. Some wanted to protest against risking American lives. Others simply thought the war unwinnable. The anti-war movements were at the heart of student protests because it was young people who were being called up to fight. The Beat Generation was affluent and educated and formed a counterculture in direct opposition to traditional American values, one of which was the duty to go to war for one's country. Rock and roll and folk music stars such as Pete Seeger, Bob Dylan and Joni Mitchell, all of whom had links to the Civil Rights Movement, provided the soundtrack to the anti-war movement. Bob Dylan provided occasionally baffling leadership. This all came together in the 1967 Summer of Love, a wave of music festivals and protest movements set in a drug-fuelled haze, which also rejected consumerism. Two years later Jimi Hendrix, a former soldier, provided a psychedelic version of the Star-Spangled Banner at the Woodstock festival in New York, scandalising conservative sensibilities.

The anti-war movement was not all about music. Protestors set themselves on fire outside the Pentagon and the United Nations headquarters in November 1965. Others took to the streets. Their chants were 'Hell, no, we won't go' (especially when burning their draft cards) and, 'Hey, hey, LBJ, how many kids did you kill today?' in reference to the war. By 1968 Johnson was a virtual prisoner in the White House, able to hear the protests from his living quarters. Protests at the Democratic **Convention** in Chicago turned violent as it became increasingly clear that the anti-war movement had divided the Democratic Party. The SDS, which had begun to factionalise in 1966 as many of its members urged a violent form of protest, had lost control of the anti-war movement by the end of 1967 as violence grew across America. It continued to participate, however, and was responsible for the peaceful million-strong student strike of April 1968.

The role of the media

The media played a threefold role in protests. First, television, now utterly ubiquitous, provided an easy way for potential protestors to see actual protests. Protest banners could be made with television in mind. Seeing protests on television inspired copycat protests far more than newspaper reports. Second, the media reported establishment reactions to protests. The great mistake made by the Alabama authorities during the march from Selma had been to allow photographs to be taken of protestors being shocked with cattle prods. A picture could tell a thousand words. Third, the new media enabled some form of independent verification of what the government said. One particularly important example of this was the Tet Offensive in early 1968. The American government tried to put out the message that the Vietnamese offensive had been largely ineffective. The pictures told a different story, adding credibility to the anti-war message that the American army was outgunned, outmanoeuvred and out of hope of victory in Vietnam. A Free Speech movement began at the University of California, Berkeley, in 1964 after the university attempted to restrict student political activity on campus. By 1968 student protest was so serious that President Johnson could barely leave the White House. In 1970, when student protestors were killed by the National Guard in two separate instances (four at Kent State University, Ohio, and two at Jackson State, Mississippi), President Nixon's opinion polling found that 90% of the country was on the side of the federal troops. The protests of the youth movement seemed to many Americans to be out of hand.

There were cultural reasons for this:

- Many Americans felt the traditional unease of the older generation when the younger generation rebels.
- Some Americans also felt that it was un-American to protest when the economy was failing and the country was at war.
- Others felt that any form of protest was contrary to the WASP work ethic, showing these students (with all this free time) to be over-privileged.

The Peace Movement, as the Free Speech movement became, was characterised by draft-dodging (fleeing to Canada or burning your draft card could carry a six-month prison sentence) and by protest songs, hippies, 'flower power' (a joking alternative to alternative forms of power available; hippies often wore flowers in their hair or on their clothes) and drugs.

The calls for peace were strengthened by the media. The American army now deployed with journalists embedded within it; occasionally these journalists did not prove compliant when the army tried to censor their output. Word got out of American disasters, the massacre of civilians, indiscipline in the ranks and the messiness of war. Journalists were forbidden from covering the repatriation of the bodies of dead American soldiers, in case the images fuelled further unrest. When Walter Cronkite, a respected journalist, was openly critical of American strategy after the Tet Offensive in 1968, LBJ was heard to remark that if he had lost Cronkite he had lost America.

ACTIVITY 4.9

These two photographs, the first from the Berkeley Free Speech Movement in late 1964, and the second from an anti-war march in Berkeley in 1967, illustrate the pace of change in youth culture. Make a list of what appears to have changed in three years in Berkeley. Account for the changes.

ACTIVITY 4.10

Divide into pairs. One of you should make the case that 'The protest movements of the 1960s were all connected'. The other should make the case that 'The 1960s was a time when different protest movements separately came to prominence'. Which of you has the better case?

Figure 4.6: Two contrasting images from the Berkeley campus.

 Thematic link: democracy

Practice essay questions

1. 'The protests of the 1960s did not cause very much to change.' Assess the validity of this view.
2. How far do you agree that Johnson had no real choice other than to escalate American involvement in the war in Vietnam?
3. 'Overall, Johnson wasted the economic prosperity which he inherited.' Do you agree?
4. With reference to Voices from the past: Johnson on the Great Society, Voices from the past: Lyndon Johnson, and Extract A, how valuable are these sources in explaining what President Johnson thought was the most important issue he had to deal with as president?

Extract A

President Lyndon B. Johnson, speech at Johns Hopkins University, 7 April 1965.

We fight because we must fight if we are to live in a world where every country can shape its own destiny. And only in such a world will our own freedom be finally secure

North Vietnam has attacked the independent nation of South Vietnam. Its object is total conquest. Over this war and all Asia is another reality: the deepening shadow of Communist China. The rulers in Hanoi are urged on by Peking.*

This is a regime which has destroyed freedom in Tibet, which has attacked India, and has been condemned by the United Nations for aggression in Korea …

We are there because we have a promise to keep. Since 1954 every American President has offered support to the people of South Viet-Nam … We are also there to strengthen world order … We are also there because there are great stakes in the balance. Let no one think for a moment that retreat from Viet-Nam would bring an end to conflict. The battle would be renewed in one country and then another. The central lesson of our time is that the appetite of aggression is never satisfied.

*Peking is now called Beijing. It is the capital city of China.

Taking it further

When you have finished the course, think about this: 'Johnson's was the most effective presidency from 1945–80 at home, and the least effective abroad.' Do you agree?

Chapter summary

By the end of this chapter you should understand:

- the economic argument about how effectively prosperity was shared among Americans, and why the American economy became less successful during Johnson's second term
- the way in which protest movements fed into ideas of American identity, and what the protest movements and their successes reveal about the nature of American democracy
- why there were competing ideas about what it meant to be American by 1969
- why the era of organised civil rights protest was effectively over, even though little had changed for the lives of African Americans in the North
- why the Democratic Party was losing its popularity in 1968.

End notes

1 Schama S. *The American Future: A History from the Founding Fathers to Barack Obama.* Vintage: 2009; 131.

2 Baldwin J. 'Fifth Avenue, Uptown: A Letter from Harlem.' In *Nobody Knows My Name: More Notes of a Native Son:* Dell Publishing Co.; 1961.

3 Halpern S. *On the Limits of the Law: The Ironic Legacy of Title VI of the 1964 Civil Rights Act.* Johns Hopkins University Press: 1995; 287.

5 Republican Reaction: the Nixon Presidency, 1969–1974

In this section, we will examine the presidency of Richard M. Nixon, a man whose view of the extent of presidential power built him up, enabled him to achieve great things (although arguably not always good things, in a moral sense) and eventually knocked him down. His domestic policy was essentially to roll back some of Johnson's reforms and be as conservative as he could be. He successfully steered the USA through difficult economic times and his success in realigning American relations with China could be seen as one of the greatest achievements of any US president. We will look into:

- The presidential election of 1968 and the reasons for Nixon's victory: divisions within the Democratic Party; the personalities and policies of the Nixon administration.

- The restoration of conservative social policies; the reaction to protest movements and forces of social change; economic change and the end of the post-war boom.

- The limits of American world power: peace negotiations and the continuation of the war in Vietnam and Cambodia; the influence of Kissinger on US policies towards the USSR, Latin America and China.

- The Watergate Affair and its aftermath: the role of Congress; the resignation of the president; Nixon's political legacy.

Introduction: the president, not a crook

The presidency of Richard Nixon was remarkable in that both president and vice president had to resign in disgrace. The **Watergate** scandal that brought Nixon down, and will always be the first item mentioned in any discussion of him, obscures an otherwise effective presidency. Nixon realigned American foreign policy in a way that enabled America to break out of an unhelpful set of foreign policy assumptions. He rebuilt his party to enable it to become the natural party of the presidency. He helped to soften the effects of an economy in the doldrums. He restored some sort of order to American cities; although there were still protest movements there was never again a situation where the president feared to leave the White House. Can a case be made for the rehabilitation of the reputation of Richard Nixon?

If so, it will take some work. Arguably, Nixon's presidency was considerably less effective in his second term, which was spent almost entirely bogged down by Watergate. It was Nixon's appointees who kept the show on the road while Nixon brooded and attempted to cling on to power. It was his successor who would supervise the final fall of South Vietnam, abandoned by American troops whose long presence in the country had ultimately caused rather than averted a war. It would be his old Republican rival Ronald Reagan who would restore the fortunes of his party, the presidency and, some would say, the country. Richard Nixon, the man who had coveted the presidency for so many years, would be chiefly remembered for the suffix '-gate' that for so long afterwards affixed itself to the name of any scandal.

Nixon was not the first president to try underhand tactics to secure an election victory. He was not the first whose aides seemed overmighty, whose words and views were not necessarily fit for public consumption and who had a foul temper. He was not the first president to be threatened with impeachment (a predecessor, Andrew Johnson, had actually been impeached over a century earlier). But he was, and always will be, the first president to be forced to resign, and his nickname, Tricky Dick, which dated back to when when he was a candidate for Congress, will always be his soubriquet.

The presidential election of 1968 and the reasons for Nixon's victory

The presidential election of 1968 has been seen as a transformational, realigning election. Four years earlier, Johnson had won in a **landslide** but against a divided Republican Party and with the vote-gathering powers of the dead Kennedy to help him. Four years before that, Nixon had lost narrowly to Kennedy himself. It would be 1992 before the Democratic Party won another presidential election, with the exception of the election that followed Nixon's second term, over which he cast a long and fatal shadow for the Republicans. Part of the reason for the Republican victory in this election, and for the subsequent decline of the Democratic Party, was the collapse of the Democratic coalition. Part of the reason was that Americans feared the assault on traditional family values, and notions of respectability and authority, from the new permissive society. Nixon offered himself as a man who had lived the American Dream by raising himself from poverty and as a firm defender of morality, true patriotism and social order.

The election was very closely contested. The Democratic governor of Alabama, George Wallace, ran as an American Independent in the South and took enough votes (and states) from the Democrat Hubert Humphrey to enable Richard Nixon, the Republican candidate, to come through to win. Figure 5.1 shows this. Wallace ran as an Independent because the Democrats would not nominate him (except in Alabama, where he controlled the Democratic Party himself). He channelled the pent-up resentments of that segment of the white working class that felt undermined by civil rights and the Great Society.

Nixon's victory in the **Electoral College** was substantial, but he polled only half a million more votes than Vice President Humphrey. Nixon won comfortably among rural and affluent urban voters, and narrowly among middle-income urban voters. One explanation for his victory is the demographic change that meant that, even though the economy was faltering, there were more of these types of voters than there had ever been before.

The context of the election also helped to determine its outcome. In 1968 America was a fractious place. Nixon campaigned on an end to the Vietnam War – not a surrender, but peace with honour – economic issues, and law and order. He spoke directly to what he called the 'silent majority' of people tired of the protests and implicitly tired of the excesses and unpatriotic attitudes of the young. One reading of the election result is that Nixon narrowly won in 1968 for precisely the reasons why he had narrowly lost in 1960. Then, he had lost because he was old, stern and represented the past. Now was precisely the right time for someone dependable, experienced and no-nonsense. The war certainly played a major part in the electorate's decision to back him. Shortly before election day, Johnson declared that he had negotiated an end to the war. Nixon made a very carefully worded statement in which he said that he had been told, but did not of course believe, that Johnson had made this announcement only to help Vice President Humphrey. This was a transparently political thing to say but it had the desired effect of making sure that everyone believed it, although Nixon had not said that it was true. In fact, Johnson's announcement had been carefully timed: he was being disingenuous. However, so was Nixon, who had privately been putting pressure on the South Vietnamese to try to scupper the deal. Both Johnson and Nixon had played politics with the Vietnam War.

Divisions within the Democratic Party

Perhaps it is an error to look for positive reasons why Nixon won. The divisions within the Democratic Party were the real reason why Humphrey (and Wallace) lost. After all, the South (which had formed the basis for every successful Democratic administration to date) had fallen away from the party leadership. Local Democrats could still be elected – the House and the Senate remained in Democratic hands for Nixon's whole time in office – but the national party was unable to agree on a platform or a candidate. This was both a new problem and something that had been coming for some time. The collapse of the New Deal coalition had been on the cards; the Solid South had been self-consciously

Key terms

Electoral College: where each state is assigned a number of electors based on its population. To win election as president, a candidate needs to win more votes in the Electoral College – this means a few big states or lots of small states. Most states award their votes on an all-or-nothing basis. Winning a state worth ten Electoral College votes (ECVs) by a narrow margin is more useful to a presidential candidate than winning three states worth three ECVs each by huge margins. It is possible to win fewer states and fewer votes and still win the presidency.

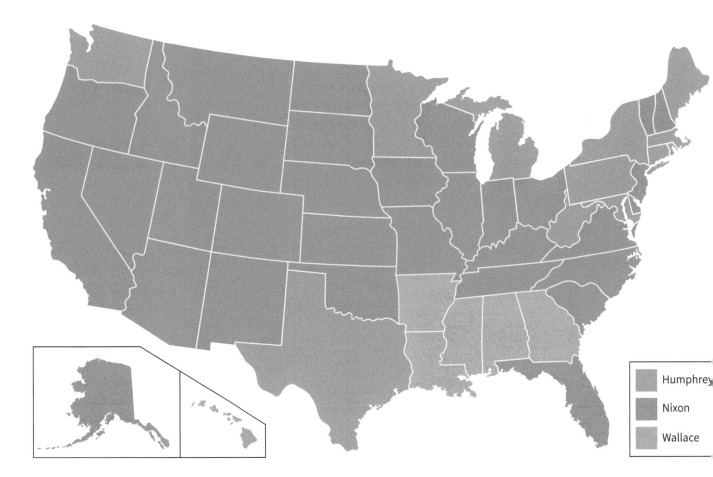

Figure 5.1: This map shows what state voted for which candidate in the 1968 presidential election. You can see that the Democrats were largely reduced to the urban northeast.

sacrificed by Lyndon Johnson. Wallace ran against Humphrey and in doing so ran against Johnson's liberal ideas. There were too many white people in the South who disliked the outcome of the Civil Rights Movement, and too few black people to vote for a non-segregationist Democrat. Nixon's 'Southern Strategy', a deliberate attempt to target the South, was the final nail in the Democrats' coffin. The South was lost to the Democrats as a result, with the exception of Texas. It is hardly a surprise that Humphrey lost the South but how did he win Texas? One answer is that Lyndon Johnson had not quite lost his influence in his native state and was able to deliver its votes to his vice president. The American electoral system is such that there was no point in winning by a huge margin in the North, as Humphrey had, if he couldn't win in either the South or the West.

Johnson's sacrifice of the South had been a calculated risk. He had, after all, confirmed that the northeast had switched hands. His analysis was that the Democrats would need to win the suburban West and Midwest in order to win a presidential election. Given that Johnson was still able to deliver Texas, Humphrey had not even needed to win the West and Midwest well. The reason why the Democrats could not win there was that the Democratic Party had split down the middle over the Johnson presidency. The issue was not civil rights – that battle was over, and Dixiecrats such as Strom Thurmond had already joined the Republican Party. Nor was it public protest – it was clear to everyone that Johnson had lost control. The issue was the Vietnam War. Senator Eugene McCarthy, running on a peace ticket, had come close to defeating the president in the New Hampshire primary. Johnson, realising that he could not win the nomination without causing extraordinary damage to his party, withdrew from the race. This left a three-way battle between McCarthy, the vice president and Bobby Kennedy. In June Kennedy won the California **primary**, putting him firmly ahead of McCarthy, and it briefly seemed that he would be in prime position to become the peace candidate as his campaign continued to pick up momentum. That he had won in California was highly significant: with its 40 electoral votes, it was the second most valuable state in the Union, Nixon's home state and the home of the Free Speech movement that had grown out of the University of California, Berkeley. It was clear that the Democrats needed to win California if they were to win the presidency. Then Bobby Kennedy was assassinated on the night of the California primary, throwing the race wide open.

The nomination went to the Democratic Convention in Chicago. Hubert Humphrey emerged victorious but there were riots outside the venue and that violence was repeated at many of his campaign stops thereafter. Humphrey was an experienced and competent candidate, a liberal leader for over 20 years, with good links to organised labour and civil rights groups. He appealed to whatever remained of the New Deal coalition but it was not enough. He lost the popular vote by 500 000 votes. In practice, about 300 000 switched votes in, for example, California, Ohio and New Jersey, all close races, would have given him victory.

Key terms

Convention: a meeting held by a political party in the late summer of an election year at which it adopts its presidential and vice presidential candidate and sets a policy platform. If the primaries and caucuses have proved decisive, conventions can be foregone conclusions, in which case they are usually stage-managed by the prospective presidential candidate. They can also be genuine opportunities to select the candidate.

Voices from the past

Nixon and the real voice of America

Extracts from Richard Nixon's speech accepting the Republican nomination for President, Miami, 8 August 1968.

Tonight I again proudly accept that nomination for President of the United States. But I have news for you. This time there's a difference – this time we're going to win. We're going to win for a number of reasons.

My fellow Americans … we're going to win because our cause is right. We make history tonight not for ourselves but for the ages. The choice we make in 1968 will determine not only the future of America but the future of peace and freedom in the world for the last third of the 20th century, and the question that we answer tonight: can America meet this great challenge?

Let us listen to America to find the answer to that question.

As we look at America, we see cities enveloped in smoke and flame. We hear sirens in the night. We see Americans dying on distant battlefields abroad. We see Americans

hating each other; fighting each other; killing each other at home.

And as we see and hear these things, millions of Americans cry out in anguish:

Did we come all this way for this? Did American boys die in Normandy and Korea and in Valley Forge for this?

Listen to the answers to those questions.

It is another voice, it is a quiet voice in the tumult of the shouting. It is the voice of the great majority of Americans, the forgotten Americans, the non shouters, the non demonstrators. They're not racists or sick; they're not guilty of the crime that plagues the land; they are black, they are white; they're native born and foreign born; they're young and they're old.

And this I say, this I say to you tonight, is the real voice of America. In this year 1968, this is the message it will broadcast to America and to the world.

ACTIVITY 5.1

Read these extracts from Nixon's acceptance speech at the Republican Convention in 1968. How useful are these to the historian studying the reasons for Nixon's electoral success in the 1968 presidential election?

ACTIVITY 5.2

Make a list of all the reasons why Nixon won the 1968 presidential election. Which seem to you to be the most important?

Hidden voices

Hunter S. Thompson

Nixon's own popularity was clearly demonstrated in his landslide victory in the 1972 election. In *Fear and Loathing on the Campaign Trail '72,* Hunter S. Thompson attempted an analysis of the reasons why Nixon was so popular: '*He speaks to the werewolf in us, on nights when the moon comes too close.*' He represents '*that dark, venal, and incurably violent side of the American character*'.

The personalities and policies of the Nixon administration

Nixon was a conservative. His view of being 'American' had been formed even before he led HUAC and he seemed to be very reassuring to the silent majority to whom he appealed. He recognised that he had an opportunity to build an electoral coalition based on American values. Although a conservative, he was a canny enough politician to know that he could not associate himself too closely with the policies of Barry Goldwater. He was helped in this by the opposition in the Republican primary of Ronald Reagan, the right-wing governor of California, and George Romney of Michigan, who campaigned to Nixon's political left on an anti-war platform. With Republicans in the field who were clearly more right-wing and more left-wing than him, Nixon was able to run as a Republican moderate.

Nixon had put some serious work into securing the nomination. He was still smarting from his narrow defeat in 1960. His own attempt to become governor of California had failed in 1962, after which he had announced to the press corps that, 'You won't have Nixon to kick around any more', signalling his retirement. By the middle of the decade he had changed his mind and become an active campaigner and fundraiser for other Republican candidates. This was always his style: he did favours for others and never forgot that he had done them. He also believed that he was the best candidate for leadership of the party and of the country, and that as president he would be entitled to take whatever measures were necessary for the improvement of America. It was that belief, and beliefs like it, which would be his undoing. Nixon believed in the imperial presidency – that the presidency should be the most powerful of the three branches of government and the president could do what he wished, without fear of the law. His domestic reforms were only part of the story. He campaigned for his own leadership as a cultural phenomenon – people thought he represented patriotism, morality and religion, and would work hard to help the silent majority.

Nixon surrounded himself with the usual mixture of trusted confidants, party grandees and experts. Of these, Henry Kissinger, the Harvard professor who had been involved in negotiations over Vietnam and who became his National Security Adviser and later Secretary of State, is the most famous. His vice president, Spiro Agnew, should also be mentioned. Picked as a Marylander to provide sectional balance (Maryland is the most northerly of the southern states), Agnew was forced to resign in 1973 after being accused of extorting bribes from contractors while governor of Maryland. The significance of this would become apparent when his boss followed him a year later.

 Thematic link: identity

The restoration of conservative social policies

In 1972 Nixon would characterise his presidency as anti-drugs, anti-abortion, pro-army and pro-peace; in contrast his opponent George McGovern was anti-'middle America'. This was true, but only because Nixon had effectively won the battle to define what 'middle America' meant. He was able to assert that the patriotic compliance of the 1950s, and the sense of duty (both personal and national) of the 1940s, were what 'normal' Americans felt, as opposed to the damaging liberalism that had enabled the protests and decline of the 1960s. Nixon's message was about self-help and local control. Accordingly he dismantled some of the more expensive federal guarantees in the Great Society, such as the Office of Economic Opportunity, and called a halt to any new spending on education, health and welfare. He announced a Family Assistance Plan to get people back to work – like FDR, he believed that there was a moral element to doing a hard day's work that had to be encouraged. He tried to slow down the pace of desegregation. In the case of *Alexander v Holmes* in 1969, which related to Mississippi, the Supreme Court overruled him, ordering the immediate desegregation of all public schools in the South. He denounced public busing of black students to schools in white areas. The reason for this was that he was trying to appeal to Wallace supporters so that they would vote for the Republicans, not the Democrats, in 1972. He wanted to keep the Democratic Party disunited. The strategy worked.

McGovern was an opponent of the Vietnam War and a left-wing activist but he had no connections with labour or with urban groups. He was nominated following the shooting (this time not fatal) of Governor Wallace, now campaigning for the Democratic nomination. Humphrey won only in Massachusetts and Washington, DC. In the midst of a serious recession in 1972, the Democratic Party suffered a humiliation far, far worse than that which Goldwater had suffered for the Republicans just eight years earlier. They still controlled Congress but they were unable to find a national candidate who could unite their party. McGovern has been heavily criticised for the manner of his defeat in 1972, and it is true that his campaign failed to catch the national mood. His nominating convention was so badly mismanaged that he delivered his acceptance speech at 3 a.m., long after the primetime slot he had hoped for on the networks. Worse, his first nominee as vice president, Thomas Eagleton, had to be unceremoniously removed which it became clear that he had undergone treatment for mental health problems, and was an alcoholic. This did not play well with the electorate; nor did McGovern's '1000%' support for him, which was delivered shortly before Eagleton was removed from the ticket.

Nevertheless, it is difficult to see how the Democrats could have won. Wallace might perhaps would have won some states in the South, but the vote in the West and Midwest depended on suburban middle America, Richard Nixon's natural constituency. It was middle America at whom the idea of a 'restoration' of conservative social policies was aimed.

Nixon's first term is problematic. He put the brakes on liberal policies, as outlined here, and tried unsuccessfully to prevent the courts from legalising others. Even leaving aside the question of how conservative his social policies actually were, what was he restoring? The dynamic conservatism of Eisenhower (the last Republican president) was a kind of New Deal for the good times. It did not have radically conservative elements. Before that were the Republican presidents of the 1920s, whose most obvious social policy was Prohibition, which had been passed under a Democratic president and Congress.

Key terms

middle America: a term used to describe conservative rural and suburban Americans, associated by Richard Nixon with the 'silent majority'. Middle America is the home of old-fashioned values and patriotism. It is a highly contentious term.

Other Nixon conservative policies that were designed to appeal to middle America included:

- 'New Federalism' – giving extra power to state and local officials rather than to the federal government. This largely failed as Congress refused to pass his legislation. Nixon was successful in eliminating the Post Office Department as a Cabinet Department in 1971. He had wanted to give grants of money directly to the states, so that they could spend their way out of recession.
- A war on drugs to cut off the supply of drugs but also to fund rehabilitation, especially for soldiers returning from Vietnam.
- Refusal to spend what he regarded as the ridiculous amount of money Congress had allocated to fund the 1972 Clean Water Act. Nixon did not disagree with the principle, just with the amount spent.

Meanwhile, he also set up the Environmental Protection Agency in 1970 and advocated comprehensive reform of medical insurance, effectively seeking to expand the provision of affordable health care. Neither of these policies was especially conservative but they were popular among significant constituencies of voters. Perhaps electoral popularity is what really mattered to Nixon.

Further reading: the new right

Conservatism, once an unfashionable subject, is now the most fertile area by far in post-war political history. The story was not just about Nixon and Reagan.

Lisa McGirr's study of political organising at the grassroots level in Orange County, California, (*Suburban Warriors: The Origins of the New American Right, Politics and Society in Twentieth-Century America. (*Princeton University Press; 2002), shows the importance of the 1964 Goldwater campaign.

Thomas Sugrue's *Origins of the Urban Crisis: Race and Inequality in Postwar Detroit* (Princeton University Press; 1996), argues that at the local level (his is a study of Detroit) competition over resources such as housing triggered an urban anti-liberalism from the 1940s on. Sugrue shows how white working-class Americans defined their security and their sense of entitlement in conservative and individualistic terms, specifically as the right to a private home (secured for many by the GI Bill) often in racially segregated neighbourhoods.

William F. Buckley, Jr, wrote *Up From Liberalism* (Hillman; 1961). He described Eisenhower as unprincipled because he tried to please everybody, and argued against the Civil Rights Movement: 'In the South, the white community is entitled to put forward a claim to prevail politically because, for the time being, anyway, the leaders of American civilisation are white – as one would certainly expect given their preternatural advantages of tradition, training and economic status.'

The reaction to protest movements and forces of social change

It might be more appropriate to consider what happened under Nixon as not so much the restoration of conservative social policies as the beginning of a movement by which conservative elements of the Republican Party came to dominate. In 1956, Nixon had been clearly on the conservative wing of the Republicans; by 1964 he was equally clearly to the left of people such as Barry

Goldwater and Ronald Reagan, his rival for the nomination in 1968. Nixon began to move towards more conservative positions but, perhaps mindful of the Democratic Congress that persisted throughout his term in office, was unable to do much in terms of legislation. Much of his domestic programme – expansion of Medicaid, further health insurance reform, affirmative action – was decidedly liberal.

Nixon's attitude towards the Supreme Court suggests that his instincts were not necessarily as liberal as they might otherwise have appeared. It was no secret that the Supreme Court, which was extremely liberal at the beginning of Nixon's first term, was working towards the legalisation of abortion throughout the United States. When the case came up, the political views of the nine justices would matter very much. Accordingly, Nixon appointed supposedly conservative justices to the Supreme Court. The new Chief Justice, Warren Burger, had a very conservative reputation for being tough on criminals; as a constitutional lawyer, he proved remarkably liberal. His appointment seems to have been a mistake – perhaps Nixon had failed to realise that now there were different types of 'conservative'. Harry Blackmun, his next appointee, became one of the most liberal justices on the Court and was the author of the opinion that legalised abortion in the case of *Roe v Wade* in 1973. Right-wing commentators even now lament how Blackmun must have been 'seduced' by liberal Washington society. Lewis Powell, the next appointee, also voted to legalise abortion; Nixon's fourth nomination, William Rehnquist, was the only one who pleased him. He eventually became a very conservative Chief Justice under President Reagan. Nixon's Court, appointed to be conservative, did not just legalise abortion. In the case of *Furman v Georgia* in 1972, it also suspended the death penalty, as it turned out for the rest of the decade. Nixon viewed his judicial appointments as massively disappointing.

As Nixon made clear repeatedly, he was on the side of the silent majority, the hard-working Americans who turned up to work every day without complaint to do their best. He viewed protestors as potentially dangerous – even worse, potentially communist. One of the worst single incidents of protest occurred during his presidency, at Kent State University, Ohio, on 4 May 1970. Members of the National Guard had opened fire on students who were protesting against the Vietnam War, killing four of them. The protest had been triggered by Nixon's announcement that the USA was bombing Cambodia. The aftermath to the protests was particularly interesting, because public opinion was mainly on the side of the National Guard. A few days later Nixon secretly went out before dawn to meet protestors at the Lincoln Memorial. His discussion was wide-ranging, discussing the war, civil rights and environmental protests. He said later, 'I just wanted to be sure that all of them realised that ending the war and cleaning up the city streets and the air and the water was not going to solve the spiritual hunger which all of us have.' Nixon characterised the students' protest as being personal rather than political, born of the desire to protest rather than motivated by any particular issue. His generation, too, had fought for its beliefs – he meant during the Second World War. A few days later Nixon went to New York City, where construction workers' hard hats had become a symbol of support for the National Guard and opposition to the Kent State protestors. Nixon wore a hard hat. Ten days after Kent State, two students were killed in similar circumstances at Jackson State University, Mississippi. The modern reaction to these killings is generally rather different, and one of horror. It is important that historians concentrate in the first instance on how things were viewed when they actually happened.

Something like 4 000 000 students – half the students in the country – protested against the Vietnam War over the next 12 months. This came to a head in April and May 1971, when students marched on Washington in an attempt to shut down the federal government. Around 12 000 were arrested. Shortly afterwards Nixon inflamed the situation by releasing Lieutenant William Calley, the officer responsible for the infamous My Lai Massacre (see the section headed Peace negotiations and the continuation of the war in Vietnam and Cambodia) in 1968, from the hard labour part of his punishment. Nevertheless, Nixon claimed, the silent majority, which did not protest, represented more Americans than this vocal minority.

Meanwhile, progress towards civil rights had slowed. In 1969 Nixon stopped the public busing of students in urban areas, which slowed down efforts to integrate schools. But he also began to enforce affirmative action among federal contractors in the construction industry, which improved the ability of African Americans to get construction work. This was the Philadelphia Plan of 1969. Progress had slowed for a number of reasons:

- Many of the goals of the Civil Rights Movement of the 1950s and 1960s had been met – for example, an end to formal, legal segregation and the right to vote. New southern governors, such as Jimmy Carter in Georgia, were opposed to segregation.
- The focus of protest had been changed to the Vietnam War, the urgency of which seemed greater to young protestors than the Civil Rights Movement.
- The problems that now faced African Americans in the North would not be solved by the methods that had worked so far for the Civil Rights Movement.
- Nixon himself sought to defuse remaining civil-rights issues in the South through negotiation rather than confrontation. Perhaps he reasoned that confrontation would no longer work; perhaps he thought that negotiation would secure him more votes in the South; perhaps both.

 Thematic link: democracy

Economic change and the end of the post-war boom

At the end of Johnson's time in office the economy had been becoming poorer for a variety of reasons (see the section headed Economic developments). Nixon was unable to end the expensive war quickly and his attempts to stabilise the economy by reining in government spending and restricting the money supply did not work. Inflation was running very high (4.7% when he took office) and unemployment almost doubled during his first term. Focusing on inflation, Nixon persuaded Congress to give him the power to impose wage and price controls. In 1971, and again in 1973, he used these powers to bring inflation down, causing food shortages and some resentment among business people, especially farmers forced to choose between selling their stock at a loss and simply not bringing it to market. Still, inflation went down, disposable income went up for the middle classes and the plight of the poorest was nothing like as bad as it had been during the Great Depression; there were no great internal migrations or banking collapses. The most obvious sign that there was trouble was the series of bankruptcies in the building industry after 1973, which began to push inflation up again. The American economy had reached an equilibrium, acquiring a robustness that enabled it to survive the end of the post-war boom.

The boom had ended for five main reasons:

- American consumer society had reached a level at which most people had what they wanted, depressing internal demand.
- The poor, especially African Americans living in the North in slum conditions with absentee landlords, were not properly integrated into consumer society.
- Other countries had recovered from the damage inflicted upon them by the Second World War, depressing external demand.
- American overreliance on oil was distorting the global market and driving up prices.
- There was a temporary lack of innovation and new products, perhaps caused by the war effort. Some revolutionary new product that might transform society in the way in which the automobile had, was needed. A young man called Bill Gates was working on it.

In 1973 the Organization of Petroleum-Exporting Countries (OPEC), whose members were largely in the Middle East, pushed up the price of oil dramatically. This was partly a response to US support for Israel in the Yom Kippur War of 1973 against Syria and Egypt, and partly the countries of the Middle East realising that they were in a position to operate a cartel. The effect on the United States, which relied heavily on cheap oil, was devastating, as oil prices quadrupled in the course of less than a year.

 Thematic link: American prosperity

The limits of American world power

The oil crisis of 1973, which quickly became an oil shock as its full implications played out, demonstrated the limits of American world power. Without sufficient oil, American policy could not be independent. The situation in the Middle East would continue to be difficult for American policymakers, stuck between a large internal Jewish constituency and the Islamic nations that controlled the price of oil and therefore that of energy. In 1973, however, this was not the Americans' major problem: that was, undoubtedly, the situation in Indochina.

Peace negotiations and the continuation of the war in Vietnam and Cambodia

Nixon was elected on a promise to obtain peace with honour in Vietnam. A timeline of the most important events in Vietnam during his time in office is shown

ACTIVITY 5.3

1. Make a list of Nixon's domestic policies. Identify them as 'conservative' or 'liberal'. If you find this difficult, think about the reasons why it was not always clear.

   Nixon's policies were related to:
   - The economic situation, which meant that he had to save money.
   - The party political situation, which meant that he had to build a coalition to be re-elected.
   - The domestic situation, which meant that he had to keep order.

2. Which of these factors was his overriding concern for each policy?

in the Timeline of the major events in Indochina during Nixon's presidency. He began the American troop withdrawal early in his time in office. This was the policy of 'Vietnamisation' – an attempt to hand responsibility for the war over to the South Vietnamese forces. It was, after all, a Vietnamese civil war. At the same time as he began his troop withdrawals, Nixon also ordered the bombing of North Vietnam, Laos and Cambodia in an effort to help his South Vietnamese allies by destroying their opposition, at the same time as Henry Kissinger began secret negotiations with the North Vietnamese. In 1970 Nixon announced the full-scale invasion of Cambodia. He had to do this because of the Hồ Chí Minh Trail, the route through Cambodia that was the most direct route between North and South Vietnam. The Hồ Chí Minh Trail was used to move men and weapons into South Vietnam. See Figure 5.2.

1969	January: Newly inaugurated President Nixon announced a policy of 'Vietnamisation' – the withdrawal of American soldiers from their positions, which South Vietnamese troops would have to take over.
1970	April: Various revelations about the conduct of American soldiers turned American public opinion even further against it. Americans bombed Cambodia to disrupt Viet Cong supply lines.
1971	February: The Americans invaded Laos to disrupt Viet Cong supply lines and the Pentagon Papers were leaked – confidential documents suggesting the US had behaved dishonourably throughout the war.
1972:	October: Henry Kissinger reached a peace agreement with his North Vietnamese opposite number, Lê Đức Thọ. December: Nixon ordered a massive bombing raid on North Vietnam. The North Vietnamese stood firm.
1973	January: The Americans announced the peaceful withdrawal of their ground troops. The South Vietnamese, with American financial aid, continued the war, at first successfully.

Timeline of the major events in Indochina during Nixon's presidency.

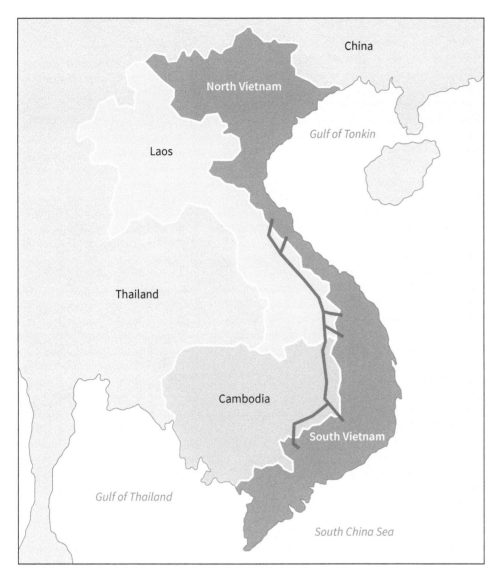

Figure 5.2: Map showing the Hồ Chí Minh Trail. Vietnam has an unusual shape, which is why the most direct route from north to south (the so-called Hồ Chí Minh Trail) is through Cambodia.

In November 1969 a story broke about events in March 1968, of which Nixon had been aware since April, in a village in Vietnam called My Lai. Lieutenant William Calley, commanding his platoon, gave the order to kill all the villagers, responding to orders he had received to 'kill the enemy'. When the scandal broke it was accompanied by a photograph taken by a journalist who had been embedded with the unit, showing the bodies of the villagers laid out along the side of the road. Women and children were clearly visible. Calley, and only Calley, was charged with murder and convicted, despite his contention that he thought he had been following orders. The life sentence caused outrage on both sides of the debate; some thought that far more people should have been punished, but many thought that Calley had been made a scapegoat. Nixon commuted Calley's sentence of hard labour in April 1971 and he was eventually released in 1974. The treatment of Calley was not the most important lesson to be learnt from My Lai. It was very clear that this sort of behaviour by American troops was not unusual, and it was

Figure 5.3: This photograph of the aftermath of the My Lai massacre is one of the iconic images of the Vietnam War.

certainly not part of the American Dream to send young Americans overseas to kill women and children. American self-confidence was shaken.

It was shaken more by the release of the Pentagon Papers in 1971. This was a set of documents put together by Secretary of Defense Robert McNamara, ostensibly designed to help Bobby Kennedy, who, McNamara had hoped, would be a future president, to avoid repeating the mistakes of the past. It revealed that successive American presidents had lied about the situation in Vietnam and cast doubt that the Gulf of Tonkin incident had actually occurred as Johnson had told the nation. The most damaging document demonstrated that Johnson had escalated the situation in Vietnam '70% to avoid a damaging defeat ... – NOT to help a friend'. Seeking to prevent the international damage this caused, Nixon tried to suppress the publication of the Pentagon Papers entirely.

In 1972, just before the election, National Security Adviser Henry Kissinger said that peace was near – the third election in a row in which a senior government figure had said this. After the election, Nixon ordered the heavy bombing of Hanoi, the North Vietnamese capital. Fifteen American bombers were lost. Hồ's government was not broken, and on 29 January 'peace' negotiations began to allow American troops to leave. The American strategy was to negotiate on the one hand while bombing the North Vietnamese on the other. Kissinger, the architect of that policy, was the front man of the negotiations. When he and his North Vietnamese counterpart Lê Đức Thọ were awarded the **Nobel Peace Prize** in 1973 for bringing an end to the bombing, Thọ turned it down. The satirist Tom Lehrer commented that, now Kissinger had been awarded the Nobel Peace Prize, there was no longer any point in satire because reality was more ridiculous.

The Americans lost the Vietnam War for a number of reasons:

- **Weaknesses of American troops**
  Most American troops were young draftees (average age 19) who had only to complete a single year of military service. They received inadequate training and never really gained enough experience to be effective. They were not trained properly for jungle warfare. They were undisciplined – supplies were often stolen and sold on by American quartermasters – and 'fragging', killing their own gung-ho officers, became surprisingly common.
- **Strengths of Viet Cong and Viet Minh**
  In contrast, the Viet Cong (northern sympathisers in the south) and Viet Minh (northern army) were fighting in home terrain. Their guerrilla warfare worked well and they could blend into the villages to avoid capture. Inexperienced American troops could not tell who were their friends and who their enemies.
- **Loss of public confidence in America**
  The American death toll – 50 000 – meant that most communities in America lost someone to the war. Photographs of the Tet Offensive of 1968 and the My Lai massacre (which happened in 1968 but came to light later) eroded much of the remaining public support for the war, as it was becoming obvious that Americans were neither winning nor acting well. The troops who were sent to Vietnam often did not want to fight and the political will to fight was eroded at home.

At least some Americans could now see that the conceited notion of America as the policeman of the world would have to end.

The influence of Kissinger on US policies towards the USSR, Latin America and China

The Pentagon Papers had also revealed the obvious, namely that the Johnson administration had considered its Vietnamese strategy as a vital part of the containment of China. Henry Kissinger, Nixon's National Security Adviser, had come up with a different strategy to contain China: he proposed to engage with Mao's government.

A German Jew who emigrated to America before the Second World War, Henry Kissinger became a professor of international relations at Harvard. As an academic he was not interested in ideology but in realpolitik, the art of the possible. Capable of tremendous charm, energetic and clearly brilliant, he had negotiated in Vietnam on behalf of the Johnson administration in 1968, then became Nixon's National Security Adviser in 1969 and later his Secretary of State (from 1973). He went on to become very controversial.

> ### Key terms
>
> **Nobel Peace Prize:** a prize awarded annually by the Norwegian Nobel Committee to those who have done the most to reduce the size of armies, promote diplomacy and bring about peace. The Norwegian Nobel Committee sometimes makes choices that do not meet with universal acclaim.

Figure 5.4: Henry Kissinger, the diplomat and political scientist who became Nixon's National Security Adviser and Secretary of State.

Kissinger recognised that the assumptions of United States foreign policy since 1945 were no longer valid for three reasons:

- The world was now tripolar – with China, there were now more than two sides.
- Ideologies, such as communism, are not fixed factors in international relations. They can change.
- America had over-extended itself. (This gave rise to the Nixon Doctrine, which stated that America would no longer take responsibility for the defence of the entire free world.)

In 1967, Nixon had written about the need to establish diplomatic relations with China. Kissinger started to make this happen in 1971, when he made a secret visit to Zhou Enlai, who was effectively Mao's deputy and concerned with foreign affairs. This went well and Nixon himself then visited Beijing in 1972. This type of diplomacy, when a diplomatic adviser makes short trips in advance of his principal, is sometimes called 'shuttle diplomacy'. In this instance the popular term became 'ping-pong diplomacy', a reference to the form of a cultural exchange happening at the same time, in which Chinese and American ping-pong teams visited each other. Nixon established friendly relations with China, which helped to calm the threat posed by Chinese nuclear weapons and to stabilise the situation in Indochina, even given the American defeat (which was clear to all parties even if it was not admitted in so many words) in Vietnam.

After China, Nixon went to Moscow. Kissinger had also been there as part of his ongoing effort to pull together talks on nuclear weapon limitation. The Soviet leader Leonid Brezhnev was keen to receive Nixon because he feared that the USA and China would become too close. The USSR and China had fought in 1969 along a small section of their very long border; there were fears on both sides that the situation might deteriorate. The USA, which had itself feared a united communist front in East Asia just as its own western European allies proved disappointing, would clearly be able to play the USSR and China off against one another. The emergence of China onto the world stage, and US engagement with the Chinese, demonstrated that the certainties of Cold War bipolarity no longer applied.

The border dispute between the Chinese and the Soviets that erupted into war in 1969 had been contained but both Nixon and Mao were aware that there were now three major players in the world. China was not a Superpower but it could be an irritant. It had (and has) far more resources along its lengthy borders with the USSR and the invasion and exploitation of Siberia appeared an obvious strategic goal for China. A shared ideology with Russia could not promote peace in the face of a shared border. Moreover, the Chinese leader, Mao Zedong, thought that the Soviets had abandoned true communism following the death of Stalin and wanted to assert global leadership for himself and for China. Richard Nixon trusted nobody but understood that negotiation could always be helpful. In the long term, his engagement with the Chinese helped to reopen the Chinese market for American companies. In the short term, it made the USSR a little more careful in its own foreign policy.

In 1972 this, and the realisation that the arms race had been unsustainable, produced two important treaties, the Strategic Arms Limitation Treaty and Anti-Ballistic Missile Treaty, which are summarised in Table 5.1. This was part of the process of détente, which was established in the 1970s as a means of reducing the tension caused by the presence of nuclear weapons in the Cold War.

Strategic **A**rms **L**imitation **T**reaty	**A**nti-**B**allistic **M**issile **T**reaty, 1972
Froze the number of strategic ballistic missile launchers. Replacement could only occur on a one-for-one basis.	Limited to two the number of locations that each of the countries could protect with an anti-ballistic missile system (ABM).

Table 5.1: SALT and ABMT, 1972: détente in action.

By 1973, when he became Secretary of State, Henry Kissinger was the only foreign policy adviser of any influence in the US government. He claims in his memoirs that by September of that year he was running foreign policy. Nixon had been distracted by the growing Watergate scandal. It was Kissinger who dealt with the Yom Kippur War. It was also Kissinger who dealt with the aftermath of his own meddling in Chile in 1970. He had used the CIA to try to undermine (or, preferably, remove) the Chilean president Salvador Allende, who had nationalised American copper mining concerns in his country. The CIA (after several attempts to organise Allende's removal at Kissinger's instigation) had offered a $50 000 reward and to supply weapons in a bungled attempt to kidnap a general who supported Allende. In the event, General René Schneider was killed by another Chilean faction. In September 1973 Kissinger, who with Nixon's knowledge had been funding the Chilean opposition newspaper *El Mercurio* to the tune of nearly $1 million, got his wish: the military coup (carried out without *direct* American aid) brought the brutal government of General Augusto Pinochet to power. This was the complete opposite of a Marxist government and demonstrated the lengths to which Kissinger and Nixon were prepared to go in order to prevent communism from establishing any sort of foothold in the West.

The Americans still held to the Monroe Doctrine, named after the country's fourth president, James Monroe (1809–17), which stated that the European powers should not seek advantage in the Americas. By the time of the Cold War, this had become interpreted as a call for American dominance over the western hemisphere. Neither Eisenhower nor Kennedy nor Johnson had been prepared to tolerate left-wing governments in the Americas. The significance of what happened in Chile is therefore twofold. First, Nixon and Kissinger were not at all unusual in their aim of preventing a left-wing government from establishing itself in Latin America. Second, the financial lengths to which they went were extraordinary, although perhaps not quite on a par with Eisenhower's and Kennedy's plans against Cuba.

Nixon had supported those plans. He maintained close links with the Cuban opposition, to the extent that in 1970 the Castro regime in Cuba asked him, via the Soviets, to promise not to attack the island. Nixon agreed in complete secrecy; naturally, the news of the agreement leaked almost immediately. At the same time – October 1970 – Nixon and Kissinger realised that the Soviets were expanding their naval base on Cuba. This clearly could not be allowed, from an American point of view – it could be the Cuban Missile Crisis all over again – and Nixon and Brezhnev agreed that the Soviets would not use this as a base for their fleet of

ACTIVITY 5.5

Kissinger claimed to practise 'Realpolitik', which is the art of the possible, refusing to bring ideology into foreign policy. Can you detect any ideological elements in his foreign policy?

'boomers' (submarines armed with nuclear missiles). From the point of view of American security, if not diplomacy, this was far more important than anything that might have happened in Chile. Kissinger later retaliated by consistently refusing to normalise relations with Cuba – a process that did not even begin to occur until 2015. It is important to note that none of Nixon's Latin American policy caused much surprise; nor did it change much. No doubt Brezhnev was trying to be awkward by expanding his facilities in Cuba at the precise time he did; the situation in Chile, however, represented the normal way of the world until the late 1980s. The USA dominated the internal politics of many countries in Central and South America.

Thematic link: American identity

The Watergate Affair and its aftermath

In 1972 Nixon formed the Committee to Re-Elect the President, known as CREEP (or CRP). Among many other activities, CREEP activists broke into the campaign headquarters of George McGovern, the Democratic presidential candidate, in the Watergate hotel, which overlooks the Potomac River in Washington, DC. The burglars were caught after a security guard noticed that they had propped a door open. This set off a series of events that led to the resignation of the president two years later. The timeline outlines some of the key dates of a scandal that became known simply as 'Watergate'.

Figure 5.5: The Watergate complex.

The burglary at the Watergate complex was completely unnecessary in terms of the election. Nixon had it won – and, for that matter, the Democrats seemed to be doing their best to lose it. Nixon and CREEP were obsessive in their attention to detail and about transcending the law. It is most unlikely that Nixon ordered the burglary himself: there might be an interesting question about the extent to which political leaders should be responsible for what happened in their names, in the cultures they had built up.

The association of the burglars with the Republican Party quickly became clear and within a week Nixon was moving to persuade the CIA to block the investigation. It was the revelation of this that ultimately pushed Nixon into resigning two years later. The tenacity of the *Washington Post* reporters Carl Bernstein and Bob Woodward, who had initially picked up the story and realised what was going on, ensured that the issue remained live. They had pressed on with their story, protected by their editor Ben Bradlee and fed by information from a mysterious informant known as 'Deep Throat'. He turned out to be Mark Felt, an associate director of the FBI, who was frustrated at the CIA's efforts to block the investigation.

The role of Congress

When, following their conviction, one of the burglars wrote to Judge Sirica to indicate that they had been heavily leaned on to commit perjury at their trial

1972	17 June: Five burglars are caught in the Democratic Party campaign headquarters in the Watergate complex. The name of Howard Hunt, ex-CIA officer and a member of CREEP, was found in the contacts book of one of the burglars.
	19 June: It was publicly reported that one of the burglars worked for the Republican Party.
	23 June: Nixon suggested using the CIA to block the FBI's investigation into the burglary. This fact did not emerge until August 1974.
1973	30 January: Judge John Sirica tried and convicted the five burglars.
	23 March: Sirica received a letter alleging that there had been perjury in the Watergate trial designed to cover up the White House's role in the break-in.
	17 April: Nixon learnt that several of his aides, including John Ehrlichman and H.R. Haldeman, two of his most trusted advisers, had been implicated in the scandal. By this stage, Nixon was fully aware of all that had happened and was creating his own cover-up.
	30 April: Haldeman and Ehrlichman resigned and White House Counsel John Dean (the President's lawyer) was fired.
	16 July: The Senate committee established to investigate discovered from Dean that Nixon had recorded conversations in the Oval Office. They asked for the tapes, as did Archibald Cox, the Justice Department's investigator, but Nixon refused, citing his executive privilege.
	17 November: Nixon told the press, 'I'm not a crook.'
1974	15 June: Publication of *All the President's Men*.
	29 April: After a long legal battle Nixon released edited transcripts of the tapes of what had been said in the Oval Office.
	24 July: The Supreme Court ordered Nixon to release the tapes. Executive privilege did not apply.
	30 July: The House of Representatives announced that it intended to impeach President Nixon on 20 August, putting him on trial in the Senate.
	5 August: The White House released the 'smoking gun' tape from 23 June 1972. Nixon had clearly lied when claiming that he had not been involved in the cover-up and had not known about it until March 1973. He admitted that the tape contained information 'at variance with my previous statements'.
	7 August: Leading Republican senators advised Nixon that he would certainly be convicted in the Senate.
	9 August: Nixon resigned.

Timeline of the Watergate Affair.

by neglecting to mention their Republican Party links, the break-in came fully into the public consciousness. Nixon knew that he had to rid himself of several of his senior aides, preferably in a way that did not make it clear how much he knew. Meanwhile, the Democratic Senate used the scandal to launch a thorough investigation into Nixon. They did not uncover much about Watergate, but they did reveal that Nixon had been spending public money on his private homes, trading political favours for campaign contributions and filing fraudulent income tax

ACTIVITY 5.6

What, if anything, can the extract from *All the President's Men* in Voices from the past: Deep Throat tell us about the Watergate scandal?

returns. Some senators undoubtedly saw an investigation into Nixon in political terms. Others saw it as their duty under the constitution, particularly because the *Washington Post* had courageously run the story in some detail, despite concerted efforts by the administration to suppress it. From the *Post's* point of view, this made up for the way in which the *New York Times* had trumped them with their own scoop on the Pentagon Papers.

Meanwhile the House of Representatives had been secretly negotiating articles of **impeachment** – the only means by which the president could be fired. The special prosecutor handling the case had refused to indict Nixon, believing that the president could only be removed by Congress. There was still considerable reluctance to do so in the House, After all, this was a major step, and the vice president, Gerald Ford, was a recent appointee himself, having replaced the disgraced Spiro Agnew, who had resigned after taking bribes while governor of Maryland. Was it really acceptable to replace the president of the United States (especially one who had been elected in a landslide) with a man who had only ever been elected to a seat in the House by the voters of Grand Rapids, Michigan?

For as all this was happening, Nixon became the first president ever to be forced to choose a replacement vice president. Although previous vice presidents had left office (through death, or in one case resignation to take up a seat in the Senate) none had been replaced. The Twenty-Fifth Amendment, under which Gerald Ford became vice president in October 1973, was used for the first time. Ford had never won a national election but was popular as the senior Republican in the House; Nixon was given no choice by Congress.

Amidst all this, Congress discovered the existence of the White House tapes. It was Lyndon Johnson who had insisted on recording conversations that took place in the Oval Office; Nixon let the system continue. From the moment Congress requested the release of the tapes, the remainder of Nixon's presidency became

---

 Voices from the past

Deep Throat

An extract from *All the President's Men* by Carl Bernstein and Bob Woodward, published in June 1974.

Deep Throat again told Woodward to concentrate on the other games – not the break-in at Democratic headquarters.

Still, they needed help, Woodward said. Could they say for certain that the games were White House sponsored?

"Of course, of course, don't you get my message?" Deep Throat was exasperated. He stood up.

What games? Woodward asked. One couldn't publish stories based on vague references to higher-ups, on information that might or might not have been leaked to the press by

Howard Hunt; that the Eagleton records were "somehow tied into Hunt and the White House."

"There's nothing more I can say," Deep Throat replied, and began to walk off.

Woodward said that he and Bernstein needed more – something that went beyond generalities ...

Deep Throat stopped and turned around. "It was a White House operation – done inside the gates surrounding the White House and the Executive Office Building .... This is very serious. You can safely say that fifty people worked for the White House and CRP to play games and spy and sabotage and gather intelligence."[1]

a struggle over whose tapes they were, and whether executive privilege could legitimately keep them from a legislature (and potentially a court) investigating criminal conspiracy.

The resignation of the President

The issue for people on the left was not just that Nixon was a difficult man. His nickname had been 'Tricky Dick' for over 30 years. Nor was it just that he had been caught in a lie. It was the fact that he had been caught in a conspiracy and that he had drawn the process out. From the middle of 1973 Nixon appeared a man under siege. This is why Kissinger came even more to the fore in foreign policy. Alexander Haig, Nixon's new chief of staff, was widely regarded as wielding the actual power in Washington as Nixon devoted himself entirely to remaining in office. The publication in June 1974 of *All the President's Men,* Woodward and Bernstein's account of the Watergate scandal, was of critical importance: Nixon was still the president, and his administration's underhand dealings were exposed for all to see. Equally significant was the eventual publication of the Oval Office tapes.

For people on the right, who might have believed (as Nixon did) that the power of the presidency was so great that, 'If the president does it, it's not illegal' – the ultimate statement of the imperial presidency – what the tapes revealed about Nixon's White House represented the final straw. For Nixon was recorded as he really was – foul-mouthed, racist, misogynistic and discourteous. He seemed to possess none of the personal values of the middle America he claimed to represent. He had no support left that might help him to weather the storm caused by the emergence of tapes.

When he was approached by the Republican leaders in the House and Senate, as well as Barry Goldwater, Nixon knew that the game was up. A President Ford, elected by senior members of Congress, was now preferable to a man who less than two years previously had won one of the most crushing presidential election victories in American history. In his resignation address Nixon claimed that he had always tried to do what was best for the nation, but nobody believed him. He was being honest: he believed that what the nation really needed was Richard Nixon as its president.

Nixon's political legacy

Richard Nixon dealt the idea of the imperial presidency what seemed to be a permanent blow. The presidents who succeeded him would be weak, unable to act without Congressional oversight: a return to the era of weak presidents a hundred years earlier. In reality, this only lasted eight years. Ronald Reagan, the new conservative leader of the Republican movement, recreated a powerful, imperial presidency. His ideological heir, George W. Bush (2001–09), would go even further. Nixon did not damage the presidency in the long term, and nor did he damage the Republican Party. He even demonstrated that the constitution worked, by resigning because he knew that he would otherwise be impeached, convicted and removed.

His most enduring political legacy was perhaps the ideological dispute known today as the culture wars. The unfortunately (from Nixon's perspective) liberal

ACTIVITY 5.7

What in the Voices from the past: the 'smoking gun' extract was so serious that its publication prompted Nixon's resignation within a week?

justices whom he appointed to the Supreme Court, and Justice John Paul Stevens, the liberal whom his politically weak successor Gerald Ford was forced to appoint, provided the background for the legalisation of abortion and gun control. This caused the protests of the 1960s to be reshaped into what has felt like a permanent battle between the silent majority, for whom Fox News now claims loudly to speak, and the liberal 'elite'. In 2004 Senator Barack Obama addressed this issue when he claimed, 'There is no red America, no blue America. There is the United States of America.' This is the man who would later become the president hounded by red America over his religion, his birthplace, gun control and healthcare reform, and who would comment in an unguarded moment that all some (Republican) people cared about was God and guns. The liberal court, Nixon's own appalling behaviour, and his confrontational attitude to protest combined to embed the divisions in America culture into the fabric of society for a generation to come. Reagan's truly conservative social policies, the 'Republican revolution' in 1995 that brought an end to an apparently structural bias in favour of the Democrats winning House elections, the presidency of George W. Bush and the emergence of the Tea Party can all be traced back to Richard Nixon's identification of a hard-done-by silent majority, although the new Republican policies bear little resemblance to Nixon's.

In foreign policy, the picture for bipartisan fans of Richard Nixon is far better. The USA's rapprochement with China did indeed help to stabilise Southeast Asia. It also put pressure on the Soviet Union, which became desperate to appear the better communist country and spent the next ten years quietly bankrupting

Voices from the past

The 'smoking gun'

This is an extract from the 'smoking gun' tape (23 June 1972, published on 5 August 1974). Nixon and Haldeman are talking about the investigation into the Watergate burglary.

Haldeman: Colson, yesterday, they [the FBI] concluded it was not the White House, but are now convinced it is a CIA thing, so the CIA turn off would …

Nixon: Well, not sure of their analysis, I'm not going to get that involved. I'm (unintelligible).

Haldeman: No, sir. We don't want you to.

Nixon: You call them in.

Nixon: Good. Good deal! Play it tough. That's the way they play it and that's the way we are going to play it.

Haldeman: O.K. We'll do it.

Nixon: Yeah, when I saw that news summary item, I of course knew it was a bunch of crap, but I thought ah, well

it's good to have them off on this … thing because when they start bugging us, which they have, we'll know our little boys will not know how to handle it. I hope they will though. You never know. Maybe, you think about it. Good! …

Nixon: When you get in these people when you … get these people in, say: "Look, the problem is that this will open the whole, the whole Bay of Pigs thing, and the President just feels that" ah, without going into the details … don't, don't lie to them to the extent to say there is no involvement, but just say this is sort of a comedy of errors, bizarre, without getting into it, "the President believes that it is going to open the whole Bay of Pigs thing up again. And, ah because these people are plugging for, for keeps and that they should call the FBI in and say that we wish for the country, don't go any further into this case", period!

itself. China, meanwhile, when Mao finally died in 1976, began equally quietly to abandon communist economics and to trade openly with America. The Cold War was over, at least for a time, and while the international events of Reagan's presidency were more dramatic than this paragraph suggests, it is certainly possible to construct an argument that Nixon's Chinese diplomacy helped that to happen. 'It took a Nixon to go to China,' the future speaker of the House, Tom Foley, would say in 1977. He meant that only someone with Nixon's anti-communist credentials could negotiate with communists without coming under suspicion himself. Nixon's achievements in China, unlike his conduct of the Vietnam War, attracted and continue to attract genuine praise from all sides of American political opinion.

There is another, more unpleasant postscript to Nixon's foreign policy legacy. The nation of Cambodia, which Nixon ordered to be bombed to disrupt the Hồ Chí Minh Trail, had been trying as hard as possible to keep out of the war. The bombing destabilised the Cambodian government and the communist revolution there in 1975 brought the Khmer Rouge to power. The Khmer Rouge proceeded to murder around 2 000 000 people, a quarter of the Cambodian population.

Nixon has a cultural, as well as a political, legacy. His complexities make him a good hero – or anti-hero. Oliver Stone's 1995 biopic *Nixon* portrays the president as dark, brooding and borderline alcoholic. Ron Howard's 2008 film *Frost/Nixon* tells the story of the British journalist David Frost's 1977 interviews with then ex-president Nixon. In Howard's film Nixon is a tragic hero brought low by his belief that the American president was not subject to the rule of law. In the end, of course, he was.

Perhaps Nixon's most enduring legacy is this: the system worked. Even a president with so high a view of executive privilege recognised that his time was up, that the constitutional arrangement for his removal, impeachment, was going to be applied, and was going to work, and resigned with as much dignity as he could muster. In that sense, the imperial presidency was checked although, arguably, future presidents just made certain that if they were going to be impeached, it was not for anything too serious and connected to their conduct in their public office. Did future presidents learn to modify their behaviour, or to cover it up more effectively?

Figure 5.6: Nixon left the White House with a gesture of triumph that many felt was inappropriate to the situation.

ACTIVITY 5.8

For discussion: is it possible to discuss Nixon's reputation as president without mentioning Watergate?

Practice essay questions

1. 'Nixon's foreign policy was intelligent and successful.' Assess the validity of this view.
2. 'Nixon was more interested in winning elections than in being a true conservative.' Assess the validity of this view.
3. How far do you agree with the idea that America's decline in the early 1970s was entirely economic?
4. How far do you agree that Richard Nixon's resignation was caused by the public perception of his character rather than by the public's discovery of his crimes?

Taking it further

'It took a Nixon to go to China, and it'll take a Democrat to balance the budget' (Tom Foley, 1977). How might you have argued Foley's case?

 Chapter summary

By the end of this chapter you should understand:

- the underlying solidity of the US economy, as indicated by its response to deteriorating world economic conditions
- the modification of ideas about American identity abroad, as America became more pragmatic in its foreign policy through Nixon's exit strategy for Vietnam and his realignment of relations with China
- the growing cultural conflict between liberals and conservatives in America, seen especially in the results of the presidential elections that Nixon won
- the personal and institutional factors that affect the power of the presidency and the way in which the Watergate scandal eventually confirmed that even the president was not above the law.

End notes

1   http://books.google.co.uk/books?id=Wpjqz9x2cJQC&printsec=frontcover&source=gbs_ge_summary_r&cad=0#v=onepage&q=deep%20throat&f=false

6 The USA after Nixon, 1974–1980

In this section, we will examine the way in which America recovered from the horrors of its previous ten years. Its economy seemed critical, its pride and international position were dented by defeat in Vietnam and the progressive reforms of the 1960s appeared to have stalled. Presidents Ford and Carter seemed only to make these things worse. The American society that emerged from this period was distinctive and in many ways vibrant, and the national mood would be changed by the election of a new and reassuring president in 1980. We will look into:

- Ford and Carter as presidents: responses to social divisions; political corruption and the loss of national self-confidence.

- The position of the USA as a world power: the final withdrawal from Vietnam; relations with the USSR and China; the response to crises in the Middle East; Iran and Afghanistan.

- African Americans in North and South: the impact of civil rights legislation; change and continuity in the 'New South'.

- The USA by 1980: its position as a superpower; the extent of social and economic change; the reasons for Reagan's victory in the presidential election.

Introduction: the presidency imperilled?

When he came to office, Gerald (Jerry) Ford had a problem. He had not even been elected as vice president. He had been the Republican leader in the House of Representatives when Nixon asked him to become vice president as a replacement for Spiro Agnew. His presidency was legal and in that sense legitimate but he lacked the personal mandate that every other president in American history enjoyed. The country had not voted for Jerry Ford even as a back-up. His presidency was brief and uninspiring but did at least feature an end to the unpopular war in Vietnam. America's celebration of the 200th anniversary of the **Declaration of Independence** in 1976 was muted. Ford failed to win election in his own right. His replacement, Jimmy Carter, was a man who in retrospect appears to have been ill-suited to the presidency. With the exception of one startling foreign policy achievement, Carter's presidency was ill-starred. The economy got worse, the national mood deteriorated further and Carter too lasted just one term. *His* replacement, Ronald Reagan, would use a combination of sunny optimism and extremely right-wing economic and foreign policy to transform America.

The presidency, once imperial and over-reaching, the all-encompassing seat of American power, now seemed imperilled. The two terms – imperial and imperilled – are not opposites but the pleasing sound they make together proved irresistible. Arthur Schlesinger's book *The Imperial Presidency* was originally published in 1973, as the Watergate scandal was brewing. The damage done by Nixon, the inability of Ford to escape the sense of his own illegitimacy and the inability of Carter to manage either an agenda or the national mood seemed to have signalled the death-knell for the notion of a strong president. Perhaps America would return to its roots, some commentators thought. Even those who thought that America returning to its roots would be a good thing could not agree on what that would actually look like.

Of course, this would hardly have been possible. By 1974 the agricultural nation of merchants, farmers and slaves that had produced the US constitution and its system of divided government was the master of the greatest army the world had ever seen (embarrassment in Southeast Asia notwithstanding) and of a robust if flagging economy. Its president presided over a complex network of executive departments carrying out functions that the Founding Fathers, back in 1787, would have found entirely unnecessary but which trial and (largely) error had demonstrated were important parts of the functions of government.

If the presidency had been made imperial by foreign policy – the president could act relatively independently as commander-in-chief and foreign policy was now an important part of American life – then it was hardly any less imperial now Ford and Carter, who were perhaps less competent, were in charge. As you read this chapter consider whether Nixon (and Kennedy and Johnson) had caused actual structural harm to the institution of the presidency, to the detriment of Ford and Carter. Is it more accurate to say that Nixon was a crook, Ford had no hope of mustering the political capital to exercise his powers of persuasion and Carter was a nice man far more suited to running Georgia than to running the United States of America?

Ford and Carter as presidents

Ford's presidency began with a sense of national relief and ended with a sense of unsurprising let-down. He had neither sought nor expected the presidency but he was a decent man who resolved to do his best. Without the legitimacy or impetus of a presidential election, without a manifesto for government and with a very clear sense that he was in office only because Congress had willed it (twice, in confirming him as vice president as well as in threatening the impeachment that persuaded Nixon to resign), he was never likely to find life in the White House easy.

Ford attempted to balance the budget and to minimise government intervention. In that sense he was a traditional conservative along the lines of President Eisenhower. The world had moved on since the 1950s and his policies did not work any more. He refused to countenance any progressive measures to help farm prices or create jobs, endangering two important foundations of American prosperity. He refused to help New York City, which by 1975 was begging for federal funds as it was yet again on the verge of bankruptcy (the city had a lot of very poor slums with very low incomes). Ford reversed his normal policy of non-intervention in March 1975 to attempt a stimulus tax cut, but this was too little, too late. The United States went into a recession during his presidency – but given the global situation and rising oil price it is difficult to see how this might have been avoided.

Ford had only eight days' notice that Nixon's resignation was likely – eight days to prepare for his elevation. His inaugural address, such as it was, noted that the 'long national nightmare was over' and asked a nation that had not voted for him 'to confirm me (as president) with your prayers'. Ford was stuck at first with Nixon's Cabinet but most were replaced. One of the two who served him throughout his time in office was Kissinger, although he lost his role as National Security Adviser. Ford's most dramatic changes were made on 4 November 1975. The 'Hallowe'en massacre', as it became known, was the promotion of several prominent conservatives, including Donald Rumsfeld, Nixon's chief of staff, who became defense secretary, and Dick Cheney, who became chief of staff. They would be hugely significant in the future development of the Republican Party. It was widely suspected that Ford's rearrangement was intended to signal a shift to the **ideological** right and that this was intended to enable Ford to win the Republican nomination in 1976 against the expected conservative challenge of Ronald Reagan. This challenge came and Ford narrowly survived it. Ford lost the presidential election that year, for reasons summarised here.

Figure 6.1: Carter and Ford debating on television in the run-up to the election of 1976.

Jimmy Carter had several advantages as Democratic Party candidate in 1976:

- He had no political experience in Washington and therefore nothing to do with the Vietnam War. He was able to campaign as an 'outsider' who was untainted by political corruption.
- He had been governor of Georgia from 1971 to 1975. He was an anti-segregationist 'New South' governor who defeated George Wallace in the Democratic primary.
- His surprising but overwhelming victory in the primary campaign had demonstrated that he was an excellent campaigner.

Ford had some significant weaknesses:

- He was blamed for the ongoing recession.
- His pardon of Nixon was unpopular, although the consensus later was that it was the right thing to do.
- He had come under a serious challenge from the conservative wing of his own party, which damaged him.
- He mistakenly claimed in debate with Carter that the Soviet Union did not dominate eastern Europe and refused to correct himself for a week.
- An image of him falling down the stairs of Air Force One, the presidential plane, appeared to be symbolic of his presidency as a whole.

The election was, however, a close-run thing:

- Carter won no states in the West other than Texas and Hawaii.
- Ford managed to raise serious doubts about Carter's competence and experience, especially in foreign affairs.
- Had Ford won Ohio, which he lost by less than a third of a per cent of the vote, and Hawaii, which he lost by 7000 votes, he would have won the election.

Key term

The **New South:** the term used to describe the South from the 1970s, in the post-segregation era.

Carter had campaigned in 1976 on the idea of a 'misery index', which he calculated by adding the rates of unemployment and inflation. By the end of his presidency, the misery index was higher. Carter seemed to be overwhelmed by the demands of the presidency, trying to do everything he could at the start of his term rather than planning and prioritising, and seemingly was unable to respond when his plans went awry. He had no answer to Congress's decision to water down his comprehensive programme for reducing energy usage and lost important momentum. This was a Democrat-dominated Congress; he was the national leader who had formed a new coalition, winning the New South and the industrial North; he might have expected some co-operation. Instead, Carter became an ineffective figure of fun, mocked for publicly declaring that he would save energy and wear a jumper to work and for his obvious belief, articulated notably in a speech of 1979, that American exceptionalism no longer applied and that there were limits to American progress.

Responses to social divisions

Under Nixon the social divisions in the United States had not necessarily diminished. The major focus of protest, the Vietnam War, was clearly no longer an issue as Ford was committed to ending it. Carter went on to pardon draft-dodgers in an attempt to draw a line under the issue of Vietnam. The Civil Rights Movement had stalled; the segregationists appeared to have lost in the South and in the North the problem was very clearly economic rather than just racial. Attitudinal change might persuade southern whites to give black people the vote; it would hardly persuade northern suburbanites to give urban blacks some money. The solution to the urban malaise of the North was clearly going to involve a large amount of government money; it was equally clear that there was no money to give in the late 1970s.

The women's movement found itself in a similar position. A great deal had been achieved in terms of women's rights. Abortion was legal and although there would be many, many attempts to restrict it in the future, the basic principle was clearly enshrined. Women were beginning to gain greater access to the professions, although the glass ceiling still existed. Nixon's vision of women staying at home doing domestic chores, never realistic in working-class America where a single income was not enough to live on, was no longer realistic in suburban America either – the economy saw to that. Meanwhile the pattern of the 1976 election was clear. The affluent and educated (not the same thing quite yet; the Great Society had allowed some poor people to be educated well) voted for Ford, the incumbent president. Others voted for Carter including, overwhelmingly, poor African Americans, whose vote proved decisive in New York, Pennsylvania and Louisiana and therefore in the election as a whole. The electoral cycle was driven by the economy; in a failing economy, the incumbent lost.

Ecologically driven protest in the 1970s

If the protest of the 1960s and early 1970s had been intended to promote modernisation, by the later 1970s a tradition had arisen of protest against the modern world. There had been a long tradition of environmentalism in the United States. The Sierra Club, a major interest group, had been around since 1892. President Theodore Roosevelt (1901–09) had been an environmentalist (and enthusiastic hunter) who saw the natural beauty of the American continent as an aspect of American exceptionalism. LBJ's Great Society expressed similar ideas.

During the 1950s and 1960s, Americans as a whole learnt how to protest. There were various reasons why the 1970s became a time of environmental protest:

- *Silent Spring*, by Rachel Carson (Houghton Mifflin; 1962), had prompted a ban on the insecticide DDT. Although the science behind this was a little dubious, Carson's book started a debate about whether the chemical industry should be trusted with the environment.
- In 1970 a Congressionally sponsored 'Earth Day' had resulted in the biggest single protest in American history and helped to set the tone for future American environmentalism.
- Plans to build an airport in the Big Cypress Swamp in the Everglades, the natural wetlands of southern Florida, had prompted a serious discussion about protecting the remaining American wildernesses from the impulse to develop. It was thought that the airport would have further destabilised an environment already damaged by canal building in the 1960s.
- Oil spills had reached the public consciousness. In January 1969 there had been an oil spill in Santa Barbara, California, at the time the largest in American history. This, and subsequent spills, prompted Nixon to take action, for example setting up the Environmental Protection Agency. By the later 1970s, protest movements had also developed.
- In 1976 the *Niagara Falls Gazette* discovered that the Love Canal housing estate in Niagara Falls, NY, had been built on a chemical disposal site. The company responsible, Hooker Chemicals and Plastics Corporation, was unwilling to admit responsibility. The federal government took two years to act, when Jimmy Carter declared a federal emergency. The Environmental Protection Agency suggested that there could be many more similar sites.
- In March 1979 one of the two nuclear power reactors at Three Mile Island, Pennsylvania, went into meltdown. This caused the evacuation of 100 000 people, panic and serious reflection on the safety of the new 'clean' power source.
- Most of the potential sites for dams in the United States had been built on by the 1970s. The Tellico Dam, a reservoir in the Tennessee Valley, was one of the last. Its construction was delayed in 1978 by a lawsuit (*Tennessee Valley Authority v Hill*) designed to protect an endangered species of fish called the snail darter. The Supreme Court upheld the Endangered Species Act. Ultimately the dam was built when Congress changed the law to exclude the snail darter. In the debate, Senator Howard Baker referred to 'environmental extremism', which would, if it continued, 'doom' the environmental movement.

Environmental protest had begun before the end of the Vietnam War protests but protest groups can gather only so much media attention. Environmentalists were far more effective in the later 1970s. Environmental protestors tended to be middle-class. Protests were often based in specific localities, although the American chapters of global organisations such as Greenpeace were growing.

In 1977, Jimmy Carter announced a comprehensive energy plan for the United States. He was partly influenced by the oil shock of 1973, which had forced Americans to think about alternative forms of energy, pollution and the environment. Carter set up the Department of Energy and announced plans to move towards renewable sources of energy. His plans responded to the environmental lobby and were also political. He realised correctly that energy security (that is, the ability to produce enough energy without relying on others to provide it) would be highly significant in future international relations.

Political corruption and the loss of national self-confidence

Political corruption is present to a varying degree in all political societies. In 1974 it reached an apparent high point with the resignation of Richard Nixon, accused of conspiracy rather than just of burglary, following shortly on the heels of his first vice president, caught out selling government contracts for personal kickbacks. This had two effects. The first, of course, was to emphasise that even the president could be a crook – but that as Ford said, it was a government of 'laws not men', and he could not get away with it. The second, perhaps unhelpful, effect was to mask the reality of what Nixon had done, which was to create a presidency so powerful that the concept of executive privilege had approached the level it holds in a dictatorship. Although Ford and Carter were constrained by Nixon's actions and their own personalities from acting similarly, they made no structural changes that might prevent similar corruption in the future.

Ford pardoned Nixon in September 1974. He believed that Nixon, in accepting the pardon, had admitted his guilt. Now Ford wanted to draw a line under the Watergate affair and for America to move on. His decision was unpopular and may well have cost him votes in the 1976 presidential election. There were other indications of political corruption at the time. In 1975 it emerged that the CIA had been plotting to overthrow foreign governments, including that of Salvador Allende in Chile. It also had files on individuals and had infiltrated protest movements. Ford established the Commission on CIA Activities within the United States under Vice President Nelson Rockefeller. Ford then let slip that he had seen material that simply shouldn't be in the public domain. It was generally assumed that this referred to the 1960 coup against President Patrice Lumumba of Congo. Ford accused his Democratic critics who raised the issue of crippling the American intelligence-gathering operation abroad.

If America could trust neither its presidents nor its spies to do the right thing, it had far greater problems to deal with. Its economic and diplomatic status was poor in the late 1970s. This was true of countries around the world but they did not have an inbuilt belief in American exceptionalism. In 1979 Jimmy Carter made a speech that he might have imagined was announcing the end of American Exceptionalism (see Voices from the past: Jimmy Carter's 'malaise' speech, 15 July 1979). In fact, it announced the end of Jimmy Carter, as it provided one plank of the campaigning strategy that would be used by the man who would humiliate him in the election in 1980.

Jonathan Livingston Seagull

In 1970 Richard Bach published the short novel *Jonathan Livingston Seagull* (MacMillan). It was a massive hit and became a film in 1973. The basic story is about a seagull whose search for individual authenticity leads to expulsion from the flock. Its individual journey leads to happiness and self-discovery.

Figure 6.2: Jonathan Livingston Seagull.

The novel is a fable and reflects a certain breakdown in American society. In the 1960s people seeking enlightenment and spiritual development – hippies – banded together in protest movements. In the 1970s individualism became more important.

One further point: in terms of political corruption, the example of Nixon was not that bad in one way. He sought to remain in political office because he genuinely thought that his being president was good for the country, however misguided and narcissistic that belief might have been. Nixon was not out to line his own pockets. His vice president, Spiro Agnew, had been on the take – but only when governor of Maryland. By comparison, in the 1870s and 1920s multiple members of the executive branch were corrupt and taking money for themselves.

Billy Carter: *not* an example of political corruption

Jimmy Carter's younger brother Billy, described as a 'professional **redneck**' by the press in 1979, owned a gas station and a beer company. The press loved him. He traded on his status until by the second half of his brother's presidency he was both the butt of jokes and source of comic relief (for example, he apparently urinated on a runway when leaving a plane), as well as, completely openly, a foreign agent of the Libyan government. They paid him $2 million and the press inevitably christened the resulting scandal 'Billygate'. Jimmy Carter was forced to deny that Billy had any influence at all over US government policy and there is no suggestion of any impropriety by the president, or indeed of anything except that the Libyan regime of Muammar Gaddafi (which would later become a great enemy of America) had wasted a great deal of money.

 Thematic link: prosperity

The position of the USA as a world power

The USA faced many challenges in the 1970s. The apparent decline of the USA's Superpower status led to President Carter attempting to rein in American foreign policy. The self-confident swagger of presidents since FDR was replaced by a more circumspect admission that American internationalism could not be all-embracing. In 1978 Carter persuaded the Senate to ratify the treaty that would gradually hand back control of the Panama Canal to the Panamanians over a period of 20 years: was this a sign of American decline? What if Panama were to become communist? Carter also spoke about human rights, not realpolitik: the art of the possible had been a dominant feature in Kissinger-era foreign policy. Carter proposed something more ethical – and then promptly went back on his promises, dealing with regimes friendly to the USA, like that of Augusto Pinochet in Chile, whatever their human rights record.

There was absolutely no threat to the USA's status during the 1970s (or indeed for some decades thereafter). The USSR was, we know now, entering a period of terminal decline. The powers of its leader, Leonid Brezhnev, were fading as he aged: he would be succeeded by two other members of the so-called 'gerontocracy' (that is, rule by the elderly) until 1985, when Mikhail Gorbachev realised that the Soviet Union could not survive. China was also led by an old man, Mao Zedong. Its economy was still communist and although its reach was becoming global its power was not yet impressive. The key point from an American perspective, however, was perhaps this: although some in the American government suspected that the USSR and China were weakening, nobody was willing to count on it.

Carter's policy was driven half by ideology and half by a pragmatic desire to maintain America's position. It was also driven by money: one of his first acts was to cut $6 billion from the defence budget. His plan was to evacuate all American troops from South Korea. He managed to remove a few troops and the nuclear missiles (and General Singlaub, the American commander in South Korea, who publicly disagreed with him) before Congress forced him to reconsider. It was felt – probably correctly – that his policy would certainly have led to the fall of South Korea. In other foreign policy initiatives, Carter:

- Increased arms sales to the Indonesian government, which had invaded Timor-Leste (then called East Timor) in a move condemned by the United Nations; Indonesia was a major oil producer.
- Accepted a number of Cuban economic migrants in 1980. Carter intended this as a humanitarian gesture. The Cuban president, Fidel Castro, sent prisoners and inmates from mental health facilities, and later compared what he had done to flushing the toilet on the USA.
- Created the Rapid Deployment Forces in 1979 to provide American leadership in response to global crises.
- Ended military aid programmes to some Latin-American countries because of their human rights abuses. This helped to overthrow the Nicaraguan government,

ACTIVITY 6.1

How valuable are these extracts from Carter's 'malaise' speech for the historian of 1970s America?

 Voices from the past

Jimmy Carter's 'malaise' speech, 15 July 1979

I've spoken to you on many occasions about national concerns, the energy crisis, reorganizing the Government, our Nation's economy, and issues of war and especially peace ... [But] it's clear that the true problems of our Nation are much deeper ... all the legislation in the world can't fix what's wrong with America ...

I want to talk to you right now about a fundamental threat to American democracy ... It is a crisis that strikes at the very heart and soul and spirit of our national will. We can see this crisis in the growing doubt about the meaning of our own lives and in the loss of a unity of purpose for our Nation. In a nation that was proud of hard work, strong families, close-knit communities, and our faith in God, too many of us now tend to worship self-indulgence and consumption ...

We were sure that ours was a nation of the ballot, not the bullet, until the murders of John Kennedy and Robert Kennedy and Martin Luther King, Jr. We were taught that our armies were always invincible and our causes were always just, only to suffer the agony of Vietnam. We respected the Presidency as a place of honor until the shock of Watergate.

We remember when the phrase "sound as a dollar" was an expression of absolute dependability, until 10 years of inflation began to shrink our dollar and our savings. We believed that our Nation's resources were limitless until 1973, when we had to face a growing dependence on foreign oil ...

With God's help and for the sake of our Nation, it is time for us to join hands in America. Let us commit ourselves together to a rebirth of the American spirit. Working together with our common faith we cannot fail[1] bringing in the new Sandinista regime in 1979. Carter did, however, give military aid to the El Salvadorian Revolutionary Junta in 1980 despite the protests of Archbishop Óscar Romero, who was assassinated after writing to Carter in protest. Carter was apparently concerned that the USA would not be able to cope with conflict in both Nicaragua and El Salvador at the same time.

The final withdrawal from Vietnam

Nixon had made a secret undertaking to give military aid to South Vietnam in early 1975. When Ford attempted to do this, Congress stopped him. They, and the country, had had enough. The fighting that broke out in early 1975 was halted by a complete American withdrawal. The terms of the peace treaty gave the Americans the opportunity to evacuate Saigon, the South Vietnamese capital. On 30 April 1975, after Americans had been helicoptered out of the city from the roof of the CIA's building there, the city fell and was renamed Hồ Chí Minh City. South Vietnam fell with it. Vietnam is still a single-party socialist state. So is Laos. Meanwhile, the Cambodians seized the American vessel the *Mayaguez*. The ship was rescued, but 41 Americans had died and 50 more were wounded in a final postscript to the Vietnam War. Domino theory had proved correct. The countries of Indochina were communist but the Americans had turned out to be the ones who had pushed the dominoes over. Meanwhile, in Cambodia, the Khmer Rouge under their leader Pol Pot had declared a 'Year Zero' and proceeded to build a Stalinist state that lasted four years (1975–79) and cost between 2 and 3.5 million lives. The imprecision of that figure should give some indication of the scale of the horror of the era known as the 'killing fields'. The Americans (given that they did not know exactly what was going on at the time; nobody in the outside world did) were of course utterly powerless to do anything about it.

Relations with the USSR and China

The end of the Vietnam War enabled Ford to build on Nixon's achievements in promoting détente. He met the Soviet leader, Leonid Brezhnev, in Helsinki in 1975 and produced an agreement known as the Helsinki Accords, summarised in Figure 6.2. The Helsinki Accords appeared to lay the groundwork for normalisation of relations – and of the geopolitical situation. The Cold War was accepted as permanent. The third 'basket' (see Figure 6.4), which was not seen as the most important at the time, took on a heightened significance as dissidents within the Warsaw Pact were able to use it to call for freedom – a fact that would not be lost on President Reagan, who would encourage them to do so.

In 1979 Vietnam was invaded again, this time by the Chinese, who invaded because the Vietnamese had intervened in Cambodia. The Vietnamese response was to seek Soviet aid. The great American fear of global communism uniting against the free world seemed a long way off. Nixon's strategy of playing the Soviets and the Chinese off against each other had been a good one. Ford was unable to do very much. He had sent George H.W. Bush to be the American envoy (effectively an ambassador, although diplomatic relations were not normal) to China essentially on a watching brief to see what would happen once the ageing Mao Zedong died. Bush had been the American ambassador to the United Nations responsible for trying (unsuccessfully) to keep the People's Republic of China out

Figure 6.3: This iconic photograph is of the final evacuation of the CIA station in Saigon, Vietnam, in April 1975.

of the UN Security Council. Now he sought an opportunity to build relations with the PRC.

Mao died in September 1976 and it fell to Carter to take the next action. In late 1978, Mao's successor Hua Guofeng saw his influence fall within China. As the Americans had hoped, Deng Xiaoping came to the fore and began to reorganise the economy along more capitalist lines. Carter rewarded this on the first day of 1979 when the Americans officially recognised that the People's Republic of China, rather than the Republic of China (Taiwan) was the 'real China'. Sino-American relations have improved steadily ever since, although Carter's hope that Chinese capitalism would bring functional democracy with it has not been realised. There were other benefits, however: both Boeing and Coca-Cola announced major trading deals with China in late 1978, and Deng visited America to meet the president, the first Chinese leader to do so. He visited Boeing and Coca-Cola, too, and also insisted on meeting Nixon, whose diplomatic efforts had originally made this possible. Deng made it clear on his return to China that American business models should be adopted. Deng also stopped encouraging communism in Southeast Asia, perhaps as a way of excluding Soviet influence in the region and perhaps under pressure from the highly successful capitalist microstate of Singapore.

The Soviet Union was still led by Leonid Brezhnev, whose mental and physical health was failing. Its economy was in the doldrums because it was exporting luxury goods to the rest of the Warsaw Pact in an attempt to keep up appearances. The French, in particular, had started to manufacture goods and export them to Eastern European markets (especially Romania) – in response the USSR began to do the same, at great cost, and causing discontent in the USSR where people

Figure 6.4: The Helsinki Accords, 1975. The description of these Accords as 'baskets' was used at the time.

realised that they were not benefiting from their own manufacturing output. The USA had to decide what to do about the USSR. Ford met Brezhnev in Vladivostok in November 1974. This lay the foundations for a summit meeting at Helsinki in 1975, where the two countries accepted the need to respect each other's boundaries, allow freedom of travel and information and respect human rights. At the time, the headline was that both sides had accepted the iron curtain. In fact the idea of respecting human rights would turn into a rallying cry for Soviet dissidents and support Carter's human rights rhetoric.

Carter's regime was divided over what to do about the USSR. Secretary of State Cyrus Vance wanted to continue the policy of détente and conciliation; the National Security Adviser Zbigniew Brzezinski (who was of Polish origin) wanted to take a tougher line. Carter veered between the two, toning down his emphasis on human rights while moving towards further talks on the reduction of nuclear arms. The second set of strategic arms limitation talks (SALT II, see Figure 6.6) produced an agreement that both sides would reduce bombers and missiles, although they still retained massive destructive capacity. Carter faced a battle to get this through the Senate, until the Soviets invaded Afghanistan, which brought a sudden halt to détente in late 1979. It was therefore never ratified. The general intention of SALT II had not been to reduce the amount of nuclear weapons available to either side. Instead, it aimed to limit the building of new weapons – a relief, potentially, for the leaders of both the USA's and the USSR's weak economies.

The response to crises in the Middle East

For all his inconsistencies, weaknesses and faults, Jimmy Carter will always be the American president who managed to broker the Camp David peace agreement between Israel and Egypt. There had always been serious friction in the Middle East between the state of Israel, established in the 1940s as a Jewish secular state, and its Islamic Arabic neighbours. This particular conflict had begun in 1967 when, in the Six-Day War, Israel had responded to Egyptian aggression with a pre-emptive strike (or outrageous invasion, depending on your point of view) that had led to its capture of the Gaza Strip and the Sinai Peninsula, as well as the West Bank and the Golan Heights, from Egypt's allies Jordan and Syria respectively. In 1973, in the Yom Kippur War (so called because its beginning coincided with Yom Kippur, the Jewish Day of Atonement), Egypt, assisted by Syria, launched a war with the public aim of annihilating the state of Israel. This time the war lasted 19 days. After various UN-brokered agreements over the next two years, Israel returned around a third of the Sinai Peninsula. The peace agreement was needed because Israel controlled a large amount of Egyptian territory and Egypt had been trying to lead a coalition of Israel's neighbours to wipe out the country.

Carter had seen his efforts in the Middle East as a direct refutation of Kissinger's shuttle diplomacy; Kissinger had sought merely to contain the situation. Carter wanted to find a permanent solution. In 1977 Carter toured the Middle East trying to make sure that he would have the support of all the heads of state. Then, in 1978, he invited Israel's prime minister Menachem Begin and Egyptian president Anwar Sadat to the presidential country retreat at Camp David.

Figure 6.5: Deng Xiaoping and Jimmy Carter at the White House.

Carter argued that peace and prosperity were the best routes to a shared future. He took both sides to the battlefield at Gettysburg (a major site of the American Civil War) and lectured them about the perils of war with one's neighbours. He persuaded Begin and Sadat to create settlement areas for the Palestinian populations of Israel in the West Bank and Gaza (the Palestinians were furious: nobody had proposed consulting them over the plans being made for their future). Carter negotiated Israel's withdrawal from the Sinai Peninsula; he guaranteed that America would supply Israel with oil if the Egyptians chose not to, correctly recognising that it was modern oil rather than biblical history that explained the Israeli government's attachment to the place. Meanwhile, Carter bolstered Sadat by promising him protection against a hostile reception in the Arab world.

What was Carter up to? There were a number of benefits to the United States:

- The Arab-Israeli conflict was destabilising religious relationships in the United States. In particular, the Jewish vote was becoming strongly pro-Israel.
- If Egypt could be brought closer to NATO, this would be strategically and economically significant.
- Israel could be helped if this large Arabic nation was at peace with it.
- The Middle East was a major source of oil and America needed to be able to rely on that oil as a source of energy. Peace in the Middle East would greatly help this. (Carter's real aim was to reduce American reliance on foreign oil but that was a long-term plan.)
- The Middle East as a whole risked polarising – picking sides in the Cold War – because the value of oil there had become obvious to all. Carter wanted to ensure that America had a foothold when that happened.

1. Parity in, and reduction of, numbers of strategic nuclear delivery vehicles – that is, missiles and bombers with worldwide reach.
2. A freeze on numbers of intercontinental ballistic missile (ICBM) launchers.
3. A ban on mobile ICBM launchers.
4. Limitations on testing of new ICBM types and new warheads.
5. A ban on quick reloading ICBMs.
6. Notification of test launches.

Figure 6.6: SALT II would, if ratified, have agreed to limit the USA's and the USSR's nuclear proliferation in these ways until 1985.

Perhaps Carter also hoped to secure his own place in history. He managed it. He did not maintain good relations with both sides. In 1980 he vetoed a United Nations resolution to make Israel dismantle settlements it had put on the West Bank; he then withdrew his veto. The end result, far more typical of Carter's presidency, was that he gained enemies but no friends and looked indecisive and foolish.

Figure 6.7: Begin, Carter and Sadat together at Camp David. It was Carter who had persuaded the other two leaders even to be in the same room together.

Iran and Afghanistan

The Camp David accords destabilised the Middle East by disrupting the Arabic consensus about Egyptian leadership of the Arab world. This had previously been uncontested. Egypt was the largest Arabic nation and, like several other Arabic nations, its territory was directly threatened by Israel, which controlled Egyptian, Jordanian and Syrian land and had subsumed the entire state of Palestine. Now, Egypt had made a peace with Israel to its own advantage if not to its allies'. In Iraq, Saddam Hussein made a play for leadership. This stirred up all sorts of religious issues – Hussein's regime consisted of Sunni Muslims, while Muslims elsewhere in the Arab world were generally Shi'ite. One consequence of the increased Shi'ite religious feeling was an Islamist revolution leading to the removal of the American-backed Shah of Iran in 1979. Iran, under the Shah, had long been an American client state in the region. Iran is culturally Persian rather than Arabic; it forms a useful buffer between Soviet territory and the oil-rich Middle East, also controlling large amounts of oil itself. The Americans had been so worried about a communist revolution that they had failed to see a religious revolution coming. Carter accepted the Shah into America for 'medical treatment' – in fact, life-saving treatment as this was really a plot designed to prevent his being shot by the revolutionaries. In revenge, Iranian forces seized the US embassy in Tehran, the Iranian capital, on 4 November 1979. In April 1980 the attempt by US marines to rescue the hostages failed before it had even started, costing the lives of eight marines. This was yet another humiliation for the United States.

The Iranian Revolution was partly a reaction to the OPEC crisis – the Shah had talked tough, to an extent alienating his western allies without producing real improvements in the quality of life for the majority of people in Iran. Meanwhile, the movement that would later become known as Islamic fundamentalism was taking hold, providing a religious flavour to a more general opposition to western, American values and ways of life. Ruhollah Khomeini, the leader of the revolution, had been a long-standing opponent of the Shah. Nevertheless, the revolution had appeared to come as a complete surprise to the CIA, which was present on the ground and specifically denied that anything was likely to happen less than a month before it did.

At the same time, the Soviet Union had done something apparently extraordinary in invading Afghanistan over Christmas 1979. There were various reasons for this – one of them fear of the expansion of Islamic theocratic governments like that recently established in neighbouring Iran. Carter had to react. The Soviets were also concerned about the apparent friendliness of America with Egypt, Israel and Saddam Hussein in Iraq. It seemed that the polarisation of the Middle East was well under way. The worst case from the Soviets' point of view now seemed to be a bipolar Middle East consisting of American allies on the one hand and Islamic fundamentalists on the other, with Soviet communists completely excluded.

Afghanistan was not a particular friend of America's and was in the Soviet sphere of influence. The Soviet Union had let America get on with its war in Vietnam. Carter must have realised that Afghanistan might prove useful in bogging the Soviets down in their own unwinnable war, as the mountains of Afghanistan provided just as much cover for guerrilla opposition as the jungles of Vietnam had. America did not need to overreact but nor could it simply sit back and let the Soviets carry on. Something had to be done. The SALT II Treaty was formally abandoned as a gesture of protest (although Carter and Brezhnev quickly agreed that its provisions should be adhered to). Carter also embargoed grain sales to the Soviet Union, correctly reasoning that this would hurt the Soviet Union more than it hurt American farmers. and announced that American athletes would not compete at the 1980 Olympic Games in Moscow. He also began the programme of secretly selling weapons to the Islamist resistance to the Soviet invasion of Afghanistan, the Mujahideen. His successor Ronald Reagan would send the CIA to help to train their leaders, including men such as Osama bin Laden. His aim was to make the Soviets spend as much money fighting the war in Afghanistan as possible.

ACTIVITY 6.2

Create a mind map of American foreign policy in the period 1974–80.

Use the mind map to decide how much of American foreign policy was consistent and how much changed. Was the replacement of Ford by Carter the major difference?

Figure 6.8: The Iranian hostage crisis was ultimately solved by Carter and was to be the final act of his presidency. The hostages were released on 20 January 1981 – a few moments after Reagan had been inaugurated to begin his term as president.

ACTIVITY 6.3

How far was Carter's foreign policy motivated by:

- human rights concerns
- economic concerns
- a desire to maintain American's prominent global status?

African Americans in North and South

By 1980, 30% of young African Americans were unemployed. The rate of black unemployment was overall twice that of whites. Even college graduates were having difficulties finding a job and city welfare funds were unable to cope. Although there were, finally, black political leaders in positions of power in some northern cities (and some southern cities too), the state of the national finances in general and urban finances in particular was so bad that they could not afford to do very much to improve matters. There were black mayors in the 1970s in Detroit, Washington, Newark, Los Angeles, New Orleans and even Birmingham.

Carter said during the 1976 campaign that he would not allow the government forcibly to integrate white (or black) neighbourhoods but nor would he be surprised if this happened naturally, or equally naturally did not happen at all. The expression of this belief did not particularly help Carter's cause, which was a difficult one. He was accused of race-baiting, looking for blue-collar white votes in Indiana and Michigan to help him win the primary against George Wallace. In fact, this was Carter's expression of how southerners of the New South viewed the situation in the North, which was, perhaps, rapidly being echoed in the South.

The impact of civil rights legislation

There was no new civil rights legislation between 1974 and 1980. Instead, attention was focused on reactions to existing legislation, in particular the Civil Rights Act of 1964 and the Voting Rights Act of 1965. The Voting Rights Act was effective. Across the South (and in areas of the North, such as the New York City boroughs of Brooklyn, Queens and the Bronx) the political barriers to African-American suffrage declined, as did incidents of violence. The economic barriers to voting remained; they were the same for black and white people. It was still true that poor people were less likely to vote than rich people. This is still the case.

Legally, civil rights in the 1970s was centred on the issue of affirmative action, as legislation came to be tested and refined by the Supreme Court, whose activist judges had already legalised abortion and suspended the death penalty in the 1970s, under their right to judge the constitutionality of laws and executive actions. The famous case *Regents of the University of California v Bakke* (1978) established that although affirmative action was in theory acceptable there must be no explicit quotas. In 1980 in the case of *Fullilove v Klutznick*, the Court found that some modest quotas were in fact acceptable – that is, quotas were fine as long as they were small (in this case, around 15%) and flexible. In employment law the case *United Steelworkers of America v Weber* (1979) established that as long as white workers were not entirely excluded from opportunities for advancement, it was acceptable to give African-American workers preferential access to training opportunities.

Change and continuity in the 'New South'

One hundred years after the first Reconstruction following the abolition of slavery in the Southern states, there was another New South. Jimmy Carter was a non-Dixiecrat Democrat, anti-segregationist but still southern, whose presidency was founded on his status as a 'favourite son' of the South. He was the first deep southerner to be president in nearly 120 years. The South was changing. One of the big issues in historians' thinking about the 1970s is the idea of 'Dixie Rising', the story of the invention of the air-conditioning unit and the rise of the Sun Belt that followed. The South now ran from Virginia to California. The historian and conservative strategist Kevin Phillips, in *American Theocracy: The Peril and Politics of Radical Religion, Oil, and Borrowed Money in the 21st Century* (Viking; 2006) has argued that the South was a national trendsetter rather than a backwater. The Atlanta of the 1970s, seeking a status of leadership in the South, became the classic new southern city – it was insular, privatised and centred on shopping malls and automobiles. From 1974 it also had its first African-American mayor, Maynard Jackson, who focused on neglected black neighbourhoods and received violent criticism from the white business community and press. In 1978 Dutch Morial became the first African-American mayor of New Orleans, Louisiana, another great African-American cultural centre. Morial promoted affirmative action in the city's hiring practices and secured federal aid for urban rebuilding projects. A state of uneasy tension prevailed over his relationship with the police department. Morial's efforts to combat police brutality (mostly against African Americans) largely failed and he was forced to cancel the Mardi Gras festival in 1979 because of a police strike. Mardi Gras in many ways defines New Orleans so this was a very big deal.

How was the South a trendsetter? How were southern values becoming national values? Here are some ways:

- Unions declined across America, beginning in the South.
- Southern redneck (not an insult – a badge of pride!) culture became mainstream – hard-working, sport-watching, anti-benefits, anti-establishment.
- Football, stronger in the South, overtook baseball, stronger in the North, in terms of popularity.
- There was a rise in evangelical Christianity in the South, which coincided with anti-abortion feeling.
- Southern opposition to gun control took on national significance in the 1970s. Southern hunting culture became iconic within America.

Every single president elected between 1964 and 2004 came from the Sun Belt, although only Carter and Clinton (1992 and 1996) were from the Deep South. Carter had been one of the first of the 'New South' governors in 1971.

The New South implied equality for African Americans. In terms of voting, there was equality. There was no longer state-condoned (or organised) violence against African Americans. Nor was there economic equality, however. In 1991 Robert D. Bullard et al. argued that the experience of African Americans had not particularly changed for the better in major cities from Houston, Texas, to Tampa, Florida (*In Search of the New South: Black Urban Experience in the 1970s and 1980s*. University of Alabama Press; 1991). The New South governors – of whom Carter was one – had enforced integration. Linwood Holton of Virginia, who perhaps went the furthest of all, placing his own children on integrated school buses, was the only Republican among them – and he was ostracised by his party as a result. Instead, across the South, the Republicans became dominant, just as they had been during

Voices from the past

Evel Knievel

Evel Knievel (1938–2007) was a motorbike rider and stunt jumper who exemplifies the idea of southern redneck chic. He was everything the liberal (northern) elite was not – sexist, drunken and irresponsible. He was also passionately anti-drugs and believed in keeping his word. He was patriotically American, usually dressing in red, white and blue. He was the last of the 'good ol' boys' and wildly popular. His reputation was international – he travelled the world with his stunts, for example jumping over 13 London buses in 1975. Although from Montana, he came to be identified with the culture of the New South. During his lifetime, songs and movies were made about him; one of his motorcycles is in the Smithsonian (the national museum in Washington, DC). His stunts were just as popular – perhaps more popular – when they were disastrous: he first came to prominence in a jump in Las Vegas in 1968 that left him unconscious for a month.

Figure 6.9: Evel Knievel.

ACTIVITY 6.4

1. Suggest three policies that would have actively improved the lives of African Americans in the 1980s.

2. Identify and evaluate the potential barriers to these policies.

the first 'New South' a hundred years earlier. This time, though, the Republicans formed voting blocks that effectively excluded African Americans, while there was an urban 'white flight' in the South to rival that of the North decades earlier. Rich people living in southern cities, who then moved to the suburbs, had almost all been white. With white suburbs and black cities, the problem of integrated schooling became less urgent; everyone went to their local school.

In economic terms, African Americans in the New South found themselves in a similar position to those in the North. There were middle-class, wealthier African Americans in the South; they did well, fully enfranchised and economically solvent. The urban poor, however, were more likely to be black than white and had few prospects of advancement. Even New Southern culture did not really appeal to African Americans. Black and white religious life remained largely separate. Although football was increasingly played by African Americans (including at the highest level) it was largely supported by white people. Gun control was an issue that mostly exercises white people (and still is). Hunting is a white activity: in fact it was a redneck activity. The New South's redneck culture excluded black people by its very name.

 Thematic link: identity

The USA by 1980

By 1980 the USA appeared to be a nation in decline but it was only the appearance of decline. The energy crisis of 1979 was serious but the American economy remained fundamentally sound. The world situation appeared to be deteriorating but the Soviet Union was sowing the seeds of its own destruction with its costly war in Afghanistan, and the Americans retained their position as leaders of the free world, a position they had held since 1941, when they entered the Second World War. All Americans now participated in American democracy if they wanted to and the emphasis in future decades would be on whether illegal Hispanic immigrants should be allowed to participate. The protest movement of the 1960s had developed into something a little different; middle-class liberal America developed a new obsession with self-help and psychoanalysis. A plain-speaking, popular ultra-conservative called Ronald Reagan would be able to harness all that and emerge with a reputation as one of the great American presidents.

What of the American Dream? Could any American achieve anything they wanted to through sheer hard work? The simple answer is: no. But they were working on it. The numbers of people trapped in serious, structural poverty were still large but they were not as large as they had been. The expanding middle class and large parts of the working class, supported by social security, were able to withstand economic difficulties without ruin. The Baby Boomer generation who were born in the late 1940s came of age in the 1960s, started families of their own in the 1970s and had considerable advantages in terms of economic and educational opportunity. They had money to burn. In the South, African Americans were now allowed to vote and institutional racism was dissipating: even Governor Wallace of Alabama announced in the late 1970s that he had repented his previous support for segregation. Like many of his countrymen, especially in the South, he had become born again.

The position of the USA as a Superpower

Defeat in Vietnam – and for all the talk of a peaceful, negotiated settlement, it was defeat – had rocked America's self-confidence. In truth, however, there was no particular reason for any other nation to be self-confident either. The world had moved on. Nixon had shown that the world was not bipolar. It was more complex. Two nations could not dominate again. There were five nuclear powers, each in various stages of decline. Despite weak political leadership and a stuttering economy America remained the dominant Superpower. But it was not plain sailing.

In reality, the USA retained its Superpower status *and* its comparative advantage over the Soviet Union, although this might not have been apparent at the time. The five nuclear powers had all suffered in the 1970s. Britain had been beset by strikes and economic depression and by 1980 was under the leadership of the confident prime minister Margaret Thatcher, who was reforming the economy. Her predecessor, Jim Callaghan, had presided over the 'winter of discontent', as rubbish piled up on the streets because of strikes and dead bodies at funeral parlours went unburied, even as Carter was bemoaning his nation's malaise in the States. France had been affected by the depression of the 1970s and had begun to accept its reduced influence in the world. China was undergoing economic reforms but was new to the principles of capitalism. The Soviet Union was terrified by the prospect of a strong China to its southeast and an Islamic Iran assuming leadership of the Middle East (and control of all that oil) to its southwest, and the realisation that it would not be able to do very much about rebellions in the Warsaw Pact, should they occur. The Soviet leadership knew that the Brezhnev Doctrine, which stated that the Soviet Union would use force to oppose rebellions in the Warsaw Pact, would be practically unenforceable if there were more than one rebellion at a time. The war in Afghanistan would turn out to be a costly nightmare for the Soviets, not least when the United States trained Islamic warriors such as Osama bin Laden to resist the Soviet invasion. Economically, militarily, politically and culturally, the USA was still a Superpower.

The extent of social and economic change

By 1980 more Americans were middle-class than ever before. In part this reflected that the old class system had broken down and the definitions had changed; in fact, the working poor, especially in the South, were still in a precarious economic position. Nevertheless, the USA in 1980 seemed very different:

- In 1940 there had been 95 million Americans; by 1980 there were 226 million.
- By 1980 most immigration to America was Hispanic and it was often illegal. The actual rate of population growth was around 1% a year, which was very low by American standards.
- By 1980 Americans on the whole had vastly more modern living standards than they had in 1945. By 1980, average life expectancy was 74.
- There was an urban crisis by 1980. Not only had the cities run out of money but they were increasingly violent. 'Urban' in this context was still often a synonym for 'black' because housing in the cities had become cheaper as the desirable suburbs had opened up, and on the whole black people were still considerably poorer than white people.
- By 1980 half of all Americans lived in suburbs, where the infrastructure was car-dependent. In most suburbs there was simply no mass transit apart from the iconic yellow school bus.
- There were only two million farmers left by 1980, generally working on large farms. Mechanisation had made a major difference. The era of 'mom and pop' farmers (which had actually been largely mythical since the middle of the 1920s) was over.
- Union membership had declined drastically. Only around 25% of workers were in unions. Even those unions were not particularly effective.
- Only a third of American workers were 'blue-collar' manufacturing or primary production sector workers.
- In 1980 America ran a budget deficit of $50 billion. As yet there were few voices opposed to such a structural deficit.

There were also clear social differences. The Culture Wars were coming – an expression of fundamentally different values along liberal and conservative lines. Liberals had prevailed over abortion and divorce and were slowly prevailing over gay rights. Conservatives were prevailing over women's economic rights – the Equal Rights Amendment failed in the early 1980s. Meanwhile there was an increase in religious feeling, often originating in the South and associated with evangelicalism, the Baptist church, the Moral Majority and the Republican Party. Jerry Falwell led the TV evangelists and Billy Graham was also a significant figure. Church membership rose in 'middle America', the small-town home of Nixon's 'silent majority'.

This was the period of the rise of the white ethnics. The 1970s saw the creation of things like the Italian-American Civil Rights League and the Jewish Defense League, and a re-assertion of Irish identity in response to the growing troubles in Ireland. It was the end of the melting-pot narrative, the decline of WASP culture and the vision of national identity. In parts of the South that identity was reborn along with born-again religion. In areas where, contrary to national trends, white-collar workers were outnumbered by blue-collar workers, where poor white people – not the 11% of Americans who were genuinely below the poverty line, but poor nevertheless – lived in mining towns or agricultural towns, a **fundamentalist** evangelical awakening was under way. At its heart were Christians who described themselves as having been 'born again', baptised as adult believers in Christianity.

These evangelicals entered politics. They were anti-establishment. They reacted against permissiveness, abortion and gay rights: they were not impressed by the 100 000-strong Gay and Lesbian Civil Rights March on Washington in 1979. They were overwhelmingly Republican. The first born-again president of the United States was Jimmy Carter, a Democrat. He was an exception.

In 1976 a Baptist preacher named Jerry Falwell began to tour the country promoting the idea that those who had Christian values should bring them into their politics. The failure to do this was responsible for the moral decline of the nation (abortion, gay rights, judicial opposition to compulsory prayers in government-funded schools, divorce). Falwell's movement, formally set up in 1979, was called the 'Moral Majority'. It clearly took its name from Nixon's 'silent majority' and shared the 1940s-Nixon's opposition to compromise with communists, opposing the SALT talks as immoral. The Bible was the portal for the Word of God; it was important to be 'born again' with a personal conversion experience (note the similarities with the liberal emphasis on finding oneself, as Jonathan Livingston Seagull did). Perhaps inspired by the coming of the third millennium, the Moral Majority became associated with millennialism, the belief in the imminence of the second coming of Christ. For the Moral Majority and its successor organisations, for television evangelists ('televangelists') such as Billy Graham, it was important to prepare individual Americans for the coming of Christ. Over time evangelical religion became associated with an assertive foreign policy, suggesting that America's role was to prepare the world for the second coming of Christ. It has also become associated with a mission to reconstruct America in preparation for that event. For the new Christian right, American Exceptionalism had become a divinely ordained mission.

What was society like in the 1970s? The radical protest of the 1960s burned itself out to be replaced by the 'me' generation, focused on self-help, psychotherapy and personal development. Health foods and fitness became popular – organic brown rice was the fashionable totem of the health-food movement. Individuals searched for authenticity through New Age spirituality and organised religion. The consumer movement became politicised. Ralph Nader, a future presidential candidate, began to investigate poor standards and corruption in car manufacture, Congress, air travel and conservation. The Watergate scandal and the release of the Pentagon Papers had shown the strength of investigative journalism. On the other side of the coin, *Rolling Stone* magazine became a respectable place for journalists to work.

The self-help culture of middle America was not the picture for everyone. There was an urban crisis and very little money to deal with it. Slums caused crime. The cheap solution of urban renewal usually meant beautification, which just involved taking housing out of city centres and moving the problems elsewhere. Suburban

Key terms

fundamentalism: Christian fundamentalism is a belief in the literal truth of the Bible. It has become increasingly common in the USA since the 1970s.

Speak like a historian

Joe Bageant on religion

You may not have heard of Reconstructionists such as R.J. Rushdoony or Gary North. But individually and together they have influenced more American minds than Noam Chomsky, Gore Vidal and Howard Zinn combined. Since the 1970s, through hundreds of books and college classes, the doctrine of Reconstructionism has come to permeate not only the religious right, but mainstream churches as well. Evangelical Reconstructionists lined up behind Christian media mogul Pat Robertson in the 1970s, making him rich and powerful. In return, he gave them the power and confidence to launch politically charged movements such as the effort to overturn *Roe v Wade* …

This push toward a theocracy and the infiltration of mainstream Protestantism by religious extremists was one of the biggest underreported political stories of the second half of the twentieth century … Thousands of mainstream Methodist, Presbyterian, and other Protestant churches were pushed inexorably rightward, often without even realising it … Other mainstream churches with more progressive leadership flinched and bowed to the radicals at every turn. They had to if they wanted to retain or gain members swept up in the evangelical movement. So what if the most fervent of these people … vowed to reconstruct America to fit Leviticus?[2]

dwellers were doing a lot better but there were still suburban homes, especially in the Sun Belt, where there was not a lot of money to go around. In some parts of the country – those near the Mexican border – there were large numbers of Hispanic immigrants. Numbers had tripled since the 1960s. The borders were porous and the infrastructure of Texas, New Mexico, Arizona and California was not necessarily able to cope. The immigration of the 1960s and 1970s sowed seeds that would be reaped over the coming 50 years. Native Americans, meanwhile, had benefited from an Indian Civil Rights Act (1968) but still suffered from worse unemployment, lower life expectancy, lower incomes and higher rates of alcoholism.

By 1980 there were two ways of being American. The 'me' generation looked inward, towards personal fulfilment and transformation. Those inspired by redneck culture tended to believe that mankind was born evil and got worse, with hard work the major cure for this condition. This helps to explain why many poor Americans would come to dislike the welfare state.

Thematic link: identity

The reasons for Reagan's victory in the presidential election

In 1980 Carter faced his battle for re-election. Only three incumbent American presidents had been defeated in a presidential election in the 20th century; Carter became the fourth (George H.W. Bush would be the fifth but only Carter was utterly humiliated by the result).

Ronald Reagan, a 1950s B-movie actor, had become the leader of the American conservative movement. He had first come to prominence in Goldwater's campaign in 1964, became governor of California and then in 1976 lost narrowly in his attempt to unseat the sitting president for the Republican nomination. Ford's defeat in the general election and Carter's disastrous presidency only strengthened Reagan's presidential cause. His charisma, optimism and view of American Exceptionalism, which contrasted sharply with Carter's, all served to help his victory in the presidential election. He was a Republican but he was an antagonist of the disgraced Richard Nixon (whom he had run against in 1968). The support of prominent Christian evangelicals also helped: Reagan ran on an anti-abortion platform even though, as president, there was very little he could do about it. He also campaigned for 'states' rights' – partly a refutation of the proposed Equal Rights Amendment and partly a reference to segregation and an appeal for white southern support. He also campaigned for a 30% tax cut to be spread over three years – a violent economic shock along the same lines as Thatcher's in Britain.

Reagan did not seem to be the more experienced candidate. Like Carter, he had been a state governor but Carter had also been president for three years. Reagan did not work as hard as Carter – he appeared not to need to. But he had a clear vision, which Carter clearly did not have (and had not had for the previous four years). Reagan managed to disguise his particular brand of what seemed at the time to be quite extreme conservatism (future conservative ideologies would move even further to Reagan's economic right) under a homely veneer. He spoke to the nation; the nation listened and liked what he had to say. There would be no more talk of malaise. In the single presidential debate between Carter and Reagan, there were two key moments. The first was when Carter referred to his young daughter Amy's assessment of the most serious problem facing America,

ACTIVITY 6.5

What, according to Bageant, was the impact of the evangelical revival of the 1970s?

Voices from the past

Tom Wolfe on the 'Me' Decade

The right to shuck overripe wives and take on fresh ones was once seen as the prerogative of kings only, and even then it was scandalous. In the 1950s and 1960s it began to be seen as the prerogative of the rich, the powerful, and the celebrated (Nelson Rockefeller, Henry Ford, and show-business figures), although it retained the odor of scandal. Wife-shucking damaged Adlai Stevenson's chances of becoming president in 1952 and Rockefeller's chances of becoming the Republican presidential nominee in 1964 and 1968. Until the 1970s wife-shucking made it impossible for an astronaut to be chosen to go into space.

Today, in the Me Decade, it becomes *normal behavior*, one of the factors that have pushed the divorce rate above 50 percent. When Eugene McCarthy filled in the blank in 1972 and shucked his wife, it was hardly noticed. Likewise in the case of several astronauts. When Wayne Hays filled in the blank in 1976 and shucked his wife of thirty-eight years, it did not hurt his career in the slightest. Copulating with the girl in the office, however, was still regarded as scandalous … Some wiseacre has remarked, supposedly with levity, that the federal government may in time have to create reservations for women over thirty-five, to take care of the swarms of shucked wives and widows.[3]

ACTIVITY 6.6

Look at the bullet points in the section headed The extent of social and economic change. How many of them express positive changes and how many are negative?

which was the control of nuclear weapons. Carter's attempt to show foreign policy as childishly simple backfired, as he just seemed not to be taking the issue sufficiently seriously. The second was when Reagan, seeking to characterise Carter as a doom-monger with nothing positive to say, shook his head and said, 'There you go again'. The moment seemed to resonate.

Figure 6.10: The body language of the two candidates in this photograph from the debate between Carter (left) and Reagan is interesting. Reagan went into the debate 2% ahead; a week later he had won by 10%, a landslide, in the election.

Carter had very little chance. The economy was in a worse state than it had been when he took office – Reagan simply asked, 'Are you better off than you were four years ago?' to make that point. Carter had been challenged for his own nomination by Senator Teddy Kennedy and it was widely thought that Kennedy had only lost because of a murky incident in in 1969 when he appeared to have been responsible for the death of a young woman in a car accident at Chappaquiddick, Massachusetts. It was Carter's misfortune that the day of the election was the one-year anniversary of the beginning of the Iranian hostage crisis (which he eventually solved so that the hostages were released two hours before Reagan's inauguration, although their release was not reported until after it). As Americans went to vote on 4 November 1980, with newspaper headlines reminding them of their president's incompetence, they naturally voted for the man who promised change. Reagan won in a landslide, with eight million more votes than Carter, who won only six states plus DC – and only DC, Rhode Island and his home state of Georgia comfortably. Carter suffered the humiliation of seeing the creation of a campaigning group called 'Democrats for Reagan'.

Practice essay questions

1. 'The "New South" of the 1970s was very different from the South of the 1960s.' Assess the validity of this view.
2. How far do you agree that the United States was the dominant nation in the world during the 1970s?
3. 'The major problem faced by presidents Ford and Carter was the damage done by Nixon to the presidency.' Do you agree?
4. With reference to Voices from the past: Jerry Falwell, Voices from the past: Tom Wolfe on the 'Me' decade, and Voices from the past: An Interview with President Ronald Reagan in the *Los Angeles Times*, 21 January 1982 and your understanding of the historical context, which of these three sources is most valuable in explaining American attitudes to women and family life in the late 1970s?

ACTIVITY 6.7

How valuable is this source (Voices from the past: an interview with President Reagan) for the historian studying what went wrong in America in the 1970s?

Taking it further

To what extent did Americans live the American Dream in the 1970s?

Voices from the past

President Reagan

An Interview with President Reagan from the *Los Angeles Times*, 21 January 1982:

I believe that we have started government on a different course, different than anything we've done in the last half century and since Roosevelt began with the New Deal, and that is the recognition that there is a limit to government – must be a limit to government size and power – and that there has been a distortion of the relationships between the various echelons of government – federal, state, and local … Now, this does not mean that we don't recognize government's basic responsibilities – the things that it is required to do … That prime function has been one that has been sadly neglected in recent years. …

We're spending a smaller percentage of the gross national product on national defense that we used to do years ago in what we considered normal times. But, we're playing catch-up. We are restoring something that was allowed to diminish and deteriorate … The people have heard so much … that their troubles are due to the deficit. In part they are. It's harder to explain that reducing the tax rate can result in even the government getting more money, that the tax cuts aren't just simply to relieve an individual of a tax burden. They are to restore a balance in government and private spending that will increase productivity, broaden the base of the economy and help provide the jobs for those people who are unemployed, and when that all happens, as it did in the Kennedy years, the government itself ended up getting more money.[4]

Chapter summary

By the end of this chapter you should understand:

- arguments about the extent to which American prosperity was in genuine danger by 1980
- the reasons why Reagan's candidacy in 1980 was so attractive, including a loss of national self-confidence arguably made worse by Ford and Carter
- competing ideas of American identity at home and abroad (America retained its dominant international status)
- the way in which the position of African Americans became more characterised by economic rather than social inequality.

Voices from the past

Jerry Falwell

'Listen America': speech by Jerry Falwell, founder of the Moral Majority, 1980

We must reverse the trend America finds herself in today. Young people between the ages of twenty-five and forty have been born and reared in a different world than Americans of years past. The television set has been their primary baby-sitter. From the television set they have learned situation ethics and immorality – they have learned a loss of respect for human life. They have learned to disrespect the family as God has established it …

There is no excuse for what is happening in our country. We must … have a return to biblical basics. If the Congress … will take its stand on that which is right and wrong, and if our President, our judiciary system, and our state and local leaders will take their stand on holy living, we can turn this country around.

I personally feel that the home and the family are still held in reverence by the vast majority of the American public …

I believe that Americans want to see this country come back to basics, back to values, back to biblical morality, back to sensibility, and back to patriotism.[5]

End notes

1 Extracts from Jimmy Carter's 'Malaise Speech', 15 July 1979 http://www.pbs.org/wgbh/
  americanexperience/features/primary-resources/carter-crisis/

2 Bageant J. *Deer Hunting with Jesus*. Random House: New York; 2007: 167f.

3 Extract from Wolfe T. 'The "Me" Decade and the Third Great Awakening', 23 August 1976 issue of *New
  York magazine.* http://nymag.com/news/features/45938/index8.html

4 Extract from Nelson J. 'Presidential Text: From the Mashed-Potato Circuit to the White House', 21
  January 1982 issue of *The Los Angeles Times*.

5 http://www.wwnorton.com/college/history/archive/resources/documents/ch36_02.htm

Glossary

A

Affirmative action
Affirmative action is a deliberate decision, usually by a government contractor or an educational establishment, to give priority to under-represented workers. In an American context, this is often African Americans.

Amendment
An amendment is the only way in which the United States Constitution can be changed. Amendments are most commonly passed by two-thirds of the House, two-thirds of the Senate, and three-quarters of the states.

American Dream
The American Dream is the idea popular in America that any American can, through hard work, achieve anything they want to.

Attorney General
The Attorney General is the chief legal officer in a democratic government. In the USA, he is a member of the Cabinet.

B

Baby Boomers
The generation born in the years immediately following the Second World War, and which came of age in the 1960s, is known as the Baby Boom generation because it was larger than the generation immediately above it; a lot of families had waited until the end of the Second World War to have children.

Bipartisanship
Bipartisanship is both major parties, Republicans and Democrats, working together on a particular issue.

Black Power
Black Power was a term popularised by Stokely Carmichael to describe a sense of proactive solidarity among African Americans.

Brinkmanship
Eisenhower's Secretary of State Dulles defined brinkmanship in this way: 'The ability to get to the verge without getting into war is the necessary art. If you cannot master it, you inevitably get into war. If you are scared to go to the brink, you are lost.'

C

Cabinet
The Cabinet is the group of departmental heads appointed by the US President. They are known as Cabinet Secretaries. Examples include the Secretary of State and the Secretary of the Treasury.

Central Intelligence Agency
The Central Intelligence Agency (CIA) is the American foreign spy agency.

Cold War
The Cold War is the name for the undeclared hostility and tension between communists and capitalists that began after the Second World War and ended in 1990. During the Cold War the USA assumed a position of leadership of the free, democratic, capitalist world.

Communism
Communism, or revolutionary socialism, is a political system based on the writings of Karl Marx, a 19th-century German economist and philosopher. Communists seek to have a society of equals, with no class structure and ultimately no leadership. They seek to overturn capitalism through a violent revolution, and to expand their socialist system throughout the world.

Congress
Congress is the name of the American legislature. It consists of the House of Representatives, whose members (representatives) are elected by constituencies with roughly equal populations, and the Senate; there are two senators per state.

Constitution
A constitution is the set of ideas about how a country should be governed – its institutions, and the rights and responsibilities of its government and people.

Containment
Containment is the idea that communism should not be allowed to spread to other countries. It is an important part of Cold War doctrine.

Convention A convention is a meeting held by a political party in the late summer of an election year at which it adopts its presidential and vice presidential candidate and sets a policy platform. If the primaries and caucuses have proved decisive, conventions can be foregone conclusions, in which case they are usually stage-managed by the prospective presidential candidate; they can also be genuine opportunities to select the candidate.

D

Declaration of Independence The Declaration of Independence is the document written in 1776 in which the American colonies announced their intention to break away from the British Empire. Written largely by Thomas Jefferson, it argues that people have rights and should not be subject to tyranny.

Deep South The Deep South is the core area in which Southern culture can be found in the USA. It consists primarily of the states of Louisiana, Mississippi, Alabama, Georgia and South Carolina.

Deficit A deficit is the amount by which a country overspends in a year. When a country is in deficit, its debt increases.

Democracy Democracy is a political system run by the people, for the people, and of the people. It involves regular elections, and some protection for the rights of minorities.

Dixiecrat A 'Dixiecrat' is the name given to a southern Democrat who did not accept the need for civil rights legislation. An example is Strom Thurmond of South Carolina.

Domino theory Domino theory is the idea that if a country became communist, other nearby countries might also 'fall' to communism, like dominoes.

Doves (and Hawks) In the 1960s it became common to refer to those who advocated peace as 'Doves' and those who advocated war as 'Hawks'. The terms are more widely used now, so that a politician who wishes to take aggressive action to bring down the deficit might be called a 'deficit hawk'.

Draft-dodgers Draft-dodgers were Americans who avoided conscription in the Vietnam War era using various means.

E

Executive Privilege Executive Privilege is the doctrine that the president and other members of the Executive should be exempt from some of the normal democratic standards of openness and transparency because they might need to keep secrets to do their job well. Nixon believed in this.

F

Federal government The federal government is the central government of the United States, as distinct from the state governments. Its head is the president.

Fifth Amendment The Fifth Amendment to the US Constitution guarantees various rights, most famously the right not to incriminate oneself. To 'plead the Fifth' means to refuse to answer a question under oath on the grounds that to answer it honestly might reveal guilt in a criminal activity.

Free Speech Movement Originating in the University of California, Berkeley, the Free Speech Movement was an influential protest movement that immediately preceded the Vietnam War, some of the protest against which it helped to inspire.

Freedom Marshals Freedom marshals were federal law-enforcement officials sent in to support civil rights protestors and protect them from violence.

G

Gross National Product (GNP) GNP is a measure of the total amount produced and traded by a country in a year. The higher the GNP, the wealthier the country.

H

House of Representatives The House of Representatives is part of the Congress of the United States. It contains representatives elected by districts throughout the country. Its members are sometimes called 'congressmen' (or 'congresswomen').

House Rules Committee	In normal circumstances any legislation to go before the House of Representatives has first to pass through the House Rules Committee. This gives the Chairman and members of the House Rules Committee considerable influence.
House Un-American Activities Committee	The House Un-American Activities Committee (or HUAC, as it was known), had been set up in the 1930s to guard against fascism; its Republican members enthusiastically investigated communist influences on the New Deal and in the labour movement; in the 1940s and 1950s it sought to investigate worrying rumours of communist infiltration, while at the same time defining being a good American as not merely being a capitalist but being actively anti-communist.

I

Impeachment	Impeachment is the process by which high-ranking American officials, including presidents, may be removed. The House of Representatives is entitled to impeach, which means sending the impeached official to the Senate for a trial on charges specified by the House.
Imperialism	Imperialism is the idea and practice of a country extending its power over other countries and building an empire.
Inaugural address	By tradition, the incoming president makes a speech at his inauguration in which he sets out his agenda. Some of these addresses – Franklin Roosevelt's first and J.F. Kennedy's – have become iconic.
Iron Curtain	The Iron Curtain was Churchill's term for the border between capitalist 'western' states and communist 'eastern' states in Europe during the Cold War.
Isolationism	Isolationism is the foreign-policy doctrine of refusing to engage in world affairs except when absolutely necessary, refusing positions of world leadership.

K

Ku Klux Klan	The Ku Klux Klan was, by the 1950s, a group of racist secret societies based in the South.

L

Laissez-faire	Laissez-faire is a French phrase meaning, essentially, 'let it happen'. Laissez-faire capitalism is an economic system based on capital that is unregulated by the government.
Landslide	A landslide is an overwhelming victory in an election.
Lend-lease	Lend-lease is the practice adopted by FDR during the Second World War of giving military, economic and food aid to America's allies in return for the right to future military bases.
Liberalism	Liberalism is an ideology that emphasises freedom from restraint by government: people should be allowed to do what they want. It has also come to be used in an American context to indicate a belief in change in society.

M

Marxism-Leninism	Marxism-Leninism is the form of communism practised in the early USSR. It is distinct from the more brutal Stalinism.
McCarthyism	McCarthyism is named after Senator Joseph McCarthy, Republican of Wisconsin, who made his name as an anti-communist campaigner. From the moment in February 1950 when McCarthy claimed that he had a list of 205 communists working in the State Department, the anti-communist movement was associated with him. Throughout his career, McCarthyism did not uncover a single actual spy.
Medicaid	Medicaid is a Great Society policy that provides free healthcare for low-income individuals and families.
Medicare	Medicare is a key Great Society policy, originally proposed by Truman but then passed by LBJ. It provided free medical insurance for the elderly; Truman received the first Medicare card in 1965.
Mid-term elections	Mid-term, or off-year, elections, are Congressional elections held in years when there is no presidential election.

Military-industrial complex President Eisenhower coined the term 'military-industrial complex' to indicate his belief that, by the end of his presidency, a large part of the American economy depended on military production.

Missile gap The missile gap is the term used to describe the fact that one nation had more, or more powerful, or longer range, missiles than the other. For most of the Cold War, the Americans were ahead.

N

NASA The National Aeronautics and Space Administration was set up by President Eisenhower to coordinate American efforts to get into space.

National Security Council The National Security Council (NSC) was set up by President Truman as a way of co-ordinating the work of the various agencies and government departments responsible for American national security, and ensuring that the vice president was aware of major issues.

Native American Native Americans were the inhabitants of the USA before the phase of European settlement began in the 16th century. There were many different Native American tribes, many of whose names survive in the names of states such as Massachusetts, Connecticut and the Dakotas.

New Deal The New Deal is the name for FDR's efforts to restructure and support the failing American economy in the 1930s. Historians are divided on whether there was one New Deal or three separate New Deals. In modern American thought the New Deal is seen as a cornerstone of liberal politics.

P

Parliamentary Privilege Parliamentary Privilege is the law common to most democracies that members of the legislature (in the US, Congress) cannot be held accountable in court for anything they say in their role as legislators. In practice this means that senators and representatives cannot be sued for libel for anything they say on the floor of the House or Senate, or in committees.

President The president of the United States of America is the head of state and the head of the executive branch of government, elected every four years.

Primary A primary election is an election in which voters choose between different candidates from the same party, competing for their party's nomination for the general election later in the year.

Purple Heart The Purple Heart is a prestigious military honour awarded to American service personnel wounded or killed in battle.

R

Red Scare A Red Scare is a cultural and political reaction to fear of domestic or foreign communism. Red Scares occurred in the USA in the 1920s and 1940s to 1950s.

Redneck Redneck is a term used for American working class people, often in the South, who identify with a particular culture. Originally the term referred to the sunburnt necks of those who worked the land outside.

Rights Rights are specific guarantees given by governments to people. An example is the right to freedom of speech, which is guaranteed by the First Amendment to the US Constitution.

Rollback Rollback is the opposite of containment, and is the doctrine favoured by General MacArthur during the Korean War that communist countries should be invaded to bring down their communist governments.

S

Secretary of State The Secretary of State is the most senior appointed member of the US Cabinet. US Secretaries of State are in charge of foreign affairs and diplomatic relations.

Segregation Segregation is the deliberate separation of black from white people in public and private areas.

Senate The Senate is a branch of the US Congress. It contains two senators from every state.

Silent majority The silent majority was Nixon's term for those Americans who did not protest against the Vietnam War, and who exhibited conservative values without feeling moved to demonstrate them publicly.

Stare decisis — *Stare decisis* is a Latin phrase meaning 'Let the decision stand'. It refers to the practice of the US Supreme Court of not overturning previous Supreme Court decisions.

State Department — The State Department, the leader of which is the Secretary of State, is an American executive (cabinet-level) department, responsible for diplomacy and foreign affairs.

States' Rights — States' Rights refers to the political doctrine that states should set their own social legislation. In practice, the term is often used as a shorthand for legislation designed to promote white interests at the expense of black people.

Sun Belt — The Sun Belt refers to the whole of the southern United States as defined by geography rather than culture, from California in the west to Virginia and Florida in the east.

Superpower — The USA and the USSR were superpowers during the Cold War, as they dominated other countries through their political, economic and military power.

Supreme Court — The Supreme Court is the group of nine Justices who head the American judiciary. They have the right to declare laws passed by Congress or by states, and actions of the president or state governors, unconstitutional.

T

Tariff — A Tariff is a tax placed upon the importation or exportation of goods. Higher tariffs are usually seen as good for industrialists, and lower tariffs as good for consumers

Term-limited — Presidents since Eisenhower have been 'term-limited'. This means that they are constitutionally barred from serving more than two four-year terms as president (plus half of someone else's term, if as vice president they had assumed the presidency mid-term). This means that presidents are forced to retire after eight years; in the period covered by this textbook, this only happened to Eisenhower.

Tyranny — Tyranny is the arbitrary and unconstrained use of power. It has become associated in American thought with any government action that deprives individuals of their rights.

U

U-2 — The U-2 is an American spy plane. Supposedly unbreakable, one was shot down by the USSR in 1960, causing an international incident. U stands for Utility (it was felt that to call the plane an S- (for Spy) 2 would have been a little obvious).

V

Veto — The president is entitled to veto legislation of which he disapproves, which prevents it from becoming law. He can be overridden by a vote of two-thirds of both the House and the Senate.

W

Watergate — The Watergate Hotel is a plush hotel and office complex in Washington, famous as the site of the burglary that ultimately brought down Richard Nixon.

White Anglo-Saxon Protestant — White Anglo-Saxon Protestant, or WASP, became a shorthand term with obvious racial overtones to describe Americans who were from particular white communities, in particular the Scots-Irish communities of the working class North and South.

White Citizens' Councils — Formed in 1954, in response to the *Brown v Board of Education of Topeka* decision that ended school segregation, White Citizens' Councils were a network of white supremacist organisations that opposed integration and the Supreme Court decision. They attracted their members primarily from among middle-classes voters and were careful to distinguish themselves from the (violent) Ku Klux Klan, preferring to use political, economic and social pressure to oppress African Americans.

White House — The White House is the building in Washington that functions as the President's residence and as his office. It was built in 1800.

Bibliography

Chapter 1:

Friedman N. *Fifty-Year War: Conflict and Strategy in the Cold War*. Naval Institute Press; 2007.

Gaddis JL. *The Cold War*. Allen Lane; 2005.

Kennan G. The Sources of Soviet Conduct. *Foreign Affairs*; 1947; 4(25).

Williams WA. The *Tragedy of American Diplomacy*. WW Norton; 1959.

Chapter 2:

Greenstein F. In The *Hidden-Hand Presidency: Eisenhower as Leader*. Johns Hopkins University Press; 1982.

Harrington, M. *The Other America: Poverty in the United States.* The Macmillan Co.; 1962.

May ET. *Homeward Bound: American Families in the Cold War Era.* Basic Books; 1988.

Chapter 3:

Gaddis JL. *The Cold War*. Allen Lane; 2005.

Schlesinger A. *The Imperial Presidency*. Mariner; 2004; 176.

Chapter 4:

Baldwin J. 'Fifth Avenue, Uptown: A Letter from Harlem'. In *Nobody Knows My Name: More Notes of a Native Son.* Dell Publishing Co.; 1961.

Davies G. *From Opportunity to Entitlement: The Transformation and Decline of Great Society Liberalism.* Kansas University Press; 1996.

Halpern S. *On the Limits of the Law: The Ironic Legacy of Title VI of the 1964 Civil Rights Act.* Johns Hopkins University Press; 1995.

Schama S. *The American Future: A History from the Founding Fathers to Barack Obama.* Vintage; 2009.

Chapter 5:

Bernstein C, Woodward B. *All the President's Men*. Simon & Schuster; 1974.

Buckley WF Jr. *Up from Liberalism*. Hillman; 1961.

Evans E. *Wars Without Splendor: The U.S. Military and Low-level Conflict.* Praeger; 1987.

Lapham, LH. *Harper's Magazine*; May 1985.

McGirr L. *Suburban Warriors: The Origins of the New American Right*. Princeton University Press; 2002.

Sugrue T. *The Origins of the Urban Crisis: Race and Inequality in Postwar Detroit.* Princeton University Press; 1996.

Thompson HS. *Fear and Loathing on the Campaign Trail '72.* Straight Arrow Books; 1973.

Chapter 6:

Bach R. *Jonathan Livingston Seagull*. Harper Thorsons; 2015.

Bageant J. *Deer Hunting with Jesus: Guns, Votes, Debt and Delusion in Redneck America.* Random House: New York; 2007.

Bullard R. D. *Search of the New South: Black Urban Experience in the 1970s and 1980s.* University of Alabama Press; 1991.

Carson R. *Silent Spring*. Houghton Mifflin; 1962.

Phillips K. *American Theocracy: The Peril and Politics of Radical Religion, Oil, and Borrowed Money in the 21st Century*. Viking; 2006.

Acknowledgements

The authors and publishers acknowledge the following sources of copyright material and are grateful for the permissions granted. While every effort has been made, it has not always been possible to identify the sources of all the material used, or to trace all copyright holders. If any omissions are brought to our notice, we will be happy to include the appropriate acknowledgements on reprinting.

The publisher would like to thank the following for permission to reproduce their photographs (numbers refer to figure numbers, unless otherwise stated):

Cover Corbis: Bettmann. Chapter 1 opener Alamy Images: Tom Carter. **1.2 Alamy Images:** Underwood Archives. **1.3 Alamy Images:** Pictorial Press. **1.5 TopFoto:. Chapter 2 opener Getty Images:** Howard Sochurek/The LIFE Picture Collection. **2.1 Alamy Images:** Stocktrek Images, Inc. **2.2 Alamy Images:** Everett Collection Historical. **2.3 Alamy Images:** Everett Collection Historical. **2.4 Getty Images:** Allan Grant/The LIFE Picture Collection. **2.6 Getty Images:** Sovfoto. **2.7 Corbis:** Bettmann. **2.9 Alamy Images:** Mug Shot. **Chapter 3 opener Alamy Images:** dpa Picture Alliance. **3.1 Getty Images:** Buyenlarge. **3.2 TopFoto:** United Archives. **3.4 Alamy Images:** Everett Collection Historical. **3.5 Getty Images:** Joseph Scherschel/The LIFE Picture Collection. **3.6 Getty Images:** Pressefoto Kindermann/ullstein bild. **Chapter 4 opener Alamy Images:** Everett Collection Historical. **4.1 Alamy Images:** Pictorial Press Ltd. **4.4 Alamy Images:** World History Archive. **4.6 Alamy Images:** Everett Collection Historical. **4.7 REX Shutterstock:** Sipa Press. **Chapter 5 opener Getty Images:** John Dominis/The LIFE Picture Collection. **5.3 Alamy Images:** World History Archive. **5.4 Alamy Images:** ITAR-TASS Photo Agency. **5.5 Alamy Images:** Travelwide. **5.6 Getty Images:** Rolls Press/Popperfoto. **Chapter 6 opener Getty Images:** Andrew Harrer/Bloomberg. **6.1 Alamy Images:** World History Archive. **6.3 Corbis:** Bettmann. **6.5 Alamy Images:** World History Archive. **6.7 Alamy Images:** ZUMA Press, Inc. **6.8 Getty Images:** GAMMA/Gamma-Keystone. **6.9 Getty Images:** Michael Ochs Archives. **6.10 Corbis:** Bettmann

The publisher would like to thank the following for permission to reproduce extracts from their texts:

Extract Chapter 1 THE IMPERIAL PRESIDENCY by Arthur M. Schlesinger, Jr. Copyright © 1973 by Arthur M. Schlesinger, Jr. Reprinted by permission of Houghton Miffin Harcourt Publishing Company. All rights reserved. **Extract Chapter 2** Michael J. Klarman. How Brown Changed Race Relations: The Backlash Thesis. Journal of American History. Oxford University Press June 1, 1994. Reprinted by permission of Oxford University Press; **Extract Chapter 3** The Papers of Earl Silas Tupper and Brownie Wise, Archives Center, National Museum of American History, Smithsonian Institution; **Extract Chapter 3** J. L. Gaddis. The Cold War. Published by Allen Lane; Extract Chapter 3 THE IMPERIAL PRESIDENCY by Arthur M. Schlesinger, Jr. Copyright © 1973 by Arthur M. Schlesinger, Jr. Reprinted by permission of Houghton Miffin Harcourt Publishing Company. All rights reserved. **Extract Chapter 4** AMERICAN FUTURE by Simon Schama Published by Bodley Head Reprinted by permission of The Random House Group Limited; **Extract Chapter 4** James Baldwin. Fifth Avenue, Uptown: A Letter from Harlem. From Nobody Knows My Name: More Notes of a Native Son. Published by Dell Publishing Co; **Extract Chapter 4** Halpern, Stephen C. On the Limits of the Law: The Ironic Legacy of Title VI of the 1964 Civil Rights Act. p. 287. © 1995 The Johns Hopkins University Press. Reprinted with permission of Johns Hopkins University Press; **Extract Chapter 5** Reprinted with the permission of Simon & Schuster, Inc. from ALL THE PRESIDENT'S MEN by Carl Bernstein and Bob Woodward. Copyright ©1974 Carl Bernstein and Bob Woodward; **Extract Chapter 6** Tom Wolfe. The 'Me' Decade and the Third Great Awakening. From New York Magazine, 23 August 1976; **Extract Chapter 6** Los Angeles Times article "Presidential Text: From the Mashed-Potato Circuit to the White House" written by Jack Nelson that published January 21, 1982; **Extract chapter 6** DEER HUNTING WITH JESUS: DISPATCHES FROM AMERICA'S CLASS WAR by Joe Bageant, copyright © 2007 by Joseph L. Bageant. Used by permission of Crown Books, an imprint of the Crown Publishing Group, a division of Penguin Random House LLC. All rights reserved; **Extract Chapter 6** LISTEN, AMERICA! by Jerry Falwell, copyright © 1980 by Jerry Falwell. Used by permission of Doubleday, an imprint of the Knopf Doubleday Publishing Group, a division of Penguin Random House LLC. All rights reserved.

Index compiled by Indexing Specialists (UK) Ltd.

Index

Lightning Source UK Ltd.
Milton Keynes UK
UKHW050905220420
362024UK00006B/115